Novel Writing Tips and Techniques

From Authors
of Second Wind Publishing

Running Angel Books
Published by Second Wind Publishing, LLC.
Kernersville

Running Angel Books
Second Wind Publishing, LLC
931-B South Main Street, Box 145
Kernersville, NC 27284

First Running Angel Books edition published
July 2012.
Running Angel Books, Running Angel, and all production design are trademarks of Second Wind Publishing, used under license.

For information regarding bulk purchases of this book, digital purchase and special discounts, please contact the publisher at
www.secondwindpublishing.com

Cover design by Tracy Beltran

Manufactured in the United States of America
ISBN 978-1-938101-25-0

Novel Writing Tips and Techniques from Authors of Second Wind Publishing is the 100th book published by Second Wind.

This book is dedicated to everyone who made the accomplishment possible: our authors, readers, friends, and followers. Thank you.

Table of Contents

A Publisher's Top and Bottom Five:
What We're Looking For vs.
What We're Watching For
By
Mike Simpson,
Chief Editor

Is there a more discouraging document in our postmodern world than the impersonal rejection letter an author receives from a major publishing house? *"We're sorry, but your manuscript does not meet our current publishing needs."*

Second Wind Publishing has never sent a rejection message like the one above and never will (as long as I'm alive). The author is left with two cruel questions: What are the "needs" the publisher is describing and how does my manuscript fall short of meeting them? When we at Second Wind reject a manuscript, we do our best to explain to the author why it wasn't suitable for us.

In this "festschrift" commentary, my particular desire is to explain to our potential authors what it is we are looking for—what makes a book worthy of publication in our view. By spelling that out, we can simultaneously explain what we are watching for—the common "fatal" mistakes most often made by those seeking publication. Below is our list, in reverse order of priority. Please bear in mind as you read that this list only applies to Second Wind. The big New York publishing houses may have their own secret lists—but at least you'll know where you stand with us.

5. A Consistent Logical Story vs. One With Plot Holes. Recently we received an interesting submission. It was a main stream novel in which a character drops dead at the end of the first chapter. The narrator—the main character—remarks that he has never seen a dead body before. I emailed the author and asked, "Not even his

1

wife's?" I reminded him that the narrator said in the opening pages he had recently been widowed, and therefore very likely had seen his wife's body. A similar problem occurs when a writer has something happen or even has a character say something that is implausible. For instance, in a crime/mystery submission, the main character walks over to a bullet hole in a wooden wall and pronounces that the slug is embedded two inches in the wall and that it's a nine millimeter bullet. How could he possibly know that just from looking at the hole?

You would think plot holes and non-sequiturs would be more likely to occur later on in a manuscript, especially in suspense thrillers where the clues must be laid out precisely and in a timely fashion. We constantly read first chapters where the actions, comments and decisions of the characters are simply not logical. Sauce for mysteries is also sauce for romance. Most every good romance has some mystery, suspense or thrilling action in it. If the plot is implausible, it destroys the magic spell the romance author is trying to cast. Thus we watch for plot holes and other implausibilities.

On the positive side, when we read a manuscript, we are looking for believability. This quality has not much to do with whether the book is a science fiction or a paranormal fantasy. Rather it has to do with the actions, dialogue and decisions of the characters being plausible. The old saying "truth is stranger than fiction" is a reflection of the reality that a manuscript will lose its readers when the narrative becomes unlikely or unbelievable. When we are reading submissions, we look for fiction that rings true. We are watching out for implausible storylines full of plot holes.

4. Unique, Engaging Plots vs. Hackneyed, Shopworn Plots. Several years ago I read the first chapter of a novel in which a honeymooning couple driving an RV in the mountains ran over a rolled up piece of carpet and very nearly plunged off the precipice in the process. Arriving home after their trip, they find state police waiting for them to question them as suspects in the murder of the man who was rolled up in the rug. That was my first introduction to Norm Brown's marvelous first novel *Carpet Ride*. I discovered that each new chapter and each new page was a literary breath of fresh air: no clichés, no predictable characters or story line.

I had the same experience reading Juliet Waldron's classic romance, *Hand Me Down Bride*. I remember laughing out loud as I envisioned the opening scene: a 19th century mail order bride sitting in her nightgown on her nuptial bed, staring over at her elderly groom, who had died of a heart attack during the night without consummating their marriage. By definition I suppose, all romances are predictable—but then so are all mysteries; you know the hero is going to figure out who the killer is. But just because a writer remains faithful to the genre does not mean she or he can't take some creative new ways to the destination.

On the negative side of the coin, we receive a lot of submissions that are hackneyed and shopworn: the tough, world-weary cop who suddenly takes a new interest in a case involving someone he or she knows. The lower class maiden preserves her chastity, even as she is noticed by the cavalier nobleman who turns out to be not really so bad as she had been led to believe, and who falls desperately in love with her to the point of being willing to sacrifice his fortune. Jane Austen was doing it better 200 years ago.

It all boils down to "a good story, well told." In submissions, we are looking for freshness, uniqueness, surprising new takes on common themes. We're watching out for repetitive story lines full of worn out, unexciting characters.

3. Characters vs. Caricatures. In Clare Collins masterful, award winning romance thriller *Fate and Destiny,* there are three villains trying to find and kill a beautiful young fugitive. One of the bad guys is a big, goofy simpleton. One is mob hit man. One is a psychotic killer. While we have all read books in which characters like these appear, none of Collins' bad guys are predictable or stereotypical. The bad guys "live and breathe," causing the reader to be interested in them even while fearing them.

So often, we receive manuscripts in which the characters have no uniqueness, no rich texturing or vividness to them. In reading such manuscripts I have the feeling that the writer needed to have a person ask this question at this moment so the main character would have a reason to go on to his or her next scene. This shallowness of character reduces those in the narrative to caricatures and in turn reduces the quality of the novel to merely a "what if" story that doesn't engage the reader.

When we receive a manuscript, we are looking for characters who are believable and compelling. We're watching out for characters who are just "place holders," those who aren't even disinteresting—they're just there to fill a space so the narrative can continue.

2. Beautiful Writing vs. Bad English. I remember the spring afternoon when a colleague handed me the manuscript of *Dear Emily: a Memoir.* After I skimmed the first page, I turned to my colleague and asked, "Have you read this?" When she said she had not, I began to read aloud. The prose was so beautiful, correct and well-paced it was like reading poetry. Well-written manuscripts have a visceral impact on the reader.

On the other hand, we receive submissions with lots of grammatical errors, with poor English and with terrible style choices. One of the worst mistakes submitters make is "tense shifting": starting in the past tense and moving to present tense. Another is trying to write an entire novel in the present tense. Don't do that. Write in the past tense and try to avoid using the word "was" as much as possible (not "she was throwing the rock at his head," but "she threw the rock at his head").

Another constant problem is the notorious POV shift. The author's point of view should either be that of an all-knowing person outside the story—the omniscient narrator—or one of the characters in the story. It is permissible to shift from the POV of one character to another—but not within one scene; Sherrie Hansen made this shift well in her novel *Night and Day*, the story of a steamy internet romance between a woman in Minnesota and a man in Denmark.

And there are also the problems of incorrect word usage and incorrrect spelin, aren't their?

Some authors, when confronted about their English, want to claim poetic license. Poetic license is an earned attribute, in my view. If you can produce writing of a quality equal to William Faulkner or JD Salinger, then you can get away with run-on sentences and intentional grammatical misuses. First, though, you have to demonstrate you know how to do it correctly. Meanwhile we are looking for excellent use of English and watching out for bad writing.

1. In Media Res vs. Back Story. While I suspect every publisher is attuned to whether or not a narrative begins "in media res" (in the middle of things), it is particularly significant to us at Second Wind. We proceed from the notion that the first paragraph should hook you into the first page, which should hook you into the first chapter, and the first chapter should embed the hook so deeply the reader will feel compelled to finish the entire book. This implies to us that the author should avoid beginning with back story and should weave it in gradually as the narrative proceeds, revealing only enough along the way to draw the reader through the narrative.

A splendid example of this is JJ Dare's *False Positive*, which begins with a beguiling description of a kitchen where a murder has just taken place. By the end of the first chapter, all the reader knows is that a police officer has just killed his wife. Equally well-done is the opening sequence of *A Spark of Heavenly Fire*, in which author Pat Bertram effortlessly draws the reader into the commonplace description of a woman walking to work through a park, only to have a jogger vomit blood all over her and die. Meanwhile others all around them are perishing in the same way.

One book that does a marvelous job of dealing with back-story while staying with the current narrative is J. Conrad Guest's *Backstop*. Guest uses the literary device of an ongoing World Series baseball game as his fictional stage. The essentials of what brought the main character to that point are told in flowing, compelling back story: between batters, between innings the catcher reflects on how he came to that pivotal few moments of his life. By contrast, many of the manuscripts we receive begin with a line or two of current narrative, only to shift almost immediately to the back story of how the characters got to that moment.

Another error many authors make is starting with a prologue and then shifting to current events in the first chapter. If a prologue is essential, it's your first chapter. If it's not, weave those events in during the course of the narrative. In a way, a prologue is like saying to your reader: "This part is essential to the story, but not really. I'm going to begin telling my story again from a better place."

Someone who gets away splendidly with breaking this rule is Deborah J Ledford in *Snare,* which won a nomination for The Hillerman Sky Award. Her prologue is a riveting scene showing the horrific events of young Katina's life and gives way after a few pages to the main story. Ledford's saving grace is that the prologue immediately hooks the reader into the narrative to find out what happened to the girl.

We want the story to grab us and drag us into the manuscript. Thus we look for books that start in the middle of the action, and we watch out for stories that back up quickly to explain how we got there.

I hope this is some help to aspiring authors. We often receive submissions from writers who "went to school" on the editorial comments we gave them and worked diligently to perfect their skills and styles. Of course we also receive ugly comments from people who want to know who died and made us the gods of literary evaluation. Along the way, we've discovered some major authors and novels. And we're looking forward to reading a lot more.

Interview with Mike Simpson

What made you go into publishing?

While participating in a really fine critique group made up of authors who had a lot of talent and experience, I became aware that many worthy authors were never going to see their books carried by legitimate publishers. It became clear to me that the true priority of the major publishing houses was making money. The approach of the major publishing houses was all about maximizing their profit. Meanwhile there were a great many quality writers who would never get an agent, let alone a publisher. My colleagues and I approached publishing from a different perspective. Our priority to give quality writers a chance to be published by a genuine press. For us, it was all about the literature.

What is the general background of the company?

After I complained loudly to my writer friends that somebody ought to start a company that put publishing ahead of profit and worked with and for authors, one of my colleagues dared me to start the company and I was dumb enough to take the dare. We officially became a press in May, 2008, published our first book in August of that year. The writers' handbook, of which this interview is a part, will be our 100th manuscript in print, as of July, 2012, about four years after we got our start. According to industry standards, now we are not a "small, independent press," but a "mid-sized" publisher.

Are you getting from the business what you hoped to?

Yes and no. Yes, we are achieving what we set out to do: being a "writers' publisher." We brought to publication dozens of authors who otherwise would not have had the opportunity. We are expanding exponentially in the variety of titles we publish, in our marketing ability and in our distribution. So many of our dreams about publishing have been realized. No, we have continued to operate on a financial shoestring, reinvesting our income in book contracts and corporate expansion. As a result, we are understaffed and we tend to run behind constantly. Overall we are very pleased with where the company is now and its immediate direction.

How do you decide to publish one book and not another? If some of the classics were subbed to you, would you have pubbed them or snubbed them?

While "it's all about literature" for us at Second Wind, I have to admit that we do have to sell books to stay in business. A key concept for us is that a manuscript has to be engaging: the first sentence has to draw the reader into the first paragraph; the first graph has to draw the reader through the first page; the first page has to compel the reader to read the first chapter. The writing must be of a high quality: comprehensible, consistent, engaging (and being just beautiful to read is a definite plus). The author must have a good story to tell and tell it well. The "classics" emerged from different publishing eras and the single biggest change is the expectation of the reader. Victor Hugo in the great classic *Les Misérables* devoted an entire chapter of the manuscript to the sewer system of 19th century Paris. Our editors would have "worked with him" on the degree to which that chapter "advanced the story." On the other hand you have a works like Harper Lee's *To Kill a Mockingbird*, which has an opening line that breaks a dozen of our guidelines, but is so fetching that you have to read where it's going. I have to admit that there are some really popular books today by well-known authors that we would have snubbed. As most committed writers will tell you, quality of writing does not necessarily equate with the popularity of the work.

How do you expect the rise in self-publishing to affect your business?

To deal first with print books, as opposed to ebooks, the short answer to that question is, "not much." The availability of inexpensive digital book publishing has made it possible for authors to get their manuscripts in print without spending thousands of dollars and without having to be accepted by a publishing house. Many authors are trying this venue to get their books out there. At a writer/publisher symposium in the spring of 2012, I was part of a panel discussion comparing traditional publishing to self-publishing. I expressed that the single most important distinction between the two—and I apologized to the self-published authors at the time I said it—is that books from a publisher are simply taken more seriously than self-published books. There is a great prejudice among reviewers, bookstores and readers that authors who self-publish do so because they could not find a publisher willing to print their book. There are other distinct advantages to traditional publishing over self-publishing: you work with professional editors, graphic designers and marketers; you become a part of a college of authors published by the same company; you make money from your writing instead of paying for it. If an author decides, however, to self-publish—and many will—I would like to offer a bit of advice: you do not have to pay four figure amounts to get a high quality copy of your book. I would encourage self-published authors to avoid "vanity presses" that offer "advice" and "services" beyond merely printing your book and making it available to distributors. It is a sad commentary on the digital age that many writers enter contracts with companies who charge ridiculous sums to print manuscripts, forcing authors to charge high prices—the sort of purchase price only your mom and closest friends will pay—in order to recover the cost of the printing and shipping. If you self-publish, shop around for the best per-book cost and skip the "expert help."

Do you have a plan to survive since new ebook publishers are springing up everyday? What has the ebook revolution done to your business?

Second Wind was fortunate to enter the publishing business just as ebooks were beginning to emerge. Having seen what internet downloads did to the music and video industries, we knew there would be big changes and we intended from the beginning to ride that wave. The changes are still coming down and at this writing no one (literally) knows where they will lead. There are some truths we know and can clearly state: 1) In the coming years, print books will recede in number and availability, but not evenly across the industry; for instance, today's toddlers will have some sort of ebook platform that will contain all their "school books"; on the other hand, children's books and coffee table books (and others that depend heavily on graphics) will be slower to succumb to the ebook wave. 2) An author can give ebooks away freely, often to a great many readers, but will have trouble selling the same book when the giveaway is over. 3) Authors have more success selling when they build a clientele with multiple manuscripts of high quality as opposed to a single volume regardless of how well written it may be. 4) Just as they are attracted to print books published by a reputable publisher, so ebook readers gravitate to ebooks that are made available by a legitimate press. At this stage of the ebook revolution, we are very much learners and working diligently not to close our corporate mind to the multiple possibilities available to us as a publisher of quality manuscripts.

What is the most difficult part of being a publisher?

There are a number of difficult realities, I've learned, about being a publisher. I never envisioned myself as an "authority" in the lives of others—especially strangers; but when you're a publisher you often get treated like royalty (on rare occasions, like dirt). It's a strange thing to receive more praise and more criticism than you deserve. Another difficulty I constantly face is that there are simply not enough hours in the day: I continually stay up late, late in the night trying to keep up with my assigned duties, but never seem any closer to catching up. By far, however, the greatest difficulty is explaining to an author why we won't offer a contract on her/his manuscript. I think this is the very reason most other publishers send form rejection letters ("we regret that your manuscript does not meet our publishing needs"). We decided early on that we weren't going to do that. We explain to authors why their manuscript doesn't work for us. Lots of authors are emotionally hurt by this; their book is like a prized child and we have just told them how it is imperfect. The hurt goes both ways, because we don't like to disappoint people. The upside is that no author we've turned down can say they don't know why.

What is the most rewarding part of being a publisher?

There are a great many rewards—even though big money so far isn't one of them. It's hugely gratifying when an author takes our comments and suggestions to heart, resubmits a rewritten work and we find it much improved. It's marvelous when one of your writer's books goes viral (and I must say, although I'm never surprised by the manuscripts to which this happens, I still can't predict which one will be next). I think, however, the biggest reward comes in feeling their gratitude as you observe writers going through the wonderful steps of being published: having their work accepted, sending back their contract, approving their proof, getting their first royalty check, writing to tell you about their next book. It's great to a part of that.

Becoming an Author
By
Susan Surman
Author of:
Dancing at all the Weddings

It isn't as if I grew up knowing I wanted to be a writer. I did write, but I never considered it as a profession. I wanted to be an actress and that's what I was trained to do. And that's what I did and who I was; who I am. (Before I grew bored with acting, I experienced some highlights—London's West End; The Fringe in Edinburgh; the Sydney Theatre Company at the Sydney Opera House, and much more). That's the thing about acting. Even if you are not doing it now, you are still an actor. With writing, if you're not writing, you're not a writer.

The transition from acting to writing came about in the 70's. I was in rehearsal for a TV show and had to take the train from Waterloo Station in London (where I was living) to a church hall out in the countryside somewhere and brought my lunch in a brown paper bag. That same week, I was to meet a producer about the screenplay I had just completed. I was picked up at my flat by a chauffeur-driven white Rolls Royce and taken to lunch. That did it! I decided to stick to writing. It was a great moment to discover I felt totally different as 'the writer' than as 'the actress.' And when the producer told me, "Susan, we can get two thousand actresses to play one role, but if you can write, we bow down to you," I was sold. These words coming from a British producer with offices in London and Hollywood was all I had to hear. He optioned my screenplay titled, "You're Never Alone with Schizophrenia" and I was on my way, so I thought. The film never got made. It sits in my files. From time to time, I try giving it some life as a short play; a short story, but move on to other projects. Maybe one day, I'll pick it up again. Writing is really re-writing.

As an actress accustomed to stage speech, I first wrote plays because dialogue came easy. I wasn't so hot on plots. They were more difficult—and structure was not easy for me. However, my first play ("In Between") was optioned for New York and later for London. There were several versions of rehearsed stage readings with professional actors and directors in London, Sydney, and the States. It was later revamped, retitled, and performed as *The Nightgown* (with me as director) in Winston-Salem. At last, my play was being played. After watching the fourth performance, I said to one of the actors, "I thought I wrote a comedy. This is a very serious play." He said, "Yes, didn't you know that?" My point being, you don't always know what you've written until you hear it or someone else reads it.

My next piece, *George, a Revue*, was performed in London at a charming café theatre; commissioned by the BBC for television; and a producer was most interested in getting it on at one of the smaller theatres in London. So, within one month, I actually could have had two plays opening in the West End of London. It never happened. Remember, this was early days, and I hadn't found my voice yet. I was experimenting with different genres. Was I really a playwright? A screenwriter? For some reason, I felt like a fraud.

Around the same time, another highlight occurred when I was asked to go and see a play at the Royal Court Theatre featuring a newcomer—someone thought to be on the horizon of a major career—with the idea that I would write material for her new TV show. I went, I saw, I was blown away. It was a then unknown Tracey Ullman. We were introduced, she read some of my stuff, and wanted me to write for her. I did a few monologues (they weren't very good) and that was that. The pieces were never used (but I did get paid).

Jump a few years ahead. I was living in Sydney and acting again. But the desire to get back to writing was strong. I had an idea for a ten-minute cartoon ("Max and Friends") about an Easter bunny who wanted more than to be used just at Easter. I wrote it and, as my plan was to approach the Australian Film Commission for money, I was the producer as well. I pulled together the personnel, including an award winning animator, wrote a proposal, made the presentation to the Commission, was praised more for my producer's abilities than for the script. Didn't get the money.

Another few years passed. I returned to the States (after nearly 24 years abroad), settling in North Carolina. I wanted to write a novel version of "Max and Friends" with the hope it would be easier to interest the film industry. With dialogue, you don't have to write directions or feelings or get them to do anything more than speak—that's the director's job—now it would be my responsibility to connect the dots, so to speak. Directing on paper. By the way, this was done on my Brother electronic typewriter. Computers were out there, but I foamed at the mouth at the mere mention of the name.

In the novel, Max was no longer a black and gold Easter bunny. He's one of fourteen purple rabbits whose Papa takes them to the new world for a new life. It's about how we are all connected and in each encounter we give something away and take something, even though we might not know what it is at the time. I loved putting in all the details; getting the characters from point A to point C. The first publisher I approached was crazy about it—and voila, with 25 black line drawings, it was a go for children of all ages, even though I had written it for adults. A contemporary epic fable. (Royal Fireworks Press, 1999). I was not the illustrator; they matched me up with someone in their stable of writers, but I had a major input as to what the characters looked like. The book still sells today.

Max and Friends was in print, I was doing book signings, getting good reviews; yet, I still didn't feel like an author. One book, you're a writer. Two books, you're an author. I wanted to be an author. I don't know where it came from, but next, I was tapping out a story (still on the typewriter) about two dogs that meet online and conduct their relationship through emails. *Sacha: The Dog Who Made It to the Palace* is for adults; a story about survival and friendship. It was inspired by what really happened to my dog in London. Publication came and I was out there selling it. And people bought. I had one book signing for dogs! Of course, they had to be accompanied by a human. By the way, in 2004, I wrote to the Queen at Buckingham Palace about the book because it was inspired by what happened to my dog when I had to leave him in London with a friend who happened to be the Royal florist. I was invited to deliver the book to the Palace and received a letter from the Queen praising the work.

So now was I an author? No. I needed another book; then I'd feel like an author. I wanted to get away from animals. I knew I would never write again if I didn't invest in a word processor. It was a few years later that I hooked up to the internet. I'm still a bit technophobic.

Ernest Hemingway said you have to write what's burning up inside you. Write the first line. The rest will come. And there it was. *The Australian Featherweight*. Historical fiction. I'd been haunted by the information that a particular Australian boxing champion went to the States around the turn of the century at the age of 21 as a champ and died on the streets of New York a pauper and a drunk at the age of 56. He'd come from the toughest area of Sydney, used his fists to get what he wanted, was seen in a street brawl and ultimately mentored by a leading figure in the world of boxing. If you go to amazon.com and type in "books by Susan Surman", there's a wonderful review of the book. For this, I mixed reality with fiction. I loved writing this. It meant a lot of research about boxing and the terms, but once I put my mind to it, it wasn't difficult. To this day, I can't say what it is about this fellow that got to me. I'm happy to say, this work has been re-written and re-titled with more depth and expanded to include a love interest. (2013 publication).

While living abroad, I traveled extensively. This allows me to use different locales in my writing. I can draw on numerous real experiences. I find it extremely useful in developing characters. But I'm making it sound easy. It isn't. I'd rather do anything than write—my house is never as clean as when I'm agonizing over what to write—and once I get started, I can't do anything else.

When I began writing *Dancing at all the Weddings* (published 2011), I didn't know it would turn into a family saga. It was simply a story about a woman's journey from frenzy to peace. But the more I got to know my characters, it just grew. How did I get the title? I was invited to an event in New York but couldn't attend. My friend said, "Oh, well, you can't dance at all the weddings." What a great title, I thought. But what's the story? I dashed out a short story, did a reading for about thirty-five invited people, knew I had something, but what? And so, back into intellectual prison, I began the agonizing. This novel spans 28 years while my others spread out over a year. Not being a math whiz, it was a challenge keeping it all straight. It took two years to write, the longest time I'd spent on any piece. Using knowledge of my hometown, Boston; my theatre expertise; and my worldly gallivanting, I wrote. And wrote. Outside activities paled against my characters, their adventures, and my connection to them. I knew who I was writing about; I knew how I wanted it to end; but I had no idea how I was going to get there. In fact, in the beginning, the final chapter was my first chapter, but when I saw that wasn't going to work, I had to move it. What became my opening was buried within the manuscript. I didn't write out scenes on index cards and paste them on a bulletin board and move them around. I tried that. It worked, but it didn't really work. My characters told me where to take them.

About a hundred thousand words later, I learned about Second Wind Publishing through Barnhill's bookstore in Winston-Salem and sent off the first chapter to the publisher. After 3 months, I was asked to send the entire manuscript. And that was that. I signed the contract. I consider myself very fortunate. Compared to finding a publisher for your work, writing is easy.

Excerpt from *Dancing at all the Weddings*

Elaine stared at the flames in the fireplace, unable to look at him now. All the romance had gone out of those crackling logs burning in the fireplace.

Jake broke the awkward silence. "You're choosing your talent as a *haus frau* in Boston with David Alter over the bright lights in Hollywood with Jake Applebaum."

"Sometimes on the way to your dream, you can fall into an even better one." Did she mean it? Was she still sitting on the fence? Did she want him to imitate the final scene of *An Officer and a Gentleman* when Richard Gere picks up Debra Winger and carries her out of the factory?

"Elaine. Elaine. Elaine." He wasn't ready to end this. "This isn't only about your career. It's about being with the person you love. I thought that was me."

"Sometimes love isn't enough."

"I thought you told me you weren't getting what you needed out of the marriage."

"The receiving is in the giving."

"You didn't learn that from me."

"It's very Zen."

"It's very bullshit." It wasn't in Jake's nature to beg, but he wasn't giving up so easily. Not like before. "I believe that love is all there is."

Why did love hurt so much? She loved him with all her heart. But she had other responsibilities. She knew she was turning her back on the true love of her life. Maybe all women had a guy like Jake in their lives. The love they had tucked away so they could move forward and lead sensible, sane, and ordered lives. The lives their mothers picked out for them because they knew better and only wanted their daughter's happiness.

"I don't want to re-create you. I won't make you into who I think you should be. I'll continue to develop myself; you'll continue to develop yourself. We're good apart, but we're better together. If that isn't love, my sweetheart, I don't know what is." Jake spoke from deep within.

"You can't dance at all the weddings." God! Her mother's words and now hers.

"Where did you learn you can't have it all? Who taught you that crap?"

Elaine realized she already had the thing she'd been searching for. Constancy.

She would be forever grateful for this time with Jake instead of going through life wondering what might have been. There would always be a place in her heart for Jake Applebaum. But he was her past, not her future. Her mother had been right. David is the kind you marry.

Outside the inn, the cold air stung like an ice pack on their faces. Despite all that had been said, he couldn't believe it was over. "I have this image of us each going through our lives with other husbands and other wives and then at the end, we're together."

She couldn't let herself be swept up in his movie-esque fantasy. She had made her decision. "We have to go now." She couldn't look at him. If she had, she would have seen his lovely green eyes filled with tears.

They sat for a while in the car, watching the ocean waves beating against the sand. Every now and again, the back of their hands brushed lightly, but they didn't look at one another. They caught the deep orange and blood-red sunset, like none they'd ever seen before. It was an awesome sight as it shifted into amber and then pale apricot before fading away.

* * *

Recently, I completed the first draft of my new novel. I had no idea how or what I was going to write. I knew I wanted romance, but I wanted it to be funny. I went to my notebooks. Lots of short stories, lots of unfinished notes—that type of thing. Every writer knows about that. Be truthful, I told myself. No caricatures; real characters. *What do you really want to talk about now?* I asked myself. Through these questions and inner examination, my answer came. And I'm having a wonderful time with these new characters. Once again, I'm in intellectual prison and loving it.

What's my process? Sometimes one line from someone, a line in a movie, or something I've heard on television might help jumpstart the process. Or reading my journal. That's always full of adventure. I'm a writer who doesn't read very much; at least not when I'm writing. I like the classics. I like biographies of folks in the entertainment business and some crime fiction. But mostly, I'm a movie fan. I think my ideas come from there. And yet, writing a screenplay isn't my natural bent.

I like what I do now. I like writing the details. I like using adjectives. You have to struggle to find the word. Then you have to find the right word. Then you have to find the exact word. And then 10,000 words become 22,000 words, then 26,000 words, then 35,000 words, and eventually you're done. How did I ever do that? I rarely remember. In fact, once a project is finished, I don't remember what I went through to get there.

When I'm not writing, I get depressed. Nothing in my life is right. The furniture is wrong. The apartment is wrong. I look fat. And when I start writing again and I'm obsessed, all is well—I'm not fat; I love where I live; everyday is a good hair day.

We used to have a saying about acting: No matter how talented you are, it isn't any good if it stays in your living room. It's the same with writing. Eventually, it has to get out there doing its own thing.

17

There are contests galore now, writing groups, and the internet has completely changed the publishing business. First, you have to write for yourself; at least I think so. But the truth is I want my book read by others, and I want it to be praised and loved as much as I loved writing it. Risky business. I don't know. Maybe it's better just to write and not worry about what others think. Woody Allen is very clear about writing for himself. Out of something like forty films, he only thinks a few of them were liked and accepted by others. And he doesn't care. He keeps churning out one a year.

Not too long ago, I was one of many invited to attend an informal reading of someone's play. I asked the playwright what else he had written. The response was (and I'm paraphrasing): "It's my first play; something I've been working on in my spare time for four or five years. I've written mostly poetry, but I call myself a playwright." In my opinion, if he really believed in his play, he would have stayed with it; he would have become obsessed by it. And that's the key word: Obsession. You must be obsessed with your writing.

You can't multitask when you write. You have something to say? Write it down to the bones. Write it, rewrite it . . . repeat rewrite . . . finish it, and then move on. Connect to the work. Believe in it. Call on your own experiences, your emotions, your feelings. Use your five senses to heighten awareness of your surroundings. If needs be, take an acting class. With acting, you have to study the sub-text. As a writer, you are writing the sub-text. First, write what you know and then embellish using your imagination. Please don't write about something you know nothing about without extensive research. Look at old photographs. I love what Arthur Miller said about writing: It should be so truthful that when you read it back, you're embarrassed.

To get going, set aside two hours a day—either early morning or late at night. Don't worry about finishing it each session. Stop at two hours. It will give you something to get back to, to pick up from. Next day, re-read what you wrote. Spend another two hours. Keep this routine up as long as needed. Before you know it, you'll be writing for three hours, and then four hours. You don't know where it will take you once you begin the project. Writing is lonely. Not everyone can do it. If you can attend any writing workshops, do it.

Even the dullest presenter/leader will spark an idea.

One last word: Nothing one writes is ever wasted. Keep those notes on bits of paper; napkins; toilet paper. In one of my novels, I used part of a story I wrote when I was thirteen years old! It worked then (I got an A minus); and it works today!

Interview with Susan Surman

What is your book about?

Vivacious and talented Elaine Richman is faced with choices: A risky life in the New York theatre; an exciting life with college sweetheart, actor/director Jake Applebaum in Hollywood; a secure life in Boston with predictable lawyer David Alter, the match anointed by her domineering mother because 'he's the kind you marry.' On the way to a dream, it is possible to collide with another dream's seduction, only to learn there is no fulfillment on the path to safety. Elaine goes through the wringer to meet herself, proving there is no expiration date on talent or true love.

How long had the idea been developing before you wrote it?

I had an idea for a short story—this was maybe 4 years before I expanded it—the character was the same, but had a different name, etc. I invited an audience to a reading to get some feedback. I knew it was the germ for something more which had to be developed. That story is in the book covering several chapters.

How much of you is hidden in the characters?

I think everything I write has an element of autobiographical tones. Born in Boston, I moved to London, then Sydney, as an actress and writer as Susan Kramer or Gracie Luck. I traveled the world, returned to the US–what I've done really with all my books is fictionalized fact.

How long did it take to write Dancing at all the Weddings?

Two years. It just wasn't finished until it was finished. Eventually, it was time to let it go. You have to let all these people you've invented go out and live their own lives. Empty nest syndrome sets in so you just have to start developing new characters.

What did you do for research?

I use a lot of the places I've been, but to be sure I had updated information, I researched online; in magazines; talking to people. Mostly, I was really writing what I knew about and one of the main male characters is based solely on a real person. Perhaps the novel depicts the way I would have liked it to turn out with him. That's why it's called 'romance.' It can be anything you like. Romance, I mean. And on paper, it's safe.

What was your technique to stay on track and develop your story?

It was very hard to keep track of the ages. I'd never done anything like this before. One year was usually my time frame. This book spans 28 years. I had to go back to the 1970's. I kept lots and lots of notes. As math isn't my strong suit, it wasn't easy figuring out their ages at any given time, but I did it by working backwards with ages. I went over and over it.

Since writing your first book, what has changed?

Now people introduce me as the author or the writer. I like that.

What is the most difficult part of the writing process?

The ideas. Coming up with the ideas.

Does writing come easy?

Sometimes; usually not. But you keep going. You have to become addicted to your own words.

Where do you keep future ideas?

I've lots of notebooks with ideas. Big notebooks; little notebooks. And scraps of paper. Will I ever get to them? Who knows? Maybe just one sentence from something looms, and I'll use it.

What is the best writing advice you ever got?

The best writing advice was from author, screenwriter, Joe Schrank. When I first started writing or rather 'thinking' I was going to write,

I didn't really know how to do it. He said, "Put aside 2 hours a day to start. That's all. Clear everything off the desk, and just do it." It was actually the first draft for *You're Never Alone With Schizophrenia*. He liked the title and said if I didn't write it, he was going to steal it. That's all it took for me to sit down and do it.

What is the first story you remember writing?

I was 13; 1953. I don't remember what grade I was in. I still have it. I got an A minus. "The Will to Dance." I don't know where it came from because it's about a ballet dancer. I'm not a ballet dancer. Anyway, I actually used it in my *Sacha* book. So nothing is wasted.

What last words would you leave?

In *Weddings*, the main character is at her mother's side as she is dying. Mother's last words to her daughter: "If you use a public toilet, remember to hover." My last words are more profound: Stay curious.

Finding Time to Write & Overcoming Writer's Block:
Two Sides Of The Same Coin
By
Mairead Walpole
Author of:
A Love Out of Time

In some ways, this article falls into the "if you can't be an example to others, then you can be a cautionary tale" category. It seems that if I can find the time to write these days, then I sit at the keyboard struggling to weave a story worth reading, or writing. When the ideas flow effortlessly, I can't seem to find the time to set them down before they drift out of reach.

Finding time to write depends somewhat on how you write. Are you the type of writer who has to go old school with lined paper and pencil/pen? Are you tied to a desktop computer? Do you have a laptop or some other form of mobile device (tablet, netbook, etc.) that makes it easier to take your writing on the go? Then there is the question of environment. Are you able to curl up anywhere or do you need to be sitting in more of an office type structure—desk chair, desk or tabletop surface? Can you tune out what's going on around you or do you need to have silence?

If you are the type of person who is tied to a desktop computer and requires the surroundings to be just so with absolutely no interruptions or distractions, finding time to write if you are juggling family and career can be problematic. Not impossible, but you will have to work harder at establishing boundaries and carving out that time than a person who "has laptop, can travel" and could block out the sounds of two young boys reenacting the battle scenes from every war prior to WWI in the same room.

I've used several strategies to find time to write.

Kickin' it Old School

From time to time, like once baseball season starts back up, I find that reverting to the legal pad or spiral notebook and a decent mechanical pencil is a lifesaver when it comes to writing. Then when I sit down at the computer to transcribe what I have written, I can perform the basic editing and re-writes to put the scene(s) into the story. I prefer the paper and pencil to my laptop in this setting for two reasons: theft prevention and preventing interruptions. Very few people are going to be tempted to steal or "borrow" my trusty legal pad, but my laptop might be a bit too tempting. Since I have two sons playing ball and in different divisions, I am often walking back and forth between two fields to watch the games. Carting a legal pad or notebook and a pencil is a lot easier than taking a laptop and I can leave the legal pad unattended if I need to. The second is the interruption factor. For some reason, writing in something that looks like a journal or on a legal pad appears to be more private that typing on a computer. No one ever walks up to me and starts chatting if I am writing in a notebook, but if I am typing on the computer— people want to see what I am doing or strike up a conversation about whether or not I have found a wi-fi hot spot or what's on YouTube.

I always have a notebook in my car for those moments like waiting in the doctor's office for an appointment or waiting for Tae Kwon Do classes to end. For Christmas, a friend gave me a lovely leather bound journal with lined pages for my writing. It is large enough to write it comfortably and still fit in my purse or my son's bat bag. I'm looking forward to using it this year when I can carve out a moment here and there to write.

What's for lunch?

If you have a job with a company owned computer, purchase a flash drive and put your manuscript on it. (Incidentally, this serves a dual purpose of being a back-up copy.) Take the flash drive to work and pack your lunch instead of going out or working through lunch, plug in and work on your manuscript. Or take your own laptop or tablet to work with you and work on your manuscript during your break. You don't need to do this every day, but perhaps pick one day a week that you set aside for writing through lunch.

Mommy/Daddy needs to decompress

This one is sometimes harder to finagle, but everyone needs an hour or so to recharge the mental batteries. Most nights, I read a book or watch something on TV to wind down before bed. When I need to do some writing this is often one of the easiest blocks of time I can carve out. I have a laptop, so I just prop myself up in bed with a laptop desk and write until I am sleepy or my husband complains about the clicking of my fingernails on the keyboard. If I am in a spot where I can't stop working, it is relatively easy to move to the den or some other spot in the house.

The Muse will see you now

For some odd reason, if I schedule an appointment to do something, I keep it even if it's with myself. There is something about writing down that appointment on the calendar that makes it unbreakable. If you can't squeeze out an hour of time somewhere in your life, block an hour of time and use it to write. If you have kids, you can order or put in a movie and set them up with popcorn and juice boxes. This will give you about an hour and a half to shut yourself away and write. On nice days, I often send my kids outside to play and then I set myself up on the porch with my laptop. I can keep an eye on them but also get some writing in. When play time is over, I've gotten some writing done and they have burned off some of their energy so everyone is happy.

And now for some other ideas

My brother-in-law recently bought voice recognition software for his job because he was finding the amount of paperwork and writing overwhelming. While he is a pretty good two fingered typist, the amount of paperwork he inherited with his new managerial position that came without any administrative assisting was about to bury him. He loves his "Dragon" is how he puts it. We were talking about it at Christmas dinner and he strongly suggested I try it out for my writing. According to him, I could put it on my laptop and dictate sections of the book while driving to/from work, on long car trips to visit family, or even while chauffeuring the kids around town. I plan to research this a bit, but thought I would pass the idea along.

I used to use a handheld Dictaphone or tape recorder in the car for capturing my ideas or working through scenes and character development. The downside of this is transcribing it later.

I've never needed complete silence to work, nor have I needed to be seated at a desk in a proper chair, but I do have some friends who require that. What one friend does is negotiate with her spouse. He gets to go hunting/fishing with no complaints from her, if he will take the kids out that evening or the next day so that she gets a couple of hours of down time to write. The barter system seems to work quite well for them. Another friend stays late or goes in an hour early to work one day a week so that she can get some writing done.

I've found the time to write but I got nuthin.

We've all been there. Two hours go by and all you have written is "Chapter One" and you've changed the font type twice and the size once. You have developed a severe case of Writer's Block. Don't panic, don't toss your computer out the window, and don't write yourself off as a writer, this too will pass. And, when you least expect it, it will happen again so find some strategies that work for you.

A creative writing professor of mine in college told us that the best way to overcome Writer's Block was to write your way out of it. Write your way out of Writer's Block? Er, really?

Yes, really. When I am dealing with a bout of that wretched state, I write. I will admit that most of what I write is absolute dreck that will never see the light of day, but just like a walk on the beach after a storm, amid the sea foam and debris one can find the occasional treasure. On occasion, what I write about evolves into a blog article or a completely new storyline. On other occasions, the only response is to hold down the backspace key or use the highlight CTRL X combo.

I limit the amount of time that I will spend writing my way out of the block. Usually 15 to 30 minutes a day. (I don't want to develop any repetitive stress injuries from the deleting or highlight CTRL X maneuvers.) Some folks may need more than that, but this time frame works for me. I also allow the Muse to lead me down creative paths that weren't in my original storyline. Writer's Block can be a good thing. It can help you see a plot that has stagnated or a character that you originally thought was a minor one should be expanded.

One of the first things that I will do is go back to my original notes and any outlines I put together. I tend to do an analysis of the basic plot. Does it make sense? Do the characters seem flat or unbelievable? I look at the outline from a reader's perspective to see if I can find any gaps or flaws in the logical progression. Then I re-read what I have written. If still am not getting anywhere, I will ask a trusted friend or critique partner to read what I have done thus far and give me some feedback. And, I continue to write. Eventually, the block will lift and I am back on track, perhaps with a different story than the one I started out with.

Excerpt From *A Love Out of Time*

"Would it be too much to ask for a hand out of this?" he asked with a wry grin on his face. Trying to keep her mirth from bubbling back to the surface, she came to the edge of the pool reaching out her hand to help him. As soon as he grasped her hand, she knew what was going to happen. Perhaps it was the mischievous smile he gave her or perhaps the knowledge of what she'd do in his stead. In any event, feeling him tug her into the pool on top of him she had one of those—duh—moments where she truly doubted her intelligence. This was the oldest trick in the book and she fell, literally, for it.

Splashing water into his face, she growled, "Oh you, you...you are in some kinda trouble buster. I had to get this dress specially made." Then she remembered one of the reasons she had gotten the dress made rather than buying a vintage dress. "Damn, my cell phone and my car keys!!" Reaching in the hidden pocket she pulled out her sodden phone and keys. "Guess the key-less entry isn't going to work tonight..." She leaned over to kiss his cheek but noticed that look was back on his face. "What? I'm not really mad. It will be a pain to replace them but it's okay."

Alden swallowed his fear and asked, "Where am I?"

"What do you mean, 'where are you?'—where do you think you are? You are in a reflecting pool in the formal gardens at Lindsay House."

"Maybe my question would be better phrased as, when am I in a reflecting pool at Lindsay House?" he said in a strained voice.

"When?" she asked, confused by the emphasis he'd placed on the word.

"Please, you have to tell me—it may sound odd—but please." A chill went down her spine that had nothing to do with the water temperature. The timber of his voice was familiar to her; a sensation like déjà vu was sweeping over her. I know him, she thought, I know him well. He is my...my what? But that wasn't possible, she had never laid eyes on him until tonight, she was sure of that. One did not forget a man who looked, or kissed, like that.

"Olivia, please answer my question. What is today's date?"

Her chill increased to full-blown shivering, "It is Saturday, May 26th 2006."

Alden was quiet as he helped her out of the pool and wrapped his arms around her. Holding her tightly, his chin resting on the top of her head, he whispered, "For me, the year is 1877."

Interview with Mairead Walpole

What is your book about?

A Love Out of Time is a time travel paranormal romance between a pair of soul mates separated by 129 years.

How long had the idea of your book been developing before you began to write the story?

Almost a year passed between when the idea came to me and when I decided to put it down on paper.

What inspired you to write this particular story?

It came out of a strange dream I had about a week before I delivered my second child. I'd had a series of really odd dreams the last few weeks of my pregnancy and they all revolved around this character pulled out of his time by his soul mate to join her in her time. The idea stuck with me and I couldn't let it go. I spent about a year turning it around in my head.

The catalyst for actually writing the story instead of thinking about writing the story came from my sister-in-law. Annie was living with us at the time while she got back on her feet financially. One night, frustrated by all the "follow your dreams not the money" talk between her and my husband while I was juggling the family finances and struggling to climb the corporate ladder, I sort of had a meltdown and questioned when exactly would it be my turn to "follow my dreams" instead of doing the corporate grind to support the family. In my defense, I was sort of in an overwhelmed, overworked, and overcommitted place. I had just finished my MBA, which my boss said I needed to have for him to promote me to the next pay grade, while working 50+ hours a week all while renovating our house and putting on an addition. Looking back, I am rather amazed it was only a minor meltdown and not a full on nervous breakdown or psychotic break.

In any event, after I was done with my histrionics, she just looked at me and said, "So, quit yer bitchin' and do it." I started tossing out my excuses about the time constraints of my job and trying to be a good mom and wife. She pointed out that I had just finished an intensive program for my MBA, so if I could make time to do that while working and being a wife/mother, then I could certainly find some time to write. To seal the deal, she made a bet with my husband that I wouldn't do it. Anyone who knows me will tell you that (within reason) I don't like being told I am not capable of doing something and taking a bet against me for something like that is a good way to lose some money! Long story short—she came home a few days later with the information about the Gather.com First Chapters contest and that was all it took. I was off and writing.

How much of yourself is hidden in the characters in the book?

None intentionally, but I am told by those who know me that parts of my personality appear in most of the characters. I don't know that it is possible to write without including pieces of you in the characters.

Tell us a little about your main characters. Who was your favorite? Why?

Merlon "Taly" Taliesin is my favorite. I guess because I have always loved stories about Merlin and he's a fun character to write about. He will be in all of the books that are following the first in this series.

Alden, the hero, and Olivia, (the heroine) are tied for second place in terms of favorites. Alden is something of a fish out of water, poor guy. He's trying to get over the loss of the woman he believes to be his soul mate and taking a simple stroll down a garden path tosses him 129 years into the future where he meets the reincarnation of that woman. 19th century colliding with the 21st century, he had to adapt quickly and the situation gave me lots to play with.

Olivia is something of a jaded romantic (and I admit that this is definitely a trait of mine) and she thinks that life would have been simpler in Alden's time, but she soon realizes that she's not a misfit in her own time. Then there are Moira and Karl, Alden's relatives. First cousins a number of times removed I guess. I'm a Virginian, but darned if I could tell you what the exact familial classification would be.

There is a villain, of course, Olivia's former boyfriend Jack. Jack is your basic garden variety sociopath. While he isn't a favorite character per se, I am not done with him yet, or rather, he is not done with Alden, Olivia, or Taly. He'll be back in at least one later book.

Who is your most unusual/most likeable character?

Taly is unusual, but maybe not the most likeable unless you enjoy slightly twisted characters who are neither wholly good nor evil. I suppose I would have to say that the most likeable character is Moira. She's that sorta quirky, loyal best friend who has your back no matter what and won't hesitate to tell you that if you wear that outfit, the proper accessory will be a "wide load" sign across your butt. Just being with Moira will banish the blues and have you smiling.

How long did it take you to write your book?

The first draft was 30 days from typing the first word to the last. It took an additional year to get it edited and polished enough to publish it.

How much of a story do you have in mind before you start writing it?

For *A Love Out of Time*, all of the basic storyline and the main characters had been created in my head. Once I started writing, the rest came together almost seamlessly. I had some minor detours and a few subplots that popped up during the writing, but the muscular-skeletal structure was all there at the beginning.

I can't say that is the case for all of my stories though. Some start as a chapter. I'll write it and then leave it to "jell" as I work through the plotline. Once I have a basic outline, then I might start to work.

Did you do any research for the book? If so, how did you do it? (searching Internet, magazines, other books, etc.)

Yes, I used the internet primarily but also relied on Bullfinch's Mythology and some other non-fiction books around Celtic mythology or legends.

How do you develop and differentiate your characters?

It might sound a wee bit crazy, but in general the characters come into existence in my head. Whenever a new character appears, I write out a page or two about each of them. What they look like, height, weight, build, hair and eye color—so that I can clearly see them in my mind. Then I capture their basic personality traits—optimist, pessimist, witty, jaded, or some combination. If they have any odd habits, or mannerisms, I will note those as well. I essentially create an entire history for them—what they do for a living, where they grew up, what their family was like. Much of this backstory never appears in the writing, but it helps ground me.

Do you have specific techniques you use to develop the plot and stay on track?

I sketch out a rough outline but it is not an exact science by any means. Sometimes my outlines are tossed out early on in the process and other times—I can't write the story without them.

How (or when) do you decide that you are finished writing a story?

To me, that is sort of like asking how do you know you're in love. You just know. Before I start writing, I do have an idea of where the story is going to end and in a few cases, I even write the ending before I start the first chapter. Then it just becomes a matter of connecting A to Z.

What is your goal for the book, ie: what do you want people to take with them after they finish reading the story?

My goal is to entertain. I don't care about writing "the great American novel" or some masterpiece of literary fiction, which strikes some people as odd given my background. If I can provide someone with a bit of mind candy to take them to another time and place, if only for 15 minutes here and there between the job, the housework, the chauffeuring of kids—then I have achieved my goal.

What challenges did you face as you wrote this book?

Making the time to write was the biggest challenge. As I mentioned above, I was working 50+ hours a week. My husband was working as a catering chef for one of the premier catering companies in the area, so I was for all intents and purposes a single mom where the house/yard work and child care was concerned. My kids were 4 and 1 at the times so I wrote whenever I could find or squeeze in a few minutes and used most of the tips mentioned in my article.

What was the most difficult part about writing the book?

I don't do vulnerable comfortably or easily and there is something about the writing process that I find triggers a sense of being vulnerable. Whether or not you intend it, your writing reflects quite a bit about you. I am selective about what I reveal to people about myself, it's not that I am an intensely private person because I am not, but I do like being able to control what I reveal and to whom. Once you publish your work, be it formally or through blogs and interviews, that control is gone. It's something I struggle with and probably always will. And, it is probably why I write under a pen name.

Do you think writing this book changed your life? How so?

It has made me more comfortable with being vulnerable. At first, I was very careful about having any connections between my pen name and my real name. Now, if someone really wanted to find out who Mairead Walpole really is, it isn't difficult.

How does your environment/upbringing color your writing?

I think that anyone reading my work would pick up on some themes that give a hint about my upbringing. It's unavoidable. Family dynamics tend to pop up in my writing. I also had a very close relative who was a true sociopath, so there is usually a character somewhere in my writing with similar traits. Sometimes they are the villain, sometimes the anti-hero/heroine, and sometimes they are a minor character.

What's your writing schedule like? Do you strive for a certain amount of words each day?

I can't say that I have a "schedule" of any kind. When the muse is on me—I have to set limits or I'd write all day and night, stopping only to feed my kids and the pets. I try to allow an hour at a sitting. At the end of the hour—I force myself to get up and do something else, laundry, play a game with the kids, run errands, clean something, then I can go back to the writing for another hour.

Do you prefer to write at a particular time of day?

Early morning, if I have the luxury of a choice but anytime will suffice.

Do you have a favorite snack food or favorite beverage that you enjoy while you write?

Coffee, black, or Chai Tea with raw honey.

What are you working on right now?

I have a couple of projects in the works right now. One is the sequel to *A Love Out of Time*. This one is Jocelyn's story. To those unfamiliar with my first book, Jocelyn is the oldest sister of Olivia, heroine of my first book. She, like Olivia, isn't entirely human but her gifts aren't the same as her sister's. Many of the characters from the first book make an appearance, and some like Taly will be main characters as Jocelyn finds her soul mate in another paranormal being. If you like vampires, this will be a slightly different take on what they are and what they want.

The second project is a story called *Love, Blood, and Hunting*. It is not a paranormal romance although some of the characters from my paranormal romance series make cameo appearances. This is a story about vengeance and redemption. My heroine is a former prosecutor turned judge with a reputation for always getting the bad guy or girl and putting them down—in the purely legal sense. Her beliefs and her character are challenged when her brother-in-law gets away with the brutal murder of her sister. The first part of the book lays the groundwork for the sister's relationship with her killer and the heroine's unsuccessful attempts to help her sister escape an abusive relationship. The second part of the book deals with the investigation, trial and aftermath. Sometimes, who we think we are and who we really are will surprise you.

The third project is a tongue in cheek account of my journey with becoming a mother on the other side of 35, (the far other side, like celebrating the big 4-0 with a newborn), titled *Parenting with Hormones and Duct Tape: Confessions of a Failed Super-Mom*. From fixing a hem to patching up a "lovey"—duct tape really does have 101 uses. As for the hormones, is it peri-menopause or post-partum depression? Who knows but dark chocolate does help.

My last project is to do some intensive re-writes to the first novel I ever wrote and wasn't comfortable enough to have published. It is a legal thriller called *Violation of Privilege*. The novel centers around a paralegal who stumbles upon documents that someone is willing to kill for during a document review. Toss in a dad on the run from the feds, a chance to bring a greedy bio-medical company concerned with profit over health to justice, and a climbing body count—she's got a lot on her docket.

What was the first story you remember writing?

A short story about a little girl who falls through a mirror and finds her imaginary friend is real. It really freaked me out a bit when I saw a re-run episode of *Lost in Space* where something similar happened.

What is the most difficult part of the whole writing process?

It depends. Sometimes it is the time management thing, sometimes it is overcoming writer's block, and sometimes it is not letting the constant interruptions of my kids turn me into a shrieking banshee. I admit, I have used the phrase, "unless someone is bleeding or has bones poking through the skin, don't bug me" on more than one occasion.

What is the easiest part of the writing process?

Typing "the end" when you're done.

What's been the most surprising part of being a writer?

How good it feels when someone tells you that they really loved your book.

What do you like to read?

I am partial to Sci-Fi/Fantasy, Paranormal Romance/Urban Fantasy, and mystery/thrillers. I love to read so anything is fair game.

What, in your opinion, are the essential qualities of a good story?

It has to have characters that are believable and that you can either understand or connect with. There has to be a storyline that interests me and has a logical progression to some end. The story has to been reasonably well written. You don't need a degree in English to be a good writer, but I get a bit distracted if the writing is lacking in the technical basics of proper grammar, word choice, and punctuation.

Who gave you the best writing advice you ever received and what was it?

My 9th grade English teacher, Mrs. Martin (Hermitage High School), told me to just write and worry about the technical aspects after I got my words on paper.

What advice you would give to an aspiring author?

See above. I would also add in that put publication out of your mind. The goal is to write a story you feel good about. Once you have it done and you've gotten it polished to the point where you can let it go, then worry about publication. I think focusing on the publication piece before you get the story down can hamper your progress.

What one book, written by someone else, do you wish you'd

written yourself?

I've never thought about that before, but I don't think I would want to have written someone else's book. What I would like is to be one of those "Cinderella Stories" like Stephanie Meyer or JK Rowling!

What words would you like to leave the world when you are gone?

Who says I will be gone?

Seriously, I'm not that into leaving words behind to immortalize my existence. If I had to leave any words of wisdom to the world it would be, "Figure out how to get along with each other."

Where can people learn more about your books?

Second Wind Publishing's website.

Is there anything else you'd like to tell us about yourself or your books?

To everyone who has bought my book, thank you and I hope you enjoyed it. Oh, and I promise I will get some more out there for you. Soon.

Creating Incredible but Credible Characters
By
Pat Bertram
Author of:
More Deaths Than One, Daughter Am I
A Spark of Heavenly Fire, Light Bringer, **and**
Grief: The Great Yearning

🐦

People often tell me they feel they know my characters, as if my story people were a part of their lives, which is always wonderful to hear. It means I did my job. And it means the readers did their job. Incredible but credible characters are a combined effort. Characters are conceived in the author's imagination, but they come alive in readers' imaginations.

A character's story begins with a gleam in her parents' eye and ends with her death. The story we tell is but a fraction of that life, and where we choose to begin and where we, the writer, choose to end defines the story. If we begin with a crime and end with a resolution of that crime, we have a mystery. If we begin with a girl meeting a boy or a woman meeting a man and end with happily ever after, we have a romance. If we chronicle the rise and fall of the character's fortunes, we could have a tragedy, a family drama or any number of stories.

The illusion of a well-told story is such that, whatever the genre, by the end of the book readers know the character as well as they know themselves and their friends. Readers know, or think they know, everything in the character's life that brought her to crisis and how everything in the character's life will work out after the story problem is resolved. By giving readers the essence of the character, we give them the means to continue the character's story long after the book has come to an end.

How do we work this sleight of hand? By showing the character in action and in relationships. By defining the character through decisions in moments of crisis.

In the prologue of *Light Bringer*, Helen comes home from working a double shift at the hospital to find a baby on her doorstep. She shows her nurturing characteristics by taking care of the child, Rena. She shows the beginning of a metamorphosis from staid nurse to loving mother by putting off calling the authorities so she can enjoy the child bit longer. But what really defines her is how she acts in a moment of crisis. Rena, a magical child, or at least a precocious one, tells Helen they have to leave, that her invisible playmate says "they" are after Rena and when they find her, they will kill Helen. Helen doesn't hesitate. She packs up her car and her life and escapes with the baby.

Helen's decision defines not only her own character, but also the character of the baby, the character of the invisible playmate, and perhaps even the story itself. It is through such defining moments that we can create a character so real readers believe they know more about the character than was ever actually written.

In older novels, especially the classics, authors wrote page after page of character description, telling us who their characters are. Those authors dissected their characters' motivations, told us their every thought, explained every feeling. Today's readers, myself included, have no patience for such long drawn-out static passages. We want to get right into the heart of the story. We want to learn who the character is by what she does, who she knows, and how she acts and reacts.

Showing, not telling, is a basic axiom of writing for today's market, but it is often hard to resist the urge to explain since you know far more about your characters than you can or should put in your novel. Still, by restraining yourself and letting readers be part of the creation process, letting them find their own explanations for what your characters do, you give them a stake in the characters and the story. And so your characters come alive.

Gender

To create a character, we begin with gender. If your character is of the opposite gender than yours, make sure you know how the other half thinks, feels, and speaks, otherwise your character might seem more of a caricature than a real person.

There are basic differences between the genders. For example, women have better peripheral vision, so while both men and women ogle each other with the same frequency, men are caught gazing more often than women are.

Brain scans show that women have between fourteen and sixteen areas that evaluate others' behavior, while men have only four to six. Because of this, women are better at juggling several unrelated topics in a single conversation. They also use five vocal tones to make their points. Since men can only identify three of those tones, they often miss what women are trying to say. So men accuse women of not being direct and women accuse men of not listening.

Women ask questions to show interest in the person; men ask questions to gain information. Women find that talking about a problem provides relief; men feel that talking about a problem is dwelling on the negative. Women think that continuing to discuss the problem demonstrates support; men want to make a decision and forget it. Women provide peripheral details because they want to be understood; men just want them to make their point. Women think that talking about a relationship brings people closer; men generally think it's useless.

There is a wide spectrum of both male and female behavior, though, so you can write a character however you wish as long as you can make it work.

You make it work by ensuring there is a reason—a motivation—for your characters behavior. We learn much about characters from their actions, but what the character does is not the defining element. The defining element is *why* the character does what he does. Characters can do anything, though the actions must be psychologically true and consistent. A character who is cowardly but does not hesitant to rescue someone from danger without any reference to fear or a believable reason for the action is not a well-written character.

When it comes to storytelling, character is all. The characters and plot (what the characters do and why) should be so intertwined that we never see them as separate.

Names Matter

Scarlett O'Hara was originally called Pansy. If Margaret Mitchell had kept that name, would her epic novel ever have become so popular? A character with the name of Pansy could be sweet and biddable with rare moments of stubbornness, but since "Pansy" lacks the harsh consonants of "Scarlett," the name doesn't sound as if it belongs to an iron-willed character who could catch and keep the attention of such a worldly man as Rhett Butler.

Though Scarlett fits the name of the character in *Gone with the Wind*, it could not be the name of a medieval heroine. In those days, the most popular name was Mary, with Elizabeth coming in a distant second. I suppose if *Gone with the Wind* were written in the 1980s, Scarlett's name would have been Heather. Odd to think that in another forty years, youth will scorn that name as being old-fashioned, fit only for elderly women, like the name Effie is today.

I had fun naming my aged gangsters in *Daughter Am I*. In keeping with the times of their youth—bootlegger times, that is—I gave them nicknames that matched their characters. I called my wise old conman "Teach," my dapper little forger "Kid Rags," my ex-wrestler "Crunchy."

And then there's my hero, poor Mary. She starts out so young and innocent, and ends up on a road trip with six feisty old gangsters and one ex-nightclub dancer. I had not intended for her to keep the name Mary. It's so not the name of a heroine of today! Nor is my Mary a medieval maiden. I named the character Mary Stuart after Mary Stuart Masterson in the film *Bed of Roses* because both Marys were strong but vulnerable when it came to love, both were very smart yet a bit naive. I never did change my Mary's name. By the time I finished the book, the character and the name were inextricably entwined. At least it's fairly innocuous. Like Margaret Mitchell, I could have named my heroine Pansy. Ouch.

What Does Your Character Want?

The most compelling characters are those who want something desperately and who will do anything to get it, which is why Scarlett O'Hara is such a perennially popular character. Frankly, my dear, I find her a bit over the top—selfish and greedy and way too egocentric. Still, her wanting does make for a compelling character.

At its most basic, a story is about want. The main character wants something, and someone or something is preventing her from getting it. The want can be as simple as a good night's sleep, as personal as a lover, or as complicated as world peace. In the end, the character gets what she wants or she doesn't get it. Sometimes she gets what she needs, which is just as satisfying for the reader because such an ending gives a story a sense of rightness, of poetic justice.

BOB STARK, the point-of-view character of *More Deaths Than One*, wants serenity, though what he gets are nightmares, both the sleeping and the waking kind. Debilitated by headaches, he doesn't have the energy to discover the truth, but Kerry, a young woman he meets in a coffee shop, goads him into it. When Kerry is threatened, though, he becomes what he needs to be to keep her safe.

A Spark of Heavenly Fire has four point-of-view characters, all of whom want something.

All KATE CUMMINGS wants is a good night's sleep.

Her husband, a semi-invalid, committed suicide thirteen months ago. Many times during the years of his illness she could have treated him a little better than she did, and she is haunted by her own mean spirit.

Then the red death descends on Colorado, the entire state is quarantined, and martial law is declared. As a patient's advocate and an insomniac, forty-two-year-old Kate sees more than her share of the horror. People with bright red eyes spewing blood, then falling down—dead. Tanks and trigger-happy troops patrolling the streets. Men in biohazard suits throwing bodies into the back of delivery vans.

Now she wants not to be afraid.

All JEREMY KING wants is to leave Colorado.

He has everything. Two Oscars for best actor. A vast Montana ranch. Wife, son, daughter. He also looks better now, at fifty-eight,

41

than he did when he was young.

Having grown up poor in Grand Junction, he hates Colorado, and only came to Denver to finish a film. As soon as the director yells cut, he's in his rented Lexus on his way to the private airfield where his jet is supposed to be ready for take-off. It isn't. Instead, armed National Guardsmen inform him that airspace is restricted. Furious that he's being treated like one of the peasants, he decides to drive home, but the mountain highway is clogged with a thousand cars going nowhere. He returns to Denver, determined to leave Colorado if it's the last thing he ever does.

All GREG PULLMAN wants is to know the truth.

Since childhood he's been consumed with the need to know why creatures act the way they do. It is no different with the red death.

After discovering that the disease is a bio-engineered organism, he tries to find out who would develop such a thing, and why. He learns that despite the ban on bio-warfare experimentation, all over the world deadly organisms are being produced and stockpiled. Bubonic plague. West Nile fever. Green monkey virus. Combinations such as smallpox with Ebola and encephalitis.

Burdened by the awful truth, he turns to his friend Kate for comfort, and finds he wants her, though he is engaged to Pippi O'Brien.

All PIPPI O'BRIEN wants is . . . well, she doesn't know what she wants.

After college, she wanted a job at a New York television station, but accepted a position as weathergirl in Denver. Now, at thirty, she wants to marry handsome Greg Pullman, but when he takes the hint and proposes, she says she'll think about it. A few days later, deciding she does love him after all, she says yes. While waiting in a bar for him that very evening, she meets Jeremy King. Feeling the full force of his personality, she leaves with him, forgetting about Greg. Now she has a new dream: lovely consort to the charismatic King.

She is signing autographs with Jeremy on a downtown street when UN soldiers arrive, level their weapons at the assembled fans, and order everyone to drop to the ground. Fighting back the urge to scream, she obeys. Those who don't obey are immediately gunned down.

Now all she wants is to accompany Jeremy on his quest to escape from Colorado.

So, that's what the characters of *More Deaths Than One* and *A Spark of Heavenly Fire* want. What do your characters want? What do they need? And in the end, do they get what they want, or do they get what they need?

Purposely Flawed Characters. Or Not.

Interesting characters make interesting stories, not the other way around. An author develops interesting characters by putting them under pressure, giving them much to lose, and allowing them to change because of their experiences. And the author makes these characters at least a bit larger than life. Who wants to read about characters who sit around watching television all the time or who repeatedly have the same tiresome argument with their children or who can't resolve their problems? We deal with that every day. We don't need to read about it. On the other hand, if the traits are too idealized, characters come across as comic book silly.

Depth of character is revealed in the choices a character makes while at risk. Without the element of risk, there is no real story, only a string of episodes. Think what Superman would be like without Kryptonite—totally uninteresting and flawed in his perfection. But Kryptonite is a purposeful flaw, put there to make Superman more interesting, which makes him seem even more of a comic book character. Oh, wait. He's supposed to be a comic book character!

To offset the problem of idealized characters, many writers try to create a purposely-flawed character, such as a boozing cop or a mother who can't communicate with her teenager, but this seems an unnecessary distraction unless, of course, it is a vital part of the character's motivation. So many flawed characters, particularly heroes with a drinking problem, have been done so often they have become nothing but cardboard cutouts. There is a long tradition of hard-drinking detectives, but there has to be a more creative way of giving characters flaws. Or not. Writers are often enthralled with the idea of flawed heroes, that they are missing the point. They don't have to give their heroes obvious flaws. By making their heroes realistic, the heroes are automatically flawed.

43

A character must lose occasionally or make mistakes. Where is the suspense if every time a character attempts to do something she succeeds? And in that loss is a shadow of the flaw, because the setback must be realistic. Did the character lose because of arrogance, assuming she knew what to do when she didn't? Did the character lose because she wasn't physically fit or knowledgeable enough? Did the character lose because she didn't plan correctly, because she was unfocused, because of her inner conflicts? Such losses force a fully realized character to change so in the end she can succeed.

In the beginning of *Daughter Am I*, twenty-five-year-old Mary Stuart has no real direction, no purpose, but when she learns she inherited a farm from her recently murdered grandparents—grandparents her father claimed had died before she was born—she becomes obsessed with finding out who they were and why someone wanted them dead. She drives halfway across the country with a feisty crew of octogenarians, friends of her grandparents, and even though she discovers they all had ties to the mob, she doesn't let her good sense override her obsession. This understandable obsession is her flaw, and if she didn't grow during the course of the story, if she didn't learn from her setbacks, the obsession could have become a fatal flaw. Fatal or not, flaw or not, Mary's obsession makes her real, makes her a bit larger than life, and makes her interesting.

To be real, a character must have strengths and weaknesses, but it's not enough simply to assign a special strength or weakness to a character—the quality needs to be tested. You can do this in one of two ways—play on the strength or play on the weakness. For example, if a character is smart but lacks physical strength, you can either place the character in a situation where the character's intelligence saves the day or you can put him in a situation where he is forced to rely on physical abilities he doesn't have.

Strengths are arbitrary and can easily become flaws. Independence can become an inability to depend on others, an ability to cope can be seen as indifference, high ethical standards can become intransigency. Which is great for a book—the resulting misunderstandings can cause conflicts among characters allows the plot or subplots to thicken. And your characters become even more credible.

Keeping your Characters Consistent

Consistency makes for a good lemon meringue pie—you don't want globules of lemon ruining the texture of the smooth filling. And consistency makes a good story—you certainly don't want globules of untruth ruining the texture of your readers' belief. I admit I'm stretching for an analogy, but still, the point is that readers will forgive a writer almost anything except inconsistencies that interrupt the flow of the story.

I once started to read a book where a man spirited away the Shah of Iran. According to the author, the Shah lived fifteen years beyond his supposed death in 1980. The operation was so secret and so successful that no one knew about it. But . . . It took only this one very high profile achievement to assure a solid client base for the man. Supposedly, word travels quickly in the very elite circles of power, and so the demand for the man's services was always in excess of his ability to produce.

What??? If no one knew that the Shah survived his death, how could word travel? And if word did travel, how could high profile clients remain "dead," especially since most of them were hiding from those in the elite circles of power? The inconsistency took me out of the story, and I never did finish reading the book.

It's almost impossible to keep inconsistencies from slipping into a story, which is why self-editing, though vital, cannot be the final editing process. We writers see consistency because we see what we meant to say. Others only see the inconsistency. I am grateful to one of my editors for finding one particular inconsistency in *Daughter Am I*. The editor wrote, "It's not clear here whether or not Mary completely removed her shirt. If she did, when she stood up and ran to the bathroom, then turned around and had the conversation with Tim, she'd have been completely topless. Given their feelings for each other, and their state of undress, it seems unlikely they would have been able to have such a lengthy conversation without biology taking over sooner."

Oops. I completely missed that. Mary took off her shirt so Tim could massage her sore back, and when the massage turned heated, Mary (engaged to someone else) runs from her feelings and hides in the bathroom. Inadvertently, I had her brazenly opening the bathroom door, standing half-naked, and starting a casual conversation—not at all what my poor innocent Mary would have done. After traveling halfway across the country in the company of seven old gangsters (well, six gangsters and one aged ex-night hall dancer) she'd lost most of her naiveté, but still, she would not have flaunted her naked breasts.

Naked breasts may pale in comparison with unsecret secret operations, but the inconsistency could have dammed the flow of the story for discerning readers. So, the moral of this tale is, if you remove your heroine's shirt or other apparel, make sure you remember her state of undress and write accordingly.

Change

Change is the reason for a story. Without change, you have an anecdote, perhaps a description of a life or a time, but no story.

Whenever there is change during the course of the story and—more immediately—during a chapter, a scene, a page, even a paragraph, it advances the story. These changes should be interesting and compelling in themselves, but they should also worsen or improve the status of a character, raise new questions in readers' minds as to the story's outcome, and prepare for scenes to come.

Changes can be major alterations in a character's life, such as the death of a loved one, or they can be as subtle as the touch of a hand. Changes can jolt the reader or give them a false sense of security so you can hit them with a major change later to better effect.

Writing doesn't just happen, nor does it happen in a vacuum. Our stories change us every bit as much as we change our stories, in an ever tightening spiral. We create episodes of change so that the characters will change, which in turn change the plot, which in turn change the whole focus of the story, which in turn changes our relationship to the story.

While writing *A Spark of Heavenly Fire*, I researched Pingfan and the human experiments that were being done there (some on American POWs) and I thought I'd found something that few others knew. Afterward, in every novel I picked up, there was a mention of Pingfan, so I had to change the focus of the book, which in turn changed the characters and how they got to the end. (The end was a given—I'd written that chapter about halfway through — I just needed to find a way to get there.) Many of the conversations I had about this Pingfan oddity ended up in the book, which gave the story an added depth.

Some psychologists say we never change in any basic way, that our characters and essential personalities are our foundation. We can only change in small ways, such as changing our habits, changing our focus, changing our perspective. This is at odds with those who say that a character must do a complete about face. That about face is possible if it is motivated, if there is a reason for your character's basic change. Normally, a smart person doesn't become stupid overnight and a stupid person doesn't become smart, though abnormal situations can create such changes. *Flowers for Algernon*, for example, or *Regarding Henry*.

Although change is important, many characters don't change— take detective novels, for example. Most of the classic detectives were the same from the first page to the last. But other characters in the stories change, and the situations change, which keep the detectives changing direction and focus. So while they themselves didn't go through any sort of metamorphosis, the stories still seemed to be about change. And perhaps the truth, as uncovered in a detective story, is a change in itself.

Sometimes a character's inability to change is the story. For example, if a character was tortured and despite the horrors, never changed, it would tell you a lot about the character, and how his non-change changed the world around him. *Forrest Gump* comes to mind.

Almost anything can bring about a change. Lies can bring about change, the truth can bring about change, a knock on the door, a trip. Even something so simple as losing weight. I had a friend, a lively teenager who was quite obese. Everyone kept telling her she would be pretty if she lost weight. She did lose a lot of weight—started a diet before school let out and spent the whole summer being active and eating right. She wasn't more attractive. And she wasn't more popular. This broke her heart. She became sullen and morose. And depressed. And regained all the weight. Which is an example of another type of change—where the character changes but ends up the same as at the beginning.

Here are some questions to ask yourself if you need to delve deeper into the changes that occur during the course of your book:

- What changes do your characters undergo?
- Do you keep the changes coming at an ever dizzying rate or do you throw small changes at your characters, changes that add up over time?
- Are your characters the same at the end of all these changes? Is their situation the same?
- Is the final outcome a major upheaval for the character or merely a change in focus?
- Do all your characters change, or just the main character?
- How do you bring about the changes?
- Are these changes logical and believable?
- Are the changes an intrinsic part of the story or just thrown in for the sake of change?

Creating Characters through Dialogue

One of the hardest techniques for new writers to handle is dialogue. When I first started out, my characters never just said something. They agreed, cautioned, reminded, mimicked, answered, contributed, guessed, explained, responded, admonished, confessed, encouraged, clarified, blurted, pointed, winced, replied, corrected, acknowledged, returned, laughed, challenged, chided, objected, contested, quipped, offered, moaned, complained, repeated, stammered, pleaded, inquired, mumbled, interrupted, confirmed, addressed, countered, advised, completed, allowed, supplied, ordered, asked, continued, chided, answered, whispered, teased, requested, hollered, echoed, declared, informed, spoke, bellowed, spit out, thundered, hissed. All within a few pages. Whew!

Even worse, I would sit and agonize over the way my characters spoke. "He responded sparingly." "She informed him haughtily." He mumbled sadly."

It was a joy to discover that modern dialogue relies primarily on "said," such a common word, the reader's gaze glides over it as if it were invisible. It was even more of a joy to discover that adverbs are frowned on. The dialogue itself, or the beat—the bit of action accompanying the dialogue—should show the character's emotion. *"I hate you", she said angrily* tells us what the character is feeling. *She picked up a rock and threw it at him. "I hate you!"* shows us what she is feeling, allowing us to become intimately involved with the character. The only time an adverb is necessary is when the character's words are at odds with his mood, such as: *"I had a great time," he said sadly.* You can also use an occasional "ly" adverb to describe the tonal quality of the character's voice. *"I hate you," he said softly.*

Besides helping identify who is speaking, beats help set the stage, tell us about the character's personality, and vary the rhythm of the dialogue. Overdone, the beats are as distracting as any other speaker attribute, so the secret is to pay attention to the flow. Do you want short snappy dialogue? Don't use beats. Do you want to slow things down a bit, keep the dialogue from seeming too disembodied? Use a few beats.

It's hard to write crowd scenes and keep each character identified without resorting to copious "said"s, but beats keep the scene moving and, if you use beats that are specific to your character, you make the various characters come alive.

This excerpt from my novel *Daughter Am I* shows the use of beats. The scene is between my hero Mary, a young woman in search of her grandparents' murderer, and a group of feisty octogenarians who are trying to help.

*   *   *

The man stopped bouncing and let his arms drop to his sides. Now that he stood relatively still, Mary could see he was skinnier than she'd first thought. A gray slouch hat tilted toward one eye, but the baggy pants cinched high above his waist and the bright flowery shirt several sizes too large marred the jaunty effect. His hands shook uncontrollably. *Parkinson's disease?*

"You must be Happy," she said.

Frowning, Happy patted his torso. "Must I be happy?" His voice deepened to what Mary assumed was his normal tone. "Can I be happy? Can anyone truly be happy?"

"His name is Barry Hapworth," Kid Rags said, flicking a bit of lint off his navy pinstriped suit jacket. "For several obvious reasons, everyone calls him Happy."

Mary glanced from the bus to Happy. "Were you driving this thing?"

Happy puffed out his meager chest. "Sure was."

"And did you almost run over Mrs. Werner's cat?"

"I'll take the fifth." Happy paused for a fraction of a second. "A fifth of bourbon."

"Did someone say bourbon?" Kid Rags removed the flask from his hip pocket, took a swig, and passed it around.

"Who are all these people?" Bill asked from behind Mary.

Mary turned, wondering how she could explain the situation to her fiancé, but Teach saved her the trouble and made the introductions. Arms still folded across his chest, Crunchy nodded to Bill, then stepped close to Mary. Happy punched the air, but stopped when Bill showed no inclination to fight.

Kid Rags shook Bill's hand. "You're a lucky man."

"What are you all doing here?" Mary asked. "I was supposed to pick you up. And why is Happy here?"

"Happy is a friend of Kid Rags," Teach began, but Kid Rags interrupted him, saying hastily, "Not a friend. Just a fellow I know."

"Happy knows someone who knows Iron Sam," Teach continued, "and since we knew your car wasn't big enough for all of us, we accepted Happy's offer to drive us in his bus."

"Who's Iron Sam?" Bill asked, sounding plaintive.

"Butcher Boy," Kid Rags said.

Bill's eyebrows drew together. "Butcher Boy? Mary, are you sure you know what you're doing?"

Mary laughed, suddenly feeling lighthearted and carefree. "I haven't a clue."

*   *   *

Dialect and regional accents are especially tricky to write. It used to be that writers tried to show dialect and accent through the laborious use of phonetic spellings and a blizzard of apostrophes.

Today, though, we readers don't like having to decipher the author's personal code. Nor do we writers need to take the time to create the code. It's better to use colloquialisms and broken language to show regional differences. For example, "I done died and gone to heaven." Not an apostrophe or phonetic spelling in sight, though you know immediately the speaker is not a high-toned college professor from Boston.

If your character has a foreign accent, you don't have to bludgeon a reader with it. All that is necessary to portray an accent is to say the character speaks with an accent. If you wish, you can use phrasing to remind the reader of the accent, such as, "We will go to the store. No?"

This snippet from *Daughter Am I* shows Crunchy's difficulty with English:

"Mary's trying to find out about her grandparents," Kid Rags said. "His name was James Angus Stuart."

Crunchy shook his head. "Don't know no James Agnes Stuart."

"What about Regina DeBrizzi Stuart?" Mary asked.

"Don't know her neither."

Dialogue is an artificial construct. Dialogue does not mimic conversation but instead gives readers the *impression* of realistic conversation.

Books on how to write dialogue often suggest listening to people talk to learn how to write dialogue. Seems like good advice, but have you ever truly listened? "We . . . um . . . we, like . . . you know . . . we stammer and like we repeat ourselves and um . . . you know."

Even when we speak coherently, we don't converse. We lecture. We tell long, boring, convoluted stories. We interrupt others and talk over them. We use clichés. We tell jokes that take forever to get to the punch line. None of which helps us write dialogue. If characters in books talked the way we talk in real life, who would bother reading? We want our characters to sound like us, just not talk like us. We also want their conversations to be witty, to the point, and conflicted.

In life, most of us cannot come up with that clever quip when we need it—it comes to mind (if at all) late at night when no one is around to be impressed. Our characters don't have to suffer from that malady because they have us and our late night epiphanies on their side. We can change their words as often as necessary to get it right.

And get it right we must. Good dialogue advances a story and shows character interacting with other characters. Good dialogue makes a reader keep reading. Bad dialogue, no matter how crucial to the story, makes readers go in search of other amusements.

The following is another excerpt from *Daughter Am I* showing the use of dialogue.

* * *

Mary noticed, for the first time, her father's receding hairline, the deep crinkles at the corners of his brown eyes. Soon he would be as old as Kid Rags, Teach, and Crunchy.

Tears stung her eyes at the thought of her father living alone in a dingy hovel, and she vowed she would not let that happen.

Realizing the silence was stretching out awkwardly, she opened her mouth to speak, but he held up a palm to forestall her.

"I don't want to know what you're doing," he said. "Whatever it is, I know it's something you feel you have to do. I thought you should be aware you're upsetting your mother."

"I don't mean to."

He heaved himself out of the chair. "That's all I came to say."

"I'm glad you stopped by," she said. "I planned on calling you later anyway to tell you I'm going to be away for a few days."

He stared at her for a moment, then shrugged. "I don't understand what you're trying to accomplish, but I suppose you know your own mind."

You are so wrong. I don't know anything.

He walked to the door, paused with his hand on the knob for a second, then turned to face her.

"I love you," he said softly.

She swallowed. "Oh, Dad. I love you too."

He opened the door. "Be careful, okay, honey? You don't know what you're getting yourself into."

Interview with Pat Bertram

What is your latest release?

My latest release is a non-fiction book *Grief: The Great Yearning*, a compilation of letters, blog posts, and journal entries I wrote while struggling to survive my first year of grief after the death of my life mate/soul mate. I wanted my fellow bereft to know that whatever crazy things they do to bring themselves comfort, others have done, and as hard as it is to believe, they will survive. I also wanted to show writers the truth of grief. They so often get it wrong, perhaps because they don't know what it feels like to lose the most significant person in their lives

What other books do you have published?

More Deaths Than One tells the story of Bob Stark who sees his mother's obituary in the morning paper, which stuns him because he buried her two decades ago before he left the country to live in Southeast Asia. So how can she be dead again?

A Spark of Heavenly Fire tells the story of how Kate Cummings, an ordinary woman, gathered her courage and strength to survive the horror of an unstoppable bioengineered disease let loose on the state of Colorado.

Daughter Am I is the story of a young woman who inherits a farm from her murdered grandparents —grandparents her father claimed had died before she was born. She becomes obsessed with finding out who they were and why someone wanted them dead.

Light Bringer: Thirty-seven years after being abandoned on the doorstep of a remote cabin in Colorado, Becka Johnson returns to try to discover her identity, but she only finds more questions. Who has been looking for her all those years? And why are those same people after fellow newcomer Philip Hansen?

What genre are your novels?

The unifying theme in all of my books is the perennial question: Who are we? *More Deaths Than One* suggests we are our memories. *A Spark of Heavenly* suggests we are the sum total of our experiences and choices. *Daughter Am I* suggests we are our heritage. *Light Bringer* suggests we are the product of history. Perhaps my genre is "identity quest," though I can't see that as ever being a big draw, so I usually call my fiction "conspiracy novels," since a conspiracy of some sort is the basis for each of them.

How do you develop and differentiate your characters?

Usually I try to do scenes with only two characters since it's easy to differentiate between two characters, but in *Daughter Am I*, I ended up with Mary Stuart driving around the country with a busload of funny and heartbreaking characters, including a con artist, a dying hit man, and a gangster's moll. Because these characters were always together, I had to give each specific characteristics, making sure those characteristics were a part of the story. For example, Happy (an ex-wheelman for the mob) has Parkinson's disease. He also carries a gun, which terrifies the others since he can't hold the gun steady. Mary ends up confiscating the gun. The weapon, Happy, and Mary's relationship to both gun and man become a part of the story. Another character, Crunchy, used to be a mob enforcer, and he becomes Mary's protector, promising to crunch anyone who does her harm. This, too, becomes part of the story, as he learns his limits and she learns to take care of herself.

How much of yourself is hidden in the characters of your novels?

Freud thought every role in a dream was played by the dreamer, and in a way, that's the way my books are. The emotions the characters feel are mine since I can only write what I feel, and their personal problems are ones I've grappled with. In the writing, though, the characters become more than I ever was as they develop in response to the needs of the story. Kate from *A Spark of Heavenly* Fire is the most like me, maybe because she was the first character I created.

How much of a story do you have in mind before you start writing it?

I know the main characters, I know the beginning of the story, I know the end of the story, and I know how I want the characters to develop, but I don't flesh out the individual scenes until I start writing them.

Do you have specific techniques you use to develop the plot and stay on track?

I don't have any specific technique, though I do fill in a timeline as I write to make sure that the events happen in a realistic framework. When I first started writing, I never had weekends or holidays in the story, just one long string of weekdays, so a timeline is very important. The timeline also serves as a brief outline of what I have written so that I can see the story at a glance. Besides the timeline, I use a theme to stay on track. If I'm not sure of the efficacy of a character trait or plot point, I check it against the theme. If the trait or plot point helps prove the theme, I keep it, otherwise I look for a stronger way of tying the ideas to the theme. I've found that a theme helps keep a story (and me) focused.

How (or when) do you decide that you are finished writing a story?

A story is finished when it is published. Otherwise, it is never finished. The more one writes, the more one learns, and the more one learns, the more one sees how earlier works can be improved. The only thing that stops this cycle of learning and rewriting is getting the book published.

What do you want people to take with them after they finish reading the story?

I would like readers to take away a slightly different way of looking at the world, perhaps seeing it in a better light or a maybe just a more truthful light. And if not that, I'd like them to feel good about having spent time with my characters. The best compliment I ever received was from someone who said he didn't want the book to end.

Where can we find out more about you and your books?

I have a website — http://patbertram.com — where I post important information, including the first chapters of each of my books, but the best way to keep up with me, my writing, and my life on a daily basis is by way of Bertram's Blog. http://ptbertram.wordpress.com

All of my books are published by Second Wind Publishing and are available both in print and in ebook format. You can get them online at Second Wind Publishing, Amazon, B&N and Smashwords. Smashwords is great! The books are available in all ebook formats, including palm reading devices, and you can download the first 20-30% free!

How to Begin and End a Story
By
Lazarus Barnhill
Author of:
The Medicine People, Lacey Took a Holiday,
and *Come Home to Me, Child* (with Sally Jones*)*

🦃

Novels, novellas and short stories are very distinct literary forms. O. Henry's short story *The Gift of the Magi* is hugely different in its construction from Tolstoy's *War and Peace*. One would be tempted to say that, as different types of literature, they have virtually nothing in common.

The longest epic and the shortest tale, however, can have two enormously important things in common: they can **engage the reader from the beginning** and they can **leave the reader satisfied but wanting more at the end**. In this brief essay I'd like to share my ideas about what makes workable beginnings and endings. I think these ideas are universal in that they apply to creative fiction regardless of its genre, setting or length.

A key idea expressed to me repeatedly by the folks at Second Wind is that my story should grab and hold the attention of the reader from the very first line. As one of the editors expressed it to me, the first line should seduce the reader deeply into the narrative. I've been told that a good example of this is the first line of my novel *Lacey Took a Holiday*:

She woke up realizing she had been sleeping in a bed smaller and softer than the one in which she made her living, and that she was wearing the sort of flannel nightgown she hadn't worn since she was a little girl.

What's good about this sentence? It begins a story with no build up (back story). Another way this is described is *in media res* ("in the middle of things"). Speaking for myself, I find that introductions, forwards, preludes, prologues or whatever you want to call them tend to slow down the process of a story. True, there are a lot of great novels with prologues (Brad Stratton's *White Lies* is one; so is Nicole Bennett's *Ghost Mountain*. These two novels, however, each use their prologue to describe a crime and they do so with no back story whatever. In this they are exceptions that prove the rule).

In the text above, the reader immediately knows something about the character being described, the setting and even a little of the history of the character. An author should be able to weave back story into the narrative as it moves along. By the bottom of the first page, the reader knows a lot more about the woman being described, but not because the author has blatantly explained it. I have found that readers will be quite attentive and sleuth out the things they want to know about your characters, which will further draw them into the story.

This leads to the concept I call "introductory mystery": the beginning paragraphs of a story, regardless of its length, deposit curiosity in the mind of the reader so that she/he will be drawn along into the narrative at least long enough to discover why a character said something or reacted in a certain manner. One example of this appears in the opening pages of *Come Home to Me, Child,* the crime/mystery novel I co-authored with Sally Jones. Within half a page the main character, Elaine, is interrupted and overwhelmed by her new neighbor, Police Chief Larry Daughtry. As the narrative continues after Daughtry abruptly walks away, Elaine asks Tim Starling, her contractor, to explain this intrusive man with whom he has long been acquainted:

"What about the chief?"

"He went into the Marines. Became a military policeman or shore patrol—whatever they call 'em. Did three or four hitches and came back to work in law enforcement around here. He started as a Cochran County deputy and, about five years ago when the chief's spot came open in Veil, he was the natural choice. I guess."

"He seemed happier to see you than you were to see him."

Starling chuckled. "I always thought Larry was a kind of a thug. He bullied me. Not that he was the only one." He began to stretch his tape measure along the yard. "It's the divine right of football players to torment band guys."

Although the contractor's explanation satisfies the introductory mystery of what sort of person has just barged into Elaine's life, the story proceeds to plant more elements to hook the reader's curiosity: why does the officer know so very much about her family; why is he so interested in her recent medical problems; and why is the police chief so interested in Elaine's plan to move her gazebo twenty feet across the yard? These seeds of mystery blossom through the course of the narrative in ways intended to gratify the reader's curiosity, but also to draw him/her ever deeper into the story.

As the police chief in his oppressive manner reveals to Elaine just how much he knows about her and her family, the reader is also learning the back story of what brought the main character to this place at this time and what is happening in her life. If, as an author, you can keep the pacing and dialogue smooth and natural—allow subject matter to emerge as it would in the flow of normal conversation—the narrative will give ample opportunity to simultaneously reveal the back story of the characters even as you develop them and their relationships.

So a good beginning 1) seduces the reader further into the story, 2) begins with narrative at the expense of back story, 3) plants elements of mystery in the reader's mind—some to be quickly revealed even as seeds of greater mystery are planted, and 4) reveals back story through the narrative process so as to introduce the reader to the characters without impeding the process of the story itself.

What about a good ending? Here are the final paragraphs of *Charlie Cherry's Ninth Step*, a work that will be coming out in the spring of 2013 from Second Wind:

* * *

Susan answered the door, barefoot and wearing the clothes she had worn to school that morning, her shirttail out.
"Charlie!"

"Hi."

"Uh—did you—did you find her?"

"Yep." He nodded. "I did."

"Are you—did she—"

He shook his head. "She's remarried."

"Oh." She tried not to show the relief that spread across her face. "What about Sloan? What about, you know, your amends?"

"Well," he said slowly, "I can tell you all about all that. But that's not really the reason I came back."

Susan slouched against the doorframe. There was a hint of anger in her voice. "Just looking for a cheap place to spend the night?"

"Not really." He looked over his shoulder at the Mazda. "You have a week-and-a-half off beginning now, don't you?"

"Yes," she replied cautiously.

"Well, I got my doings done and I've still got the better part of two weeks myself. I have a few hundred bucks just burning a hole in my pocket, and I was wondering if you'd like to go down to San Antone and walk the river with me."

For a moment she hovered in the doorway. She stepped toward him and leaned forward, looping her arms around his neck and pressing her lips to his.

She breathed at length and said, "Do you want to leave in the morning?"

"Well look. We kind of rushed into things last night. Surely we can slow down and do thing a little more romantically."

Her expression was curious. "More romantic than last night? Like how?"

"Well, let's go pack your stuff, and I'll take you for a moonlight ride with the top open on my rocket. We'll cruise on down to this barbeque house I found in Dallas. Best pecan pie I've had in fifteen years."

She was smiling, her arms a swing and her face moving gently a few inches beneath his. "Then what?"

"Well, then we'll drive on down the road 'til we find just the perfect spot to spend the night."

"Salado."

He shrugged. "Wherever you want, darlin'."

They kissed, a deep, sweet kiss. He straightened.

"Come on now. I'll help you."
She turned and went inside. He watched her graceful steps.
"Pack light. I imagine I'll be picking you out a few things. How do
you suppose you'd look in one of those white senorita dresses?"
　　"A senorita with freckles?"
　　"I love freckles. . . . Susan?"
　　"Yes?"
　　"How do you feel about stepchildren?"

* 　 * 　 *

Before we talk about what's right (I hope) with the passage
above, let's talk about what can go wrong with the ending of a story.
If we put our heart's blood into writing a manuscript, we need to
make sure we don't bleed out before we reach the end of the story.

First, there is no "happily ever after" if we are writing for adults.
In this sense, Margaret Mitchell did a better job of ending *Gone with
the Wind* than Shakespeare did with *Hamlet*. At the bittersweet
ending of *GWTW*, Scarlett is torn with grief and guilt, and yet
clinging to hope. The story has come to an end, but the reader is left
yearning for more. Indeed readers immediately and constantly
clamored for a sequel. There could never be a sequel to *Hamlet*—
everybody was dead. Killing off your main characters is often (as
demonstrated by the current most popular male romance author) just
another way of not having to deal with the complexity of human life.
Hollywood movies, of course, are the land of "happily-ever-after-
pat-ending-where-the-good-prevail-and-the-bad-get-what-they-have-
coming." But if you decide your story is going to be more real-to-life
than a Hollywood blockbuster, you as an author have to decide to
give your readers what the story allows you to give them.

In the passage above from *Charlie*, I give my readers multiple
resolutions to several issues the main character faced throughout the
story: what became of the girl he loved and was violently separated
from in high school; what will he do to the vicious adult who beat
him mercilessly when he was a teenager; what will happen between
him and the girl who secretly loved him in his youth? In each case
the result was not what the reader might have suspected. My
intention is that the reader find the ending surprising, hopeful,

plausible, uplifting and fun.

Another huge, disappointing mistake authors make is that the ending does not live up to the buildup of the narrative. There is a famous horror author who does a splendid job of building suspense and anticipation throughout his overly long novels, only to have them fall flat time and again because of really lame endings. Your ending has to be as big as the story that precedes it. When readers hear Charlie, above, promise Susan he's going to tell her what happened to him that day, they know that she will be astonished—just as they were surprised—to hear what he found out in the previous few hours.

Finally, leave your readers wanting more. All of the major questions and issues Charlie Cherry faced at the beginning of his story have been resolved by the end, but the resolution is intended to make the reader want to know what happened next in the characters' lives. I'm not suggesting that you leave yourself an opening for a sequel—although books do sell better if they are part of a series. Rather I'm saying that you want your readers, after they finish that last line, to keep wondering what will become of these characters they've come to know, with whom they've experienced adventures.

So a good ending 1) is plausible, realistic and complete enough to satisfy all the main themes of the story without solving all the world's problems, 2) has an ending that is as big and satisfying in its resolution as the story that precedes it, and 3) leaves your readers brooding about the characters and events and feeling sorry that the story has ended.

And that, I think, is a good place to end the essay.

🦃

Interview with Lazarus Barnhill

What are your books about?

There are two answers to that question. First, I'm very fortunate because my publisher allows me to have books in more than one genre. Currently I have both romance and crime/mystery titles in print. Coming up soon, I hope to have several mainstream novels in print as well. The second answer is that my books are all about believable characters facing believable issues, forming believable relationships and rising up in inspiring, creative but believable ways.

How long do the ideas for your books take to develop?

Beside my bed I keep a spiral notebook that has the outlines for two dozen books in it. Whenever I get an idea for a book, I write down a tentative title (you call the baby something when it's born, although in the long run it creates its own true name), the basic plot and the key characters. Over time I, as I brood about the stories, I'll go back to my notebook and add more detail, alter the plot, rename the characters, etc. The stories continue to grow. In a way they "become ripe" over time—that is, I get to a point where I can't help but start the actual writing process. Each ripens at its own pace. *Caddo Creek*, the sequel to *Lacey Took a Holiday*, chronologically takes place ninety years after the original story and was actually conceived after the "first sequel," *Lacey's Child.* I guess the bottom line to the question for me is that a story is a living thing: it develops within the author's being and emerges when the time is right for it.

Who are the main characters of your stories? Do you have a favorite? Is part of yourself hidden in them?

All the characters in my stories are based at least in part on people I've known or encountered. I embellish or diminish aspects of them as suits the need of the narrative. In *The Medicine People*, Ben Whitekiller, the catalytic figure whose return to the little town where he is wanted for murder sets off an unstoppable chain of events, and Robert Vessey, the detective who hated and wanted to kill Whitekiller for decades, were actually both based upon the same person: my uncle Herb, an Oklahoma peace officer and Native American who wrestled throughout his life with his own demons. Lacey, the beautiful and feisty main character in *Lacey Took a Holiday*, was based upon a very spirited artist I knew many years ago. Andy Warren, Lacey's antagonist and eventual love interest, was based upon a fellow I knew who was everything I'm not: tall, quiet, confident and patient. I have not yet written myself into a novel as a character. I'm not sure I'd give myself an even break. Because I try to breathe life into all of them, I can't say that one is my favorite. I am partial to strong-willed, bright, determined female characters like Lacey, Deena in *The Medicine People*, Elaine in *Come Home to Me Child* and Corral in *Caddo Creek*. I like creating male characters who are independent and will go their own way, yet care enough about others to make sacrifices: Dan Hook and Johnny Whitekiller in *The Medicine People*, Andy Warren and Curly the saloonkeeper in *Lacey Took a Holiday*.

Do your books have "takeaways," goals you intend your readers to grasp? How do you know when you've finished a novel?

The course of my life has exposed me to a lot of good and bad experiences, a lot of admirable and wicked people and a lot of wisdom and stupidity. I think, as we age, we discover many of the same truths in life, which is to say that a story can be true or it can be false: true in the sense that it resonates with what we learn as live; false in that the action, dialogue or development of the characters violates our sense of real life. For example, at the conclusion of Margaret Mitchell's *Gone With the Wind*, which is a great romance novel that breaks a lot of the genre's rules, the reader is confronted with a huge irony: Scarlett discovers she loves Rhett just as Rhett decides he won't squander anymore time trying to win her love. As melodramatic as the setting is, it's a "true story". So I would say my goals for my stories are 1) to write truth stuff (all the characters are believable, engaging and worth caring about) and 2) to end at a point where the specific themes of the story are resolved, but the reader is left wondering what happened to the characters next. At the end of *The Medicine People*, one of the characters has been shot, one jailed for attempted murder, one exonerated, a secret love has been revealed and two passionate but completely unconventional love affairs have begun. I want the end to be satisfying, but also compelling. Years ago I wrote a fantasy novella. It's still the first piece of my fiction that I still consider worthwhile. I sent it to my mother who read it at one setting, called me up and demanded that I write a sequel. "Ah," I thought, "I have arrived!"

Have you always wanted to be a writer?

When I was a child of four or five, Wednesday nights were "dollar nights" at the Riverside Drive In: a whole car load of people could see the movie for a buck. My parents and sister would sit in the front seat and I'd sit in the back. Periodically during the show, I would say what the character on the screen was about to say. Eventually my parents got really tired of that and forbade it. But something took root in me even back then. As an elementary school child I would constantly start stories that ended up being only a page or two long— and made me feel like a failure. When I was in sixth grade I lay awake one night and created a story that involved every child in my homeroom class. With the blessing of Miss Roach (and, no, I did not make up that name), I laboriously wrote the story down—probably thirty-five or forty pages—and was given permission on the last day of school to read it to the class. With about five pages left (I was just about to be machine gunned by the villains, having recovered the money they stole from the bank), the principal came in and said that we were free to go to the playground or to stay inside. The students immediately bolted—not one even asking how the story ended. I decided then to write the sort of stories that people would not be able to put down . . . and I'm still working on that.

Plot Twists:
Three Little Questions
By
Norm Brown
Author of:
Carpet Ride

🦃

As a writer and avid reader of mystery novels, I love a good plot twist. Like that special seasoning in a favorite recipe, they are often what turn a simple story into an intriguing tale. The unexpected is what keeps readers turning the pages. However, like the food seasoning, plot twists can be overdone or simply distracting. Whether creating the timeline for a novel or writing the first draft, I like to keep my mind open to possible twists and surprises that could be stirred in to make the story more exciting and suspenseful. Some are included in my novel and many are tossed away. To help me decide, I came up with three little questions to keep in mind as I work through each scene.

What if? As I come to each scene, usually a complete chapter, I have a pretty good idea what needs to happen in order to simply advance the plot (or a subplot) of the book, but as I'm filling in the details, I like to ask, "What if this was to happen instead of what the reader is expecting?" In my novel, *Carpet Ride*, I was surprised myself at how often the story expanded in a whole new direction. Seems to me, if you end up writing exactly the plot you started with, you probably missed some opportunities to make it better. So, turn your imagination loose and experiment with alternatives in the story.

Why? When it comes to plot twists in a mystery, I don't believe in sheer coincidence. Whatever surprising thing happens, it should happen for a logical reason. The cause does not have to be obvious to the reader right at that moment, but as the story unfolds the logic of this particular sequence of events has to be believable or your reader will feel cheated.

What then? To avoid cluttering your novel with meaningless distractions, any sudden plot twist should add something to the story. Even if it turns out to be a red herring, the twist should advance the plot toward its eventual conclusion. Otherwise, it's just filler. And nobody wants to read filler.

As an example, I have included a scene from my novel, *Carpet Ride*. In the excerpt below, John Canton and Cindy Kildeer are searching for Nathan Hanover's summer cabin in Colorado. They know Nathan was having an affair with the wife of his business partner, who was killed in a suspicious hit-and-run accident that has been blamed on John's best friend. John and Cindy intend to confront Nathan with evidence proving he also gave a large sum of money to the widow shortly before her husband's death, possibly to help pay for a contract killing. To John and Cindy, the best case scenario would be for Nathan to confess. The worst case could be a fight. Let's see how it goes.

Excerpt from *Carpet Ride*

At eight thirty on that Saturday morning, there was almost no traffic on the little two-lane road leading up to Estes Park, Colorado. The annual steady stream of RV's and trailers transporting happy campers to and from Rocky Mountain National Park had not yet started. The June nights were still a bit on the chilly side at these higher elevations. John knew from personal experience the vacationers would arrive in force later in the summer when it was miserably hot everywhere else. Like a lot of Texans, he'd been in that crowd a few times.

John was doing the driving for today's adventure, having convinced Cindy they should take turns. The short drive up from Boulder in the brilliant morning sunshine had been delightful. The air had become noticeably cooler as they gained altitude in the canyons leading up into the Rockies. Snow still capped some of the higher peaks visible in the distance.

Earlier in the trip he and Cindy had talked about the climate and the beauty of the rugged countryside, like any other tourists. But once they had passed through the small town of Lyons and began to make their way through the narrow canyons leading toward Estes Park, the small talk dropped off. According to JJ's directions, Nathan Hanover's vacation house was somewhere along this section of road. The closer they got, the more uneasy John felt about their plan to confront the man on the very personal and possibly dangerous subject of his relationship with his murdered business partner's wife. Cindy was feeling the same apprehension, judging by the silence from her side of the car.

Coming out of a rock-walled canyon, the road leveled out into an open area with a scattering of houses on both sides. It seemed to fit JJ's description of the area around Nathan's place. Checking the empty road behind them in the rearview mirror, John slowed to a crawl.

"This looks promising."

"Yeah," Cindy said. "I count at least three houses with a green metal roof. Popular feature around here, I guess."

"That's the only one I see that has brown siding." John pointed at a single-story house on the left, just ahead.

"You're right." Cindy leaned closer to the windshield. "And that sure looks like Nathan's car."

She pointed toward a silver BMW parked on the gravel driveway that led up to the side of the house.

"Good enough for me." John pulled over onto the shoulder of the road and stopped. They sat there and watched the house for a moment. Nothing seemed to be moving other than a steady stream of gray smoke spiraling out of the chimney.

"Boy, must be quite a blaze he's got going in the fireplace."

They watched for a few more seconds. Then, gathering his nerve, John turned across the road and slowly drove down the driveway toward the house. From this angle of approach, he could only see the rear and left side of the structure. The main entrance faced away from the highway to better take advantage of the scenic view of the mountains. As John's rental car eased up to the house, the only sound that disturbed the morning stillness was the crunching of gravel under the tires. Even that ceased when John stopped a few feet behind Nathan's BMW.

Closely watching the house, he reached down to turn off the engine, but stopped. He thought he'd seen a curtain move in a window along the side of the house. He froze with his hand poised above the ignition switch and watched. The white cloth moved slightly again as if waving in a gentle breeze, just as the first bright yellow-orange streak appeared at the bottom of the window and began snaking its way up the curtain. Then came another. Within seconds the plain white curtains were replaced by a window-full of the brilliant color.

"Fire." John threw open the car door and put his foot out. "That place is on fire."

He jerked his cell phone off his belt and held it out toward Cindy. When she didn't immediately take it, John tore his attention away from the house and looked over at her. She was twisted completely around in the passenger seat, her back toward him, looking at something at the rear of the house. She may have spotted flames erupting back there also, but John didn't take the time to ask.

"Cindy. Here, take this."

She turned back toward him and took the phone. Her eyes looked huge. Her mouth popped open to say something, but John didn't give her a chance.

"Try to call for help," he yelled over his shoulder as he climbed out of the car. "Got to see if anyone's in there."

Slipping in the gravel, he ran toward the side of the house. He stopped a safe distance from the now curtainless window and stretched up onto his toes, but could see nothing inside. Just beyond the glass was an impenetrable wall of gray smoke. John's stomach lurched at the thought of someone trapped in there, hopelessly cornered by rising flames. He couldn't imagine a more horrifying way to die. But maybe there was still time. He jogged around to the front of the house, where he came to a set of cement steps leading up to the main entrance. He bounded up to the top step, but stopped himself before rushing blindly through the door and possibly into a raging fire on the other side.

"Hello." He banged his fist on the wooden door. "Anyone in there?"

John tried to look through the four-inch square window in the door, but from the outside the glass was like a mirror. He turned an ear toward the door and listened for a moment. There were no cries for help. If someone was in there, they may have already been overcome by smoke. And their chance for survival was quickly ticking away. It would take a while for a rural fire department, probably made up of local volunteers, to arrive on the scene. Too long to just stand there and wait.

John looked down at the brass doorknob. He lightly grazed the metal surface with the back of his hand. It felt cool. The fire had not yet reached this part of the house. He grabbed the knob and pushed the door open, and was immediately greeted by a cloud of thick acrid smoke. He turned his head away for one more deep breath of the outside air, then slipped inside.

Although it was a sunny morning outside, the living room was dark in addition to being half-filled with smoke. An old-fashioned shade was pulled down over the one window he could see. John glanced back at the sunshine coming through the open door. He wasn't particularly thrilled with the idea of closing off this connection to the safe world beyond, but providing a source of fresh air could accelerate the spread of the fire. He reluctantly gave the door a push and it swung closed with a fateful sounding click.

John turned and squinted across the smoky space he assumed to be some sort of main living room. Through the haze he could see an eerie orange glow emanating from the narrow gap at the bottom of an interior door on the other side of the room. The air temperature rose noticeably as he made his way toward the light. He stopped at the closed door and again used the back of his hand to test the heat of the doorknob. The old-fashioned glass knob felt definitely warm, but not painfully hot against his skin. He gripped it and leaned close to the door.

"Anybody in there?"

John bent his knees to get below the growing layer of smoke suspended from the ceiling and listened. What he really hoped to hear was the sirens of approaching fire engines, but no such luck. He did hear something, though. Was that a faint groan? A dry hacking cough from beyond the door settled the issue. Nathan Hanover, or some other poor soul, was in the next room. Unfortunately, so was the fire.

"Hang on. I'm coming in," John yelled out before realizing he had actually made that decision.

He shook his head. What a deal, he thought, somehow surviving the last few days of playing detective with real murderers, only to burn himself to a crisp while acting like a one-man fire rescue squad. This was insane.

He turned the knob anyway.

A gust of cool air whooshed past him and into the room. He took one small step beyond the door and froze. The heat was incredible. He couldn't see much of anything, but the flashing orange glow of the smoke engulfing him meant the flames were not far away.

John suddenly began to choke, having unwittingly taken another breath of the dense smoke. He crouched lower to get his head beneath the dark cloud, which extended considerably lower than it had in the living room. There was not much more than three feet of halfway breathable air near the floor. He wiped at his stinging eyes and squinted up into the smoke above him. Just how much time would he have before the entire room exploded into one big ball of fire? He had seen that phenomenon, called flashover by firefighters, demonstrated on a television documentary. Once the temperature reached a certain level, every combustible object in the room would simultaneously burst into flame. And the chance of survival for anyone in that space would drop to just about zero.

From his low squatting position, he could see the main blaze across the room from him. In the hazy glare he could also make out the shadowy shape of a bed. Against his better judgment, John began to duck walk across the wooden floor, directly toward the fire. The crackling of the flames got louder and he could now see that the bedspread and blankets on the bed were burning furiously on the right side. Lying on the floor near this corner of the bed was a rectangular, boxlike object. It didn't appear to be human. No living creature could have survived in this area of intense fire, anyway. John redirected his awkward waddle toward the other side of the bed where the creeping flames had not yet reached. He held one arm out for balance and with the other clamped the tail of his shirt over his mouth. The makeshift mask didn't work all that well. He was stopped by another painful spasm of coughing just as he arrived at the unburned side of the bed. He got the hacking back under control, but then heard another cough, almost like a weak echo of his own. The sound seemed to have come from above him, up on top of the queen size bed. He filled his lungs as much as possible and rose up into the smoke just high enough to peer over the top edge of the mattress. The undulating orange flame on the far side of the bed provided sufficient light to silhouette the dark form of a human body, curled up on top of the sheets in a defensive fetal position.

John leaned across the bed to get a closer look at the shadowed face, holding a hand up to shield his eyes from the bright tongues of fire springing up only inches behind the body. He blinked furiously to clear the smoke from his eyes enough to recognize the motionless figure on the bed. The man's eyes were closed and his face seemed far too relaxed considering his perilous situation. Nathan Hanover was either unconscious or dead.

"Hey." John stretched across the bed and put his hand on a shoulder. "Anybody home?"

He jerked the shoulder back and forth hard enough to bounce the entire body around on the mattress. There was no response. But looking down the bed, John noticed his shaking had caused Nathan's legs to separate. The left had fallen back and was now in direct contact with the line of fire that was munching its way across the bedspread. Before John could react, a bright new flame popped up from Nathan's lower pants leg.

"We gotta go."

He quickly pulled the limp body across the mattress and hugged the other man's head to his chest as they both flopped off the edge of the bed. They landed hard on the floor, and John immediately turned his attention to the flame whipping around the lower leg of the pants. There were probably already serious burns, but it would get much worse if he didn't take the time to extinguish the blaze. He resisted the urge to try to beat the flame down with his hands. Burning himself would only make their situation more difficult. He needed something to smother the flames. He was about to pull off his shirt when he noticed Nathan had landed on a small oval-shaped throw rug. John pulled it up and wrapped the heavy material around the burning pants leg. When he let go, the flame was gone. The blackened, shriveled cloth of the pants stuck sickeningly to Nathan's skin, but at least the spread of the damage had been stopped.

John shuffled on hands and knees back up to Nathan's upper body. His face looked completely lifeless. The tongue was visible at one corner of the slack, open mouth. At that moment John had no idea whether he was rescuing a living person or simply postponing the cremation of a corpse. Even if he had the time, he didn't think he'd be able to calm himself enough to check for a pulse. Nathan's skin still felt warm to the touch. But then, so did everything else in this bedroom from hell.

John grasped both wrists and began to drag him slowly across the floor. Nathan was fortunately not a huge man like his business partner, JJ. But it still felt like lugging a bag of cement across the floor. He would have preferred to pick the man up and try to run, but neither of them would survive long breathing the black smoke that filled the room from the ceiling all the way down to about two feet above the floor. Lying almost flat to stay within the shallow band of breathable air, John could only inch along by pushing against the floor with his feet. If he could just get Nathan into the living room, they might manage to stay alive long enough for help to arrive.

He pushed and pulled until they were a few feet away from the burning bed, then stopped to get his bearings. That few seconds of effort left him gasping in the abrasive air and coughing. The suffocating tightness in his throat got even worse when he realized he had absolutely no idea where the door was.

The visible world beneath the smoke had shrunk to a height of not much more than a foot. With his chin almost touching the floor, John squinted to focus his stinging eyes. The only identifiable feature he could make out was a section of narrow wooden trim ran along the bottom edge of the bedroom wall. Somewhere along the wall, that baseboard had to connect with the doorway that led out of the bedroom. Feeling a tiny rush of hope, he turned Nathan's body to the left and resumed the awkward sidestroke motion. He moved parallel to the wall, keeping the baseboard trim in sight.

After several feet of tortuous progress, John stopped to wipe away the stinging black tears. It took his oxygen-deprived brain a moment to register what his eyes could then see. Just inches ahead, the horizontal baseboard abruptly turned upward to form the bottom corner of a doorway.

John turned his unconscious passenger and dragged him through the opening. He didn't waste time worrying about the possibility it might be the wrong doorway. This was their last chance. If this route led into a dead-end bathroom or a big closet—then so be it. They'd just die from smoke inhalation instead of being roasted alive in the bedroom.

He moved forward a few feet and stopped. The space they had just entered was nearly as smoke-filled as the bedroom. And there was even less light. The orange glare from the bedroom door behind him didn't reach very far. John felt disoriented; there were no visible walls or baseboards to follow. His watery eyes slowly adjusted, however, and he noticed there actually was another source of light. A solitary beam pierced the smoke like a tiny spotlight. The white cone narrowed as his eyes followed it back toward its source, a small illuminated rectangle on the far side of the room. That size and shape seemed familiar. He suddenly realized he was looking at the little square window in the front door of the house. The white glow was sunshine.

John stumbled to his feet. He bent over, reached under Nathan's arms, and locked his fingers in front of his chest. Walking backwards, he began to drag the unconscious body in the direction of the spot of light. His head was now up in the smoke. He couldn't breathe or even open his eyes. He just concentrated on moving straight back and kept shuffling his feet until his back bumped up against a solid surface.

John lowered Nathan to the floor and fumbled around with one hand behind his back until he located the doorknob. When he turned it, the door suddenly swung inward with no help from him. He was almost knocked down by the sudden force of fresh air rushing into the house.

As John crouched to renew his grip on Nathan, there was an abrupt change in the room. It was like an explosion, but without the customary loud bang. He looked up at a huge ball of bright yellow fire rolling toward them from the bedroom door. It roared and expanded almost all the way across the living room before bursting like a fiery bubble only a couple of feet short of Nathan's extended legs. The smoke cleared briefly and John could see the fire-filled doorway into the bedroom. As he watched, flames boiled out of the top of the opening and began flowing across the ceiling of the living room like an upside down river.

"God . . ."

Whether curse or prayer, the exclamation was left unfinished. John grabbed Nathan's arms and put everything he had left into dragging him out of the house. He quickly passed through the doorway, and continued stumbling backward. He didn't intend to stop until he had put a safe distance between them and the burning house.

Two steps later, the world abruptly dropped out from under him. As he tumbled backwards, the edge of a roof passed through his field of vision. There was just enough hang time for him to belatedly remember the cement steps leading up to the entrance. He flew out beyond them and landed flat on his back on the hard packed earth.

John slowly opened his bloodshot eyes. A couple of fuzzy black spots swirled around in a bright blue sky.

The view was suddenly blocked by an upside down face.

"Anybody else in there?"

The inverted mouth moved with each shouted word.

"No." John noisily sucked in cool mountain air to fill the painful vacuum in his lungs. "At least, I don't think so."

Strong hands supported his neck and shoulders as he struggled to rise to a sitting position. He saw a second man in a yellow rubber coat kneeling beside Nathan, who had landed face up on top of John's outstretched legs. The firefighter was patiently trying to pry John's clenched fingers off the motionless man's wrists.

"We've got him, sir." He looked up at John. "You can let go now."

The chill was mostly gone from the morning air, but John held the heavy woolen blanket tightly closed in front of his chest. He was sitting on the bench seat of a weathered old picnic table. The first team of firefighters on the scene had wrapped the blanket around his shoulders and settled him there after determining he was not seriously injured.

Up on the roof of Nathan's smoking camp house two men in yellow protective suits were hacking away at the green aluminum with big axes. John guessed the purpose of the ragged hole they were making was to provide ventilation for the extreme heat trapped inside the structure. There didn't seem to be any reason to create a new entrance up there. Several firemen had already walked in through the front door, dragging thick cloth-covered hoses behind them.

John looked away from the activity on the roof and over to his right where two men in white uniforms were hovering over the body of Nathan Hanover. He was still lying on the stretcher the firemen had used to move him away from the burning house. The EMS team from the nearby ambulance had taken over Nathan's care as soon as they arrived. Watching them work, John was relieved to see a lack of desperate life-saving activity. The paramedics appeared to be calmly attending to the blackened and blistered area of the left leg. Nathan appeared to be still unconscious, though John had seen his head roll from side to side a few times like he was beginning to come around.

One of the paramedics rose as a man in a tan uniform walked out from behind the ambulance. The new arrival appeared to be some brand of law enforcement officer. Looking back toward the main road John saw a car with a Sheriff's Department emblem on the door. It was parked along the roadside so it wouldn't block the emergency vehicles lined up on the gravel driveway behind Nathan's BMW. It slowly dawned on John his rental car should be in that line. He remembered jumping out and running toward the burning house, leaving Cindy in the car with his cell phone. A quick pat of his hand on his empty pants pocket verified that he had also left the keys in the ignition. From his perch on the bench John looked over the area around the house. The little blue car was nowhere to be seen, and everyone bustling around the area was wearing either a uniform or firefighting gear. There was no sign of Cindy. She may have had to drive all the way into the little town of Estes Park to get help. In this remote area, it wouldn't be surprising to learn the nine-one-one service city folks take for granted was not yet available.

John's attention was drawn back to the movements of the Sheriff's deputy. After a brief conversation with the paramedics, the slightly chubby officer had ambled over to talk to the firefighter who seemed to be giving orders to all the others. He nodded his agreement with whatever the fireman had to say before turning and strolling toward the picnic table. John slid the blanket off his shoulders and piled it up on the bench beside him. He suddenly felt a little childish huddled under it.

"Hi there."

"Hey."

"Looks like you made it out in a lot better shape than your buddy over there."

"Yeah, I'm fine." John nodded toward Nathan. "Is he going to be okay?"

"They're taking him on into a hospital, but they said his vitals look pretty good." The deputy turned and, along with John, watched the EMS team making preparations to load the stretcher into the ambulance. "The only external injury seems to be the burn on his leg, and the paramedic said his lungs seem to be relatively clear. So he probably didn't pass out from smoke inhalation. The unconsciousness must be caused by something else."

The Sheriff's deputy turned back to John.

"Would you know anything about that, sir?"

"No. He was like that when I found him, curled up on the bed in there. I actually thought he was dead at first."

The deputy tugged at his belt, which was weighted down with all sorts of police paraphernalia.

"Well, they found a couple of empty whiskey bottles in there. He's not just drunk, though, according to the EMS guys. They think he's under the influence of some kind of drug, like a strong sedative or something."

John glanced over toward the door of the smoking house. Firefighters were still coming in and out, but the activity had noticeably slowed.

"Do they have any idea yet how the fire started?"

"Maybe. The chief said there was a small propane heater on the floor right at the edge of the bed. If it got knocked over somehow, it could have provided the initial flame."

John thought about the box shaped object he had noticed while crawling close to the flames.

"I think I saw that in there. I didn't realize it was a heater, though."

"Did your friend there knock it over, or did you?"

John frowned at the phrasing of the question. The deputy appeared to be working on a theory that he and Nathan had been doing drugs in the house when the fire was accidentally started.

"No, no." John shook his head. "The place was on fire when I got here. I saw flames through the window and went inside to see if anybody was in there."

"You just happened to be strolling by here at that critical moment?"

"No, sir. I came up here looking for Mr. Hanover. I just wanted to ask him about—some things."

"Could I see some identification, please?"

"Certainly."

John extracted his Texas driver's license from his wallet and handed it over. The deputy sheriff scribbled some information from it onto a small spiral notepad.

"So, how did you get here, Mr. Canton?" He looked John in the eye as he returned the license. "That BMW there belongs to a Nathan Hanover from Boulder. I've already run the tags."

"Yeah, that's him." John gestured toward the ambulance. "This is his camp house. We drove up here from Boulder to talk to him."

"We?"

"Yes. The receptionist from his office was with me. I asked her to report the fire. Guess she had to drive somewhere to do that."

The deputy flipped back a couple of pages in his notepad.

"The adult female who called in the fire didn't give a name to the emergency operator. Just reported the fire's location and hung up, like she was in a big hurry to get out of here. Any idea why she'd want to run away like that, Mr. Canton?"

Before John could answer, the police officer's focus seemed to shift toward a point somewhere beyond John's left shoulder. The look of suspicion on his face suddenly relaxed into slack-jawed amazement.

"I didn't run away."

The familiar voice came from behind John. Turning, he followed the deputy's gaze to Cindy's face. Her cheeks were tinged with a defiant pink glow. Now John understood the deer-caught-in-the-headlights expression on the other man's face. He had had the very same reaction when skewered by those intense pale blue eyes for the first time.

"Hmm?" was all the lawman managed to say.

"I said—I wasn't running away from anything. For your information, I was chasing the murderer." Cindy's eyes dipped down to take in the man's uniform. "Isn't that what you're supposed to be doing, sheriff?"

"Uh, just deputy, actually."

Cindy released her hold on the cop. Her hand lightly made contact with the upper part of John's arm as she closely studied his face.

"Are you okay?"

"Yeah." John shrugged. "I'm all right."

He thought he saw just a wisp of a grin slip across Cindy's face. Her shoulders twitched. John suspected she was struggling to suppress a giggle. He could not imagine what the girl found so amusing at the moment.

"Wait, wait, wait." The deputy was finally catching up. He held up an open hand as if directing traffic. "What did you say, Miss, about a——did you say murderer?"

"Yes, the guy who killed Nathan Hanover." Cindy spoke slowly, as if she thought the man was either hard of hearing or certifiably slow-witted. She glanced at John, obviously expecting some form of confirmation.

"Nathan's not dead," he said. "I got him out in time. They're taking him to the hospital."

"Oh. Well then, I guess I was chasing the man who attempted to kill Nathan."

*　　*　　*

What if? As the scene opens John and Cindy (and hopefully the readers) are bracing themselves for a confrontation, maybe even a fight, with Nathan Hanover at his cabin. In my original timeline sketch, those were the two probable outcomes. As a fiction author, however, I'm not locked into following probability. In real life, improbable things happen all the time. As I'm actually typing the scene, I think, *"What if the darn place is on fire when they get there?"* John instinctively rushes toward the house. He had been wishing he'd brought a gun, but now a fire extinguisher is more in order. Hopefully at this point the reader is thinking, "Wow! I didn't see that coming." All right, I may have a good plot twist here, but that leads to the second question I need to ask myself.

Why? Did lightning strike the chimney? Did a short in old wiring cause the blaze? Things like that happen, but such pure coincidence at that precise moment would be unrealistic and, frankly, insulting to my reader. I need a cause for the fire that makes sense within the plot of the story. So, while John is running toward the burning house, Cindy spots a man scrambling out a rear window. It is not Nathan, the guy they came there to accuse of financing a murder. The stranger scrambles to a hidden motorcycle and takes off with Cindy in pursuit. Okay, the house fire didn't just happen—there was no lightning bolt or spontaneous combustion. This new guy, whoever he may turn out to be, purposely started the fire with Nathan inside the house. This leads me, as the author, to the last little question to consider.

What then? I'm not adding an unexpected event solely because it's more exciting. Everything that happens should in some way advance the main plot or a sub-plot within the novel. The word itself, *twist*, implies a change in direction. In my example, the folks trying to solve a murder must now consider who else is involved and why this stranger would try to kill the man they believe financed it. Is their original suspect a villain, a victim, or possibly both? The trip to the cabin has provided more questions than answers for our determined heroes and the danger of additional killing has been ramped up. So off they go in a new, but completely logical, direction. To find out where it goes from there, you'll have to read the book.

While not very grammatical, my little test questions seem to work for me—and I do love a good plot twist.

❧

Interview with Norm Brown

What is your book about?

Near the end of their honeymoon trip across Oregon, Sam Stanley, his new wife Lynn, and her one-year-old son Andy, traverse a steep mountain road in a rented RV. In the middle of a blind curve they run over a long roll of carpeting angled across the road. Sam barely manages to avoid crashing down the mountainside. When he walks back up the road to move the obstacle—it's gone. Upon returning home to Austin, Sam learns that the crushed body of a business executive from Boulder, Colorado has been found at the site of their reported accident. The Oregon police suspect Sam in the obvious hit and run death; there is no roll of carpet. When deadly "accidents" continue in Texas, Sam realizes they were all supposed to die on that mountain.

How long had the idea of your book been developing before you began to write the story?

It rattled around in my head for over six months before I actually sat down and began to outline the plot.

What inspired you to write this particular story?

The opening scene occurred to me when my son and I were traveling on vacation in a rented RV through the Coastal Wilderness of Oregon. While negotiating a frighteningly narrow curve on a steep, lonely mountain road, I couldn't help but imagine what would happen if something suddenly blocked the way of the big, clunky vehicle. Like most book ideas, it started with that simple question: What if?

Tell us a little about your main characters. Who was your favorite? Why?

The novel actually has two protagonists, but if I had to choose my favorite it would be Sam Stanley. At the beginning of the story, newly-wed Sam feels almost literally on top of the world. When targeted by an unknown enemy, he discovers courage and strength he never knew he possessed. *Carpet Ride* is the story of Sam's evolution from vulnerable victim to desperate defender of his little family.

Who is your most unusual/most likeable character?

I was surprised by how much I enjoyed writing about the one-and-a-half year old boy, Andy. The growing bond between him and his new step dad Sam added a level of vulnerability that I think helped ratchet up the intensity of the story. The little guy is barely starting to form words, but he actually helps to solve the mystery.

How long did it take you to write your book?

I'm not a speedy writer at all. I wrote and rewrote for over a year before even considering trying to find a publisher.

How much of a story do you have in mind before you start writing it?

I know a lot of authors like to let the story unfold as they write, but I'm definitely an outliner. The basic story was laid out in my notes before I started. The details of the plot changed a lot however by the time I finished the first draft.

Did you do any research for the book? If so, how did you do it?

The action of the story takes place at locations I was already somewhat familiar with in Oregon, Texas, and Colorado. I think that reduced the amount of background research required. I do remember however nervously wandering around a local hospital intensive care unit to get a feel for the layout of a scene. I always feel like an intruder in hospital hallways, and in this case I probably was.

How do you develop and differentiate your characters?

Although I start writing with a very detailed plot, I find that my characters evolve and more or less define themselves through their actions and words as the story unfolds. One main character, Sam's best friend John Canton, didn't even exist when I started the first draft. I soon discovered that I needed him to help Sam solve the murder mystery and he went on to become a second protagonist. Starting out as a rather reckless young man, his development throughout the story is more or less the opposite of Sam Stanley's. By the last chapter he has noticeably matured and puts his life on the line to defend his friends.

Do you have specific techniques you use to develop the plot and stay on track?

I worked most of my life as a computer programmer/analyst. Just as when creating a software program, I need a fairly detailed timeline of how my novel is going to proceed before I start typing. While writing *Carpet Ride* I kept the timeline updated until very near the end. Once the editing and rewriting phase started, the timeline was still useful as a reference for details.

What do you like to read?

I read mostly mystery and suspense novels. I particularly like stories that put ordinary people into extraordinary circumstances.

Points of View
By
Juliet Waldron
Author of:
Hand-Me-Down Bride and *Roan Rose*

I recently reviewed a book by first time indie author, a gifted natural storyteller. Her book centered upon a long-ago tragedy in a small, tight-knit backwoods town. I found the story difficult to follow, because of frequent POV shifts, sometimes as often as every few paragraphs. There was a double drop between these shifts, but she also had a habit of changing voice. Sometimes the new POV is first person, sometimes third. Occasionally, I found myself stumbling from first person to third person subjective, or yanked straight out of the story by bursts of the venerable nineteenth century third person omnipresent. Many of her narrators are unreliable, as well, and there are many, many characters, almost an entire town, but few of them are well fleshed out. However, each one, Rashomon-like, has a unique piece of information about the pivotal event.

As compelling as the story was, it couldn't overcome the author's mechanical difficulties. POV can be a tricky subject for any new writer, especially to those of us who are self-taught, as are many indie authors. Just because you read widely doesn't mean you know how to handle POV. Elaborate Point of View shifts are complicated business even in the hands of experienced writers.

If you are thinking of finally writing "that book," decide who/what/where/when before you get going. Laying the groundwork, pouring the foundation, you might say, is the place where a writer truly has to start. Find the eyes (the "Narrator") through which you want to see events, and please don't, for the reader's sake, use too many pairs!

If you head over to Google and look up "POV + writing" or

something similar, you'll come up with some excellent entries on the subject, so this is a bare bones look at the subject. I'm going to talk about just a few possible ways to tell a story, and then about how to stick with it.

First, remember the grammar.

"I-we" is first person. A first person narration is like a one-way coffeeklatsch. The story will be between the protagonist and the reader. A last will is the final way a person might express themselves using first person.

"I bequeath the sum of $600 and title to the mill, commonly known as German's Mill, as well as the attached house, barn and 3 acres, to my Karl Joseph Wildbach on the condition he forswear continued use of the English alias "Joe Wildbrook." —from *Hand-Me-Down Bride*

"You" is second person. This is rare in novels, but often appears in song lyrics and greeting cards.

"He-She-it" is third person. The "person" you chose for narrator—especially if you want to keep things simple—will remain the same throughout your novel.

"Sophie went into the parlor, which was almost as dim and dingy as her room had been. After the first look around, she decided that this was where she would begin cleaning tomorrow. Farm annuals, a stack of newspapers and a ledger lay in a heap at one end of the table. The curtains were so stiff that they lifted like boards when the breeze struck them. An old serpentine-front secretary had been set by a window to take advantage of the light. " — from *Hand-Me-Down Bride*

What the limited third person perspective can*not* do is know what other characters are thinking. They also cannot see through the eyes of other characters. For instance, the limited third person can notice the "shifty eyes" of another character, but cannot comment upon his/her own eyes. For instance, Alice can see her boyfriend's "blue eyes blaze," but she cannot, from her own perspective, see her own "brown eyes spill tears." Alice may feel tears on her cheeks, but she won't comment upon her own eye color. Therefore, "Limited" means exactly that. Once inside a character's head—you mustn't hop away into another.

"When they surfaced, sputtering and laughing, Karl saw Sophie, shoes and stockings in hand, tearing way along the narrow path to the mill. Shapely legs and white petticoat flashed beneath her somber black skirts." —from *Hand-Me-Down Bride*

To refine the definition a little more, "Narrator" may be either a character within the story or simply a presence which hovers over and comments upon the action, the above-mentioned omnipresent third person narrator," and is often used in nineteenth century novels.

"The Pitchin boys went galloping to round up more help. Around about sundown, Resolve's kinfolk arrived. They brought food, blankets and a bucksaw, the quickest way to cut the huge tree and extract the dead from beneath the ruin of the cook-shed." —from *Hand-Me-Down Bride*

For today's genre novelists, an omniscient narrator is a more frequent choice than you'd imagine. Here's an example:

"While fighting the Great War, a boy surviving among rough and desperate men, Karl had learned some of life's hardest lessons . . . He'd done enough killing, witnessed enough death and dying . . . He had accepted his father's offer to manage the mill. It was noisy and dirty there, nothing that either Papa or George wanted to deal with. Karl had been thankful to keep life simple he got well and sorted out his mind about what he had seen—and done—during the long agony of that terrible war." —from *Hand-Me-Down Bride*

Many young adult novels, such as the *Harry Potter* series, switch back and forth between third person omniscient and third person limited. Third person limited is perhaps the most common—and probably most obvious—way for a beginning writer to handle building a story. Pick a single character to be your narrator; it doesn't even have to be the protagonist. This narrator/character can plan, experience, and speculate on the action. Here's a case where after a paragraph break, third person limited switches into third person omniscient.

"Still, he thought, the way my life has gone lately, even the prospect of fatherhood wouldn't be much of a surprise. If Theodore

looked up from hell and saw them, he was was probably laughing...The simple fact of marriage had not changed Karl as much as his father had imagined, but two great forces of nature— love—and the whirlwind that had devastated the McNallys—had brought revelation." —from *Hand-Me-Down-Bride*

There are several ways of creating more points of view, if you should want to complicate things. You might alternate narrators, using chapter breaks to signal the change. (The *Fire and Ice* fantasy series does this.) The danger here can be the introduction of too many characters for the reader to want to become familiar with while impatiently waiting a plot advance in an earlier narrator's story. At any rate, alternating points of view is not something you want to jump straight into without a lot of careful drafting.

Another common way to handle point of view is to use the first person. This story is told by an "I" (or rarely) "We." First person narrative has been unpopular among genre editors for a long time, although it is an excellent way to dig deeper into the perspective, emotions and beliefs of a single character. A first person narrator speaks of the past, whether long ago or recent. They are older and wiser than their younger selves, although, again, they may or may not be, the protagonist.

"I stood there expectantly, but he was awfully drunk. For an unsteady minute, he considered my voluminous skirts. Finally, he simply locked his arms around my legs and lifted. I had to duck to keep my head from being bumped as went through the door." — from *Mozart's Wife*

There is a great deal more about this subject. If you are interested in digging deeper: http://www.novel-writing-help.com/writing-in-the-first-person.html and http://en.wikipedia.org/wiki/Narrative_mode

❦

Interview with Juliet Waldron

What is your book about?

Roan Rose, my newest novel, is a story about a peasant girl who becomes a house servant to a royal family. Their wealth and power and their eventual downfall affect her life in unpredictable and sometimes terrible ways.

How long was the idea for the book developing before you wrote the story?

Perhaps four or five years. I'd wanted to write a book about the Wars of Roses since childhood, but was never sure how to approach it, especially as the subject has lately become very popular.

What inspired you to write this story?

My love for the Late Medieval period and my interest in the royals involved. I'd already researched the period pretty thoroughly.

Tell us a little about your characters. Who was your favorite?

The heroine, Rosalba, is my narrator. It is through the lens of her perception we see the events of this tumultuous, barbaric era. As a poor girl, she sees life in the castle in ways her masters do not. As a peasant woman in the 15th Century, Rosalba has a mostly insurmountable set of challenges, but she is bright and resourceful. Occasionally her emotions keep her from making the best choices, but she is always courageous and not afraid to act.

How long did it take to write Roan Rose?

About three years, which is fast for me. One thing about writing a historical based upon the lives of real people is that the plotting is done in advance. I don't think a historical writer should alter facts to pretty up—or tidy up—a story.

What do you want people to take with them after they finish the story?

I'd like them to know a little more about history and about the historical characters involved, of course. In this case, I'd like them to think about women's lives, and how perceptions of women have changed in 600 years—and how, in many ways, they haven't changed at all. Limitations placed upon women simply because they are women are present the world over. In positive and in negative ways, biology is still destiny.

How has your background influenced your writing?

My mom was an Anglophile who loved to travel. I spent my teens in Cornwall and in Barbados. An English education reinforced my interest in the UK and her history. (She is called "Britannia" after all.) I read Josephine Tey's *The Daughter of Time*, which is a classic mystery novel about the disappearance of the Princes in the Tower, before puberty. As I was nerd child who had crushes on historical figures, the idea of an unjustly accused King whose name had been blackened by the real perpetrator was appealing. My interest in this Wars of Roses story resurrected during my writing years. Somehow, I felt I "owed" the Middle Ages a book. *Roan Rose* is my take on what is becoming a favorite ground for novelists.

What's your writing schedule like? Do you strive for a number of words a day?

My schedule, when I'm deep in a story, is ideally all the time. As I'm retired, that's possible. Otherwise, I don't push. My muse—and I believe in her/him—goes back out the window when rules are set in concrete. Now, if you are a writer with lucrative contracts and books pending, you are working at a job, and need to punch the clock. Otherwise—my kind of writer sometimes needs to run the vacuum, cook a meal or clean the cat boxes.

What are you working on right now?

I've got a creature story in the works. Thank heaven no one is waiting with baited breath, because I don't have time for creativity just now. Every now and then, I'll jot down a paragraph or two, just to hold onto the images.

What is the most difficult part of the writing process?

The most difficult part is WRITING. It's one thing to have those little voices in your head and pretty images of some long-ago world, but it takes the other side of the brain to actually find the words and force them out through the tips of your fingers onto a keyboard. Left side creates; right side organizes and uses logic in order to discriminate, to pick and choose among effects you want your words to make. That takes time and lots of re-reading and re-thinking—commonly known as "editing."

What do you like to read?

History/non-fiction is my favorite, because that's where my stories come from. However, I spend a lot of time reading in order to review e-books of all kinds and historical novels through the *Historical Novel Society* magazine.

What writer influenced you the most?

At the moment, I'd say Cecelia Holland.

What do you think the most influential change in book publishing will come from?

It's here, and it's called the internet. The rise of the e-book, after a decade in which problems of software and hardware have been (more or less) sorted, is the best thing that's happened for readers since the printing press. It gives them far more books to choose from at better prices. Traditional publishing has a long way to go before it can meet the e-book prices of independents or the appetite of e-reading consumers. It's good for writers because more of us can take a crack at the market than ever before. Perhaps we can find readers in a more direct way than through the strangle point of NYC.

Where can readers learn more about you?

From my website: http://www.julietwaldron.com

Moving Smoothly:
Transitioning in Writing
By
Jan Linton (JJ Dare)
Author of:
False Positive and *False World*

❦

Ready. Set. Transition!

Developing smooth changes in writing is a matter of getting into your character's head. Visualize the action happening in and around your character. Visualize your book like a movie directed by you and starring your character.

I sit in my director's chair and think about how I want the action to proceed. I'm at the end of Chapter Two in *False World* and I need to make the reader feel comfortable with a big hop across the world. I need to establish a connection between a familiar character and an unfamiliar character. Below is an excerpt from the end of Chapter Two and the beginning of Chapter Three.

As the door quietly shut, Joe felt his body relax back onto the bed as he fell asleep before his head touched the pillow.

He dreamed of the moon.

Chapter 3

Across the ocean, a man sat on a balcony overlooking a pristine garden. A full moon illuminated every plant and tree within the landscaped field. It was beautiful and tranquil, but the man paid little attention to the moonlit scene.

Joe is the protagonist in my books, *False Positive* and *False World* written under the pseudonym JJ Dare. Shared imagery is one way to connect Joe to an unknown character. The image of the moon joins two characters and presents a transition between dissimilar chapters.

If a reader has to flip back and forth in a book repeatedly, they may eventually give up. Disjointed action is hard to follow. Well-written books join the chapters like Grandma's quilt joins scraps of fabric. Although the quilt is made from different materials, it is bound together in a unity of careful stitching and harmonious batting. A book can be like this, too.

The reader is omniscient. They have the inside scoop and the privilege of knowing what a character might not. Transitioning in this case is relatively easy. The misstep in this type of transitioning is letting the omniscient knowledge hang too long before the protagonist catches up. Following is an example of a shift change that starts at the end of Chapter Six from *False World*.

Liz and Joe had no way of knowing that while they were in their safe retreat, the world had fallen even deeper into chaos and, for quite a few people, it seemed as though the gates of hell had opened and Armageddon was upon them.

Chapter 7

Earth was under siege.

The hounds of war had been loosed and the entire world was preparing for battle. Nations were organizing their military forces to wage war against other nations, countries were already battling their neighbors, and in some areas, even cities were arming themselves against the villages close to them. Only people who were living in caves were unaffected by the changes across all lands.

I set up the beginning of Chapter Seven at the end of Chapter Six with "the world had fallen even deeper in to chaos." With those words, I was able to give the reader a heads-up on the next scene. Chapter Seven describes what went on in the world while the protagonist was out of pocket.

Instead of breaking a chapter into sections, I like to start new chapters to allow the action to gain momentum. Many chapters in my books end on mini-cliffhangers, another type of transitioning. I try hard not to delineate the action within my chapters by written stop signs, such as dashes, dots or asterisks.

I rarely use these types of paragraph break symbols. Most of my action is consistently flowing. If I need to insert a few days of inaction in a story, I will simply note that the character was inactive for a little while. Following is an example from *False Positive*:

> *Joe was stunned. The police had closed the case and told him to go home and wait for word from his missing mother. After several tedious days of watching too much television, drinking too much beer, and waiting for a call that never came, Joe was ready to scream. Slipping on jeans that had become mysteriously too tight, he put on his shoes and was walking out the door when the phone rang.*

Here is an example from Chapter Five of *False World* of when I needed a visual break in a paragraph. The reason I added one of my rare visual breaks is because the character is sleeping and I'm letting him doze without dreams. Poor guy needed the rest:

> *Exhaustion hit both of them at the same time. With a mumbled good night, Joe lay back on the couch and was asleep before his head hit the throw pillow.*

> *   *   *

> *Pain.*
> *The day after arriving at Liz's safe house, Joe woke to aches and pains from the top of his head to the bottom of his feet. The adrenaline rush he had had the day before had quickly worn off and a bastard load of pain was coursing through his body.*

Choppy transitioning within chapters makes it hard for the reader to follow the story. Chapter to chapter transitioning is a bit more forgivable since the end of one chapter can signify the end of a scene.

Like a movie, the storyline needs to flow smoothly. A filler chapter that adds nothing to the plot is like the refreshment ads in the theatre before the movie starts. I paid for the movie, not the reminders to buy concessions. Disjointed hops and skips in a story can turn a wonderful work into a forgotten one.

Consistency is a key to successful changes in time within a story.

Jumping back and forth with too many flashbacks might turn some readers away. Below is a section from my short story, *Love Transcends*, written for the *Love is on the Wind* anthology. In a few paragraphs, the reader knows the characters evolved into a happy couple over the space of twelve years. No heavy flashbacking was involved:

> *They found bliss and comfort in each other's arms. A joy that had been missing in their lives was now filling their souls and they felt as though the angels themselves rejoiced.*
>
> *They were both content to live together forever in their own small heaven. Jack made his furniture and Annie painted her beautiful art. The most alluring and endearing painting was of a woman, not unlike Annie herself, perched on the cliff beside their home with hair blowing in the wind and arms spread out like wings.*
>
> *Although she could have thought of better pictures to love, Jack was crazy about this one. He insisted, gently, of course, that Annie hang the picture above their mantel. Every night, Jack would stand for a few minutes looking at the picture with a contented smile on his face.*
>
> *Life continued at a pace with which they both were comfortable. They were not rich, but they did not require a lot of money. Their needs were simple and as long as they had each other, nothing else really mattered. The years passed, but time did not diminish the love and passion they felt for each other. Life was good.*
>
> *Annie had been with Jack for twelve years, twelve wonderful years. The day of their twelfth anniversary dawned bright and cold as Jack left to deliver the furniture he had created the week before. He had a special surprise planned for Annie and his excitement was such, he could barely contain himself.*
>
> *Annie waved to Jack as he left. Like she did every morning, she walked to the edge of the cliff and looked out over the ocean.*

All in all, transitioning is simple if you put yourself in your story. WWMCD (What Would My Character Do) is my mantra when writing. Being the director and actor in my book helps me to focus on keeping the action shifts rolling along smoothly.

Like a movie director, look at your tale and guide the action smoothly. Whether you are writing a novel, novella or short story, smooth transitioning can make or break your work.

🐦

Interview with Jan Linton

What are your books about?

False Positive and *False World,* the first two books in the Joe Daniel's trilogy, are about deception, espionage and redemption. These are written under the pen name of JJ Dare. I'm working on the third and final book.

What inspired you to write this particular story?

I was inspired to write about hidden government agendas and their devastating aftereffects when I thought about why we, as a nation, involve our resources in other nations' conflicts. My biggest inspiration: the eternal "what if"?

How much of yourself is hidden in the characters in the book?

The aggressive part of my passive/aggressive personality is turned loose in the books. I can let myself go through my characters; I can destroy without regret, lie with a straight face and a cold heart, and generally, get away with murder.

Is there a message in your writing you want readers to grasp?

Trust no one.

Do you think writing this book changed your life? How so?

Writing my first book a few years ago gave me confidence. I believe it was an exercise to prepare me for the challenges I would shortly face in my personal life.

What has changed for you personally since you wrote your first book?

I've lost three people in my family (my brother, my partner and my mother) since March, 2010. My late partner Dan was my biggest supporter. The belief he had in me gives me the strength to keep writing.

What are you working on right now?

This interview! Oh, and a few articles, blog posts, and my perpetual 30+ novels in various stages of incompletion. One particular thing I'm working on was suggested by my late partner's brother, a Memphis novelist. He thinks I should put together a collection of my short stories.

What is the most difficult part of the whole writing process?

Inspiration. When it's not there, it can't be faked. Constipated writing can be unbearable.

What is the easiest part of the writing process?

Inspiration. When it's there, the words flow like a raging river. If the story is in my head and I've been tapped by my muse (and she stays with me), I can write a novel in a week.

Does writing come easy for you?

Short stories are much easier. I can put a short story together within an hour. All of my life I've been a "condenser." I like to pare my words down, whether written or spoken, to the bare minimum. This is a double-edged sword since to write a complete novel I have to expand the story and I detest using useless filler.

What's been the most surprising part of being a writer?

The most surprising aspect of being a published writer is the positive feedback I've received from readers. Only a few weeks ago, I had a reader ask when the third book in the Joe Daniels' trilogy would be coming out.

What, in your opinion, are the essential qualities of a good story?

The hook is the essential part of a story; with a good hook, the reader won't want to put a book down. I try to draw the reader in immediately with a one-two punch.

Have you completed any other books?

I have three completed works that need editing. Editing is so boring that I put it off for as long as I can.

Where can people learn more about your books and/or you?

Find my books at Second Wind Publishing
http://secondwindpublishing.com.
Find me on my personal Facebook page,
http://www.facebook.com/jan.d.linton

CAPTIVATING SETTINGS
By
Deborah J Ledford
Author of:
Staccato and *Snare*

One of the most important elements for any writer is to establish a "voice"—one that is recognizable, and somewhat expected by the reader as you continue to present more works. The ideal way to imprint your particular voice, cadence, tempo, tone is by setting your scenes. Once you truly place the reader at the location, whether it is a city, neighborhood, store or house, they become comfortable and willing to take the journey with the characters you present.

I write psychological suspense thrillers, therefore ominous settings are crucial in my novels. In this chapter you will find examples from *STACCATO* and *SNARE* to give you an idea of my personal writing voice when it comes to settings.

It is important to put the reader at ease and to give them a visual at the beginning of each chapter, especially the first time the location is presented.

The first scene of *STACCATO*, our hero, the twenty-year-old world-class pianist Nicholas Kalman discovers his father's journal hidden away in the music room of the mentor who has raised him for a decade:

Compelled by the words, he found it impossible to re-shelve the book, or to dismiss the pages as utter fiction. He wondered what the written implications meant for him. Reading his father's recollections, he had fallen under their spell. His father warned of the seductive elements to be cautious of—things that had already ensnared Nicholas.

Looking around, he recognized what his father had described as cunning manipulations of deceiving comfort: first edition books exhibited within walnut cases surrounding him in a ritualistic circle, the ebony Steinway grand piano that sat regally upon a platform in the middle of the music room, exactly as the writings stated. The details even noted how flames from the fireplace bathed the Pakistani rug in an amber glow.

In the introduction scene, first pages of *SNARE*, we meet eight-year-old Katina Salvo and within a few paragraphs discover the life she is burdened with in 1995:

She wished for a radio or record player, anything that might drown out the sounds. She wondered how long this fight would last. There had been so many in the past few weeks. They seemed to get worse each time.

Streaked ivory wallpaper peeled near the heat register in the cramped bedroom, furnished only with a twin-sized bed and scuffed desk. The room displayed none of the comforts the few kids she knew took for granted. A tattered, handmade quilt, passed down from her father's mother, offered the only color in the room. Its unraveling edge brushed against the frayed braided rug on the floor.

Both of these examples provide setting information for the reader, and the details show insights to what have formed these characters as people.

Every element you introduce must be used somewhere within the novel you are writing. Think of this as foreshadowing what will come. Make certain that each prop (such as furniture) introduced is instrumental and will be used later in the novel. The point is not to introduce anything that will not be useful to the reader. Be careful of "info-dumping" when it comes to creating your settings.

For instance in *SNARE*, this is the description of the stage where Katina Salvo will perform live for the first time—where chaos soon ensues:

Stage lights were now set for a mere amber glow and soon she could make out a knot of people near the stage opening at the farthest end of the wings. As she moved to them, she noticed someone had closed the main curtain and she realized the effect would add to the mystery. It would also provide a much more dramatic entrance than if the drape were already open.

In *STACCATO*, Nicholas's nemesis, Alexander Boden, is described in the setting Nicholas always thought of as home, where terror now reigns. This passage is described within the journal by Nicholas's father that the son has discovered adds to the suspense that follows:

Lips holding an easy smile. Clothes flawless and crisp, shoes polished like mirrors, cufflinks gleaming in tailored shirts. The cane tapping.

Tap. Tap. Tap. You hear it approaching, but you can't escape.

BE CONCISE IN DESCRIBING INTERIOR SETTINGS

Let the reader become comfortable. Show them the room or area your characters will inhabit. For instance, in *SNARE*, the reader learns quite a lot the first time we meet Katina's nemesis, her father who has just been released after seventeen years in prison after killing her mother:

In a flophouse off 37th Street, Karl Brandt lay on the thin mattress in his third-story room studying a discolored splotch on the ceiling. The quiet made him uneasy and restless. Muffled street sounds urged him from the bed. He wrenched the window open and sat on the radiator beneath the glass to watch the strangers below. Accustomed to seeing only prisoners' orange jumpsuits or correctional officers' bland uniforms, he still had difficulty taking in the brightly colored clothing of the passersby.

In *STACCATO*, this is what the unofficial mortician of Swain County, North Carolina, finds in his morgue:

Once inside the morgue, he wedged a straight-back chair under the knob. He flipped on the light switch and the fluorescents hummed and flickered, then bathed the room in its flat, blue light. Henri's mouth dropped open. He froze, gaping in disbelief. Six, black plastic-covered bundles seemed to swallow the light.

TAKE YOUR READER "THERE" WITH EXTERIOR SETTINGS

You have the opportunity as a writer to take readers where they may have never visited before. This is a perfect way to show exactly what you wish to convey.

In *SNARE*, Hawk experiences Katina's upbringing when he sees the traditional structures on the Taos Pueblo Indian reservation:

Two massive structures bookended a narrow creek. He counted five stories of staggered, uneven rooflines covered in more of the smooth mud, the levels stacked on top of each other like twin rectangular tiered cakes. Doors the color of turquoise marked openings in the walls.

MOOD TO CONVEY SURROUNDINGS

At the top of chapter 22 in *STACCATO* the lead investigators witness the surroundings where Nicholas's vehicle is found:

Hawk and Stiles arrived to a scene bathed in generator-driven white-blue spotlights. County vehicles were parked on U.S. Highway 74, resembling a young boy's scattered toys. The cruisers' revolving red and blue lights added to the eerie glow.

One hundred yards below the roadway, officers milled about on the muddy bank of the Nantahala River. They searched the area around the crushed vehicle, barely recognizable as a black Porsche. The sports car sat precariously on the riverbank, suspended by a cable attached to the rear of a tow truck.

White-capped ripples rushed past, glinting in the moon's light. It had been hours since the Porsche had been discovered, but the scene still buzzed with activity.

This is an example of mood conveyed within setting at the top of chapter 57 in SNARE:

Hawk's shoulder throbbed. Shooting pains that ripped to the bone brought tears to his eyes. The smell of fresh coffee and baking pie would normally be inviting, but instead, his stomach churned in a cataclysm of nerves. Every sound seemed amplified. Even the clock over the stove ticked louder than he thought possible.

IMPLEMENTING WEATHER AND ATMOSPHERE

Atmosphere is a captivating way to introduce a scene. Try

featuring weather to enhance the tone for a setting.

During one of the last chapters of *STACCATO*, Nicholas confronts the man he always thought of as his closest friends—who turns out to be the co-conspirator in the death of his love. The end of the scene takes place outside the morgue. A storm is brewing in the North Carolina night:

"Why? Nicholas shouted. "Tell me, you bastard. Why did this happen?"

Sampte kept his chin tucked to his chest, refusing to look at Nicholas.

A flash of lightning lit the area, halting all action for a moment. A deafening crack, followed by a train-like rumble resounded through the trees.

When Sampte raised his head, Nicholas searched the man's eyes for any clues. Instead, he recognized the flat, resolved gaze, rivaling a look only Alexander could brandish.

To Nicholas, Sampte's silence seemed louder than the thunder.

In *SNARE* the implication of a storm is introduced when Steven Hawk takes in a vision as he arrives in Taos, New Mexico. The danger for Katina remains and he has no idea what he will encounter in the days ahead:

As the vehicle approached the airport exit, Hawk noticed a massive billowing white cloud high in the air that encompassed a third of his vision. The formation reminded him of a natural Hiroshima bomb mushroom. He hoped the duality of beauty versus tragedy wasn't an omen of what was to come and pushed aside the troublesome thought.

There you have it—examples of settings to capture settings your readers are sure to appreciate.

Interview with Deborah J Ledford

Could you provide us with a little bio?

I am first and foremost a suspense thriller author. My latest novel, *SNARE*, is The Hillerman Sky Award Finalist. *STACCATO* is book one of the Deputy Hawk/Inola Walela thriller series and both novels are published by *Second Wind Publishing*. I'm also a three-time nominee for the Pushcart Prize. My award-winning short stories appear in numerous print publications, as well as literary and mystery anthologies.

What is your training and experience?

Before my writing career I was a professional scenic artist for movies, theatre and industrial films. Then I started writing screenplays. I see writing as an extension of the visual form, and due to my experience writing scripts my novels are quite visual and heavily dialogue driven. I also have my own independent film production company and will be writing the screenplay for *SNARE*.

Could you tell us about *SNARE*?

The tagline is: Revenge with a beat. It's the journey of popular rock star Katina Salvo who is about to embark on her first personal appearance. She's just learned she's been receiving death threats and unbeknownst to her, her father has recently been released from prison for killing her mother 15 years earlier. Her six day journey, along with Deputy Steven Hawk who is assigned to protect Katina, takes her on a path of murder, revenge, retribution and discovery.

What was the path to publication for *SNARE*?

SNARE began as a screenplay, then I went on to novelize the piece much later. It's been through so many evolutions since day one. I began to get serious about what was to become the printed version of novel before my debut novel *STACCATO* was published in 2009. *SNARE* was released 12.21.10.

What sort of research did you do for this book?

I'm part Eastern Band Cherokee and knew that I wanted the Native American element to be instrumental for *SNARE*. Once I decided on the Tribe to focus on I came into contact with the communications director on the Taos Pueblo in New Mexico. Floyd "Mountain Walking Cane" Gomez read every word of the manuscript as I composed each draft. He either approved scenes, characters and elements, or told me flat out "No, you cannot use this." (He told me this quite often!) Elements Floyd wasn't sure about were cleared by elders and the Taos Pueblo Tribal Council.

Why are the settings in your novels so important to you?

I decided if I was going to write an ongoing series the location would be every bit as important as the characters. I spent my summers growing up in western North Carolina, in the heart of the Great Smoky Mountains. Since this locale is rarely featured in print, and I know it so well, this is where I decided to set the overall main location. The characters, their motivation and journey are sparked from the areas featured in both books. For the other location in *SNARE*, I fell in love with the Taos Pueblo, New Mexico, reservation and its people after researching for the Native American tribe I wished to highlight in the book.

Could you share one of your favorite paragraphs in *SNARE*?

Sure. The paragraph below indicates the spiritual connection Deputy Steven Hawk shares with the female lead, Native American Katina Salvo. The scene appears in Chapter 48 when Hawk and Steven are on the Taos Pueblo Indian Reservation:

Hawk took in a deep breath and let it out slowly. "Well, I felt something. Kind of like when I think my dad's visiting me. He died almost seven years ago, but sometimes I swear he's in the room when I'm alone. I've got a wind chime hanging on the back porch. It's just a little copper bell, but sometimes, when it's real quiet, and not a leaf is stirring, that bell strikes a single ting."

Where do your ideas come from?

Some come to me in quite vivid dreams, but most ideas for my novels and short stories are prompted by real-life events. I love the CNN news crawl—short headline-type info that more often than not you never hear anything else about. A lot of subplots have been prompted by news related events. Also, I'm a people watcher and I try my best to implement characteristics, ticks and sometimes dialogue from actual people I've witnessed.

How can we find out more about you?

Free downloads of the first chapters to *SNARE* and *STACCATO*, as well as a few of my previously published short stories can be found on my website at http://www.deborahjledford.com. I'm also on Twitter, have a Personal Page on Facebook as well as a Facebook Book Page, and can be found on the great book site Goodreads.

Foreshadowing
By
Nancy A Niles
Author of:
Vendetta: A Deadly Win

🐦

Foreshadowing is one of those techniques that seem to come naturally and effortlessly to most writers. It is something that happens often in real, everyday life and can be blatantly obvious or so subtle that it can easily be overlooked.

Foreshadowing has been described as being hints of what's to come. These hints can be delivered by the author through narrative. They can be spoken by the characters. They can take the form of thoughts in the POV character's mind. They can be symbolic. They can come through the sense of smell, the sense of sight and hearing. Usually a writer's imagination is the limit when it comes to foreshadowing.

Verbal Foreshadowing is when the hint is said through dialogue such as one character asking the other if so and so still carries a gun, or as subtle as asking if so and so is still taking medication. These examples leave the reader wondering if that character is going to shoot someone or wondering what would happen if he/she stopped taking the medication, or if the medication could somehow make her/him change in some way, maybe become violent, or at the very least, unpredictable. The reader then expects something to happen from this foreshadowing and it cranks up the suspense. These gems can be interspersed throughout the novel to bring interest and a bit of intrigue to the story.

Foreshadowing Through Inappropriate Responses. This is done through having one or more characters react to stimuli in an inappropriate manner, such as, in a fearful situation, the character, instead of showing fear shows amusement. What is going on? Has the character set up the other character for a downfall? Has the character been scared into insanity? This type of foreshadowing tells the reader that more is going on and prepares them for the unexpected.

Foreshadowing Through Thoughts in the main character's mind can give hints of what may be coming. Such as, *"I wondered where he had been. Some said he'd been away on a vacation. But I could never find out where exactly he'd gone. Camp Fed? Or the Good Shepherd Home For The Silly? Wherever he'd gone he seemed to have gotten a new lease on life. He seemed more determined, more purposeful, as though he had plans. But for what? Revenge? Did he have murder on his mind or was my imagination working overtime?"* Well, you get the point. The main character can lead the reader anywhere through her thoughts and a little paranoia is always called for especially in the PI genre.

Foreshadowing Through a Character's Fears is closely related to foreshadowing through the character's thoughts. However, the fear factor makes the foreshadowing more ominous. And again, in the PI genre the detective is usually cynical and expecting the worst, not believing anyone or anything.

Symbolic or Paranormal Foreshadowing can be something that the main character brings to the reader's attention. In the horror genre I've noticed many times the author will tell the reader of legends surrounding certain animals. Such as, crows are the harbinger of death. They supposedly carry the dead person's spirit to the other side. And then lo and behold a flock of crows appears just as the main character is setting out on her journey. Or make it one crow who is hunched on a fence post, its beady obsidian eyes tracking the main character. In that instance, less is definitely more. Actually, the author can make up their own legends and feed them into the story. Or the more subtle approach could be an icy touch of wind on the back of the main character's neck when they look into the eyes of the antagonist.

Which leads me to another type of foreshadowing: **Bodily Reactions in Foreshadowing.** Who hasn't read a book where a chill goes down the spine of the main character, or the main character experiences a shortness of breath at the mention of a name? It is both a subtle type of foreshadowing and also rather obvious. It tells the reader to be warned, something is not quite right, and who among us has never felt a chill at certain times that turned out to be a warning?

Foreshadowing Through Smell, Sight and Hearing. This is also called setting the stage, or using setting as character. In the PI genre the setting is usually as haunting as the haunted main character. The PI is in the streets that teem with the smell of fear, violence and decay. You just know the main character is in an unsafe place and violence is expected. Sounds of people fighting, guns going off, etc., also foreshadow danger. Smell can let the reader know someone is smoking marijuana, or the stink of whisky, or even the copper smell of blood can lead the reader to expect certain things to come.

This is a great way to foreshadow. Especially with the sense of smell since smell is so closely connected to memory. The author can have the main character smell bodies being burned and then find out that it isn't bodies, but it's the Fourth of July and there are barbecues happening. The main character interpreted the smell from a memory that still haunts him of the Vietnam War and witnessing people being burned alive. This type of foreshadowing gives the reader a window into the main character's mind and past experiences. It can foreshadow a tenuous grip on reality and make the reader nervous for the main character.

Foreshadowing Using the Weather and Dreams, Or Through Finding Something Out Of Place. An impending storm or natural disaster is a good way to foreshadow a possible upcoming suspenseful event. Dreams can warn the main character and the reader of something coming and finding an article out of place can foreshadow mischief. And who among us hasn't seen that solitary shoe out of place on the highway and wondered what happened to the owner?

I'm sure there are many more ways to foreshadow. In my novel *Vendetta: A Deadly Win* I used foreshadowing throughout the book. Here are some examples:

Foreshadowing Through a Character's Perceptions. In the opening paragraph I have Paul Faraday thinking of blood as he looks at the garish neon signs on the boulevard. This alerts the reader to his state of mind, (violent) and a foreshadowing that all is not well:

The red neon lights reminded Paul Faraday of blood running down the sides of the buildings. The drops were big and small, round and oblong and flashed and blinked with the rhythm of a thousand beating hearts.

Another way to foreshadow through a character's perceptions is in their judgments about the other characters. Such as I did on page 49 where Bernie and Stella are joking around with each other and Tina is watching them:

Stella giggled loudly and I looked around the room not wanting to intrude on their horseplay. When I'd first seen them together their antics had charmed me until the next time I saw them together and Stella had been a completely different person. She had seemed to hate everything about Bernie and certainly never one to horse around. I wondered how someone could have such extreme moods. And as time went on I became concerned at her 'dark' moods and actually feared that someday she might do something to harm him or herself.

The reader is alerted that something bad is coming either for Bernie or Stella and that promise is fulfilled later on in the book.

On page 3 Paul is on his way to deliver a ransom demand and he is convincing himself that he can get the drop on the kidnapper and save his wife. This is a sample of **Foreshadowing Through Narrative of the Character's Thoughts**:

Besides, he'd brought a gun, safely nestled on top of the bills. Paul had run through his plan a thousand times.

This foreshadows violence and most likely a fight to the death with the kidnapper.

Bodily Reactions, Sight and Feelings. On page 4 as he is

nearing the destination his confidence begins to wane:
But that did not cause the shaking in his hands or the cold sweat popping on his brow. He could feel someone watching him, tracking his car. The low lying hills could hold any number of snipers and he'd never see them coming.
Is he beginning to lose it? Will he panic? Are there snipers waiting for him?

On page 8 is an example of **Foreshadowing Through An Inappropriate Response.** Faraday has just offered the kidnapper a million dollars in unmarked, small bills and tells him to take the money and run because of the type of people who would come after him if he hurt Anna or himself:
His mind scrambled to think of something, anything. "Look pal, the money is all there, just take it and leave. You can get far away on a million bucks," he reasoned. "Don't do something that'll get you killed," his words came out in a rush. "You don't know the kind of people who would come after you if you killed us. Just give me Anna...now!"
The kidnapper's chuckle sent chills down Paul's spine
He chuckles? Is the man insane? What does he know that we don't? This foreshadowing also tells the reader that the detective trying to solve the case will also have to deal with some tough characters. And the reader finds out why the kidnapper laughs in the face of death.

The endings of chapters are good places to give some **Foreshadowing Through a Character's Fears**. The last paragraph on page 22 is an example of this type of foreshadowing:
I patted his hand. "It'll be okay, Hutch," I said. But I felt not as certain of that as I sounded. In fact I did not feel sure at all.

On page 69 I give a **Symbolic or Paranormal Foreshadowing** delivered by Megan, Tina's assistant. Megan practices Santoria and has abnormal powers of perception. She is cleansing the bad vibes in the office:
"I be burning sage in here all day," she said. "I feel de discord too as soon as I come in dis morning. It's clearin' up. I tink Bernie

and Stella are okay for now."

How about later? Something is definitely brewing between Bernie and Stella and it is not good.

An example of **Setting As Foreshadowing** is on the bottom of page 74 and top of page 75 where in the middle of Wal-Mart the main character finds herself isolated, trapped and in danger:

"Can I help you find something?" He straightened up, holding the box cutter like a switchblade and took a few steps toward me.

"No, I'm just looking at these steering wheel covers."

"You were looking at more than that," he accused, blocking my passage to the main aisle. The overhead security cameras would only show an employee speaking with a customer. There were no people even near this aisle and the tall shelves made me feel claustrophobic.

Foreshadowing Through Dreams is on page 87:

In the depths of a nightmare, a brutal image appeared: Hutch's house in flames, billows of smoke choked my lungs, heat from the fire radiated over my body and I couldn't get my breath. I awoke with a start, clawing at my chest, my body covered in a clammy sheen of sweat. I took in deep breaths of air to slow the pounding of my heart.

This dream replays the scene where the stalker set Hutch's house on fire. It reminds the reader of the danger the antagonist represents and puts the main character on guard for another attack which happens very quickly. (Two paragraphs later).

On page 114 I give a **Foreshadowing Of Something Out Of Place**:

I wouldn't have seen Jason leave. He could have gone anywhere. I stared up and down the alley and noticed a beat-up tennis shoe. The sight of that shoe gave me the creeps and I headed back to my car.

Had Jason been wearing that tennis shoe? Had he been kidnapped?

Foreshadowing Through The Weather came in a couple of chapters before Megan is kidnapped and is built upon until the storm is brewing and Tina must fight it to find her assistant:

Thunder rumbled off the hills west of town. That's all we needed with the town packed with tourists who didn't understand the meaning of the words flash flooding, which happened once or twice a year when the sky opened up and dumped the annual rainfall within five minutes, paralyzing the city. I remembered the news clips of helicopter rescues that had taken place a few years back. And people died in flash floods, their cars literally swept off the road into arroyos that had suddenly been transformed into raging rivers. Now, as lightning traveled across the sky and thunder crashed overhead a stunned silence fell on the crowd at the valet parking stand, followed by nervous giggles.

These are just a few examples of foreshadowing that I used in my novel, *Vendetta: A Deadly Win*. As you can see foreshadowing cranks up the expectations of the reader and adds depth to the story. It is a promise of things to come and questions to be answered. I personally love a book with tons of foreshadowing. And believe me, I check to make sure the author fulfills her promise with each and every foreshadowing I discover while reading a novel.

🦃

Interview with Nancy A Niles

How long had the idea of your book been developing before you began to write the story?

I first came up with the idea for the novel about eight years ago. I wrote numerous drafts and with each one I came to know my protagonist a little better. The plot never really changed that much with the rewrites, but the main character and her back story were in a constant state of flux until she became very real to me about three years ago.

What inspired you to write this particular story?

Having been born and raised in Las Vegas, Nevada I wanted to show the beauty of the city through my protagonist's eyes and the devastation that the city has wreaked upon many people who have lived here, or who only have visited here. The city is a paradox.

Who is the most unusual/most likeable character?

My main characters assistant, Megan is the most unusual, likeable character. She is from New Orleans and experienced the hurricane Katrina. She is also familiar with the ancient art of Santoria and worships Damballah the Snake God. Megan has definite opinions and puts a different slant on most things.

How has your background influenced your writing? How does your environment/upbringing color your writing?

Having grown up in Vegas I've met many gangster and wanna-be gangster types. I based the gangster character, Vic Costello on someone I knew very well for many years. My main character's boss, Bernie was loosely based on a very outgoing, funny character who had been well known around town for years. Vegas is a Mecca for offbeat, outgoing, fun loving people. I think being brought up in a gambling town has caused me to realize how dangerous gambling can be and I've seen how it can affect people and families. I've also seen how people change when they come to this city and become so different from whom they've always appeared to be.

What do you like to read?

I love PI fiction, police procedurals, mysteries, suspense and even some romances. I will read anything and find some enjoyment in every genre.

What has changed for you personally since you wrote your first book?

I know I've become much more observant of people and more aware of life changing situations that are going on around us all the time. I hear life changing stories from the news, from strangers and from friends. I also have developed a habit of asking myself how different personalities would have reacted to the same problem or event. In fact, I think I am probably constantly writing in my head and developing characters now that I am a published author. I have gained more confidence in my writing. I find that I want to write more and I feel as though something is missing if I miss a day of writing.

What's been the most surprising part of being a writer?

It always surprises me when the words come – because many times I have no idea what the story is going to be about, or who the characters are. I find that if I just relax and begin to type the characters will surface and pretty much tell me the story. It is awesome and I love the process.

Do you have a saying or motto for your life and/or as a writer?

A quote from Maya Angelou and I try to remember this every day:

"I've learned that people will forget what you said, people will forget what you did, but people will never forget how you made them feel."

Timing
By
Claire Collins
Author of:
Images of Betrayal and *Fate and Destiny*

❧

Timing is everything. It can be what makes someone lucky or unlucky, a success or a failure. It also contributes to what makes a piece of writing incredible or confusing.

In the movies and on TV shows, even in commercials, music is used to set the tone and mood of the scene. Most of the time the music is sneaking around in the background, barely there so it isn't a distraction, but instead used to enhance the emotions of the audience. Watch an action movie with the sound off. The "edge of your seat" experience will be weak or maybe even missing altogether without the fast crashing musical crescendos in the background. The lonesome music in a sad scene, the slow seductive music in a love scene. Each type of music sets the tone and timing for the accompanying scene. What if an action scene had a light, lilting, happy little ditty playing in the background? Wouldn't that be confusing to the senses?

Timing, cadence, or flow in a piece of work creates the rhythm and is as important in prose as it is to music. Timing has to do with making sure the hero shows up at just the right time, as well as bringing in the villain when he or she will have the most impact. You can't kill the bad guy in the middle of the book and then do the "happily ever after" for the next 150 pages.

It's never good when climax happens too soon.

For writing comedy, the timing is in the punch line. Drag the joke out too long and you bore the audience. Cut the joke too short and you leave them wondering what's supposed to be so funny. When writing poetry, timing brings one phrase smoothly into another and creates a rhythm for the poetry interpreter. Think of how quickly you are pulled out of a poem if the rhythm and rhyme is off.

In *Images of Betrayal*, the heroine, Tysan—or Ty for short—realizes that something isn't quite right with the photographer she recently met. The scene set like a building musical tempo in the background. With the scene set, the story begins to build slowly, working up towards an important scene in the storyline.

The lighting was low and comfortable and the room was warm, so I hung my coat on the back of my chair. My purse sat in the chair next to me and Walker pulled his chair close to my other side. He clutched the envelope in his hand until we were situated. The coffee was excellent and I took a sample of the scone drizzled in honey before I looked at him expectantly.

"Are you going to show me the pictures?"

He held the envelope in both of his hands, his coffee and scone untouched. He looked a little pale, and I thought I saw one of his hands tremble. Almost reluctantly, he pulled a stack of photos from the envelope. The picture on top of the stack was apparently from the parade. The colors were beautiful, but I only got a glance at it before he moved, placing the envelope in the middle of the table and taking a sip of his steaming coffee.

"What's wrong?" I asked, holding my hand out for the pictures. "Let me guess, mine didn't come out and you don't want to tell me."

He shook his head before he pulled it away from the edge of the cup. "No, no, nothing like that. The pictures came out just fine." He thought for a moment, studying my face before continuing.

The reader should be able to feel Walker's hesitation and Ty's anticipation. Each emotion is distinct to a character and those emotions offset against each other. The scene has a mixture of dialogue and description. In the next example, Walker has shared some pictures with Ty that weren't quite what Ty expected. The scene is all dialogue and the sentences are short and swift.

I didn't look at Walker, but he squeezed my hand. This couldn't be real.

"I don't understand," I whispered.

116

"Neither do I," Walker whispered back.
"How is this possible?"
"I don't know."
We both looked at the picture in my hand. He had months to think about this. I only had the last few minutes.

I've never been a stickler about sentence structure. I'm a fragmented sentence junkie. I'm not a lazy writer, but I write suspense and sometimes a sentence of one or two words has the impact needed for a fast moving novel. I use short sentences when my characters are in stress or a scene that I want to move very fast. I like to stretch out emotional scenes with longer sentences and more detail. When humans are excited or under duress, they notice less details and when I write those types of scenes, I give less detail. When people are happy and content, they try to absorb as much as possible and to memorize details. Those types of scenes have much more information and longer descriptions.

The beginning of *Fate and Destiny* starts with a woman in the fight of her life and then flips to a normal day in the life of our hero. Descriptions are long complete sentences interspersed by short and fast emotional and stressful thoughts and actions to create the mood of suspense.

Excerpt from *Fate and Destiny*

I can't die like this.
The man reached across her and flung open the truck door. With her last ounce of strength, she opened her eyes and looked at him, trying to reach out and grab him. The giant of a man shoved her through the door as her arms flailed helplessly. Her numb body tumbled down the embankment from the road. She couldn't have stopped the momentum, no matter how much she wanted to. Her body wouldn't do as commanded and her mind wanted to follow it into the dark, unfeeling place.
Pain shot through the fog in her head as her leg cracked against something stuck precariously from the snow.
I won't die here. I won't die alone.

117

If determination alone could have saved her, she would have risen from the snow and walked down the mountain. Fate wasn't on her side.

Determination gave way to surrender as her head slammed into the landscape. Before her eyes shut to protect any remnants of sanity, she saw the truck turn and disappear down the road as barking from the hounds of hell erupted around her.

With the temperature dropping by the second, Andrew Greer slid as much as he walked, risking broken bones with every step. The end of his scarf slipped from around his neck, loosening enough to allow the demanding wind access to his nose. He glanced back wistfully at the cabin. A finger of smoke curling from the chimney beckoned to him, calling him in that direction. Warmth. Security. Coffee.

Wrapping the coat tighter around him, Andrew walked around the corner of the cabin. Across the clearing, Shadow leisurely sniffed a frozen tree stump. It must be nice to have a built-in fur coat. Although a pelt of fur ten inches thick would not ward off the cold today.

He set his mind back on getting the supplies from the shed as soon as possible before the blizzard resumed its fury. He'd been snowed in for the last two days.

Andrew cocked his head, standing still, and listening. The vehicle passing on the roadway sounded bigger than a snowmobile but it was hard to tell with the sounds echoing from snow banks and carried on a howling wind.

Assuming someone dared to clear the road, a fresh batch of slick, wet snow and ice would soon recover it, wasting the effort.

Piling the last of the provisions in the cabin, he made one last trip around the edges of the building looking for damage. Convinced the structure was sound, he pulled the scarf down from his face, piercing the frigid air with a long whistle. The sharp sound was an alert to Shadow that it was time to go back to the cabin.

The stark trees mixed with the full varieties of fir and rocks poked from the mounds of white. The wind ruffled the dunes of snow. Dog tracks disappeared into the forest, but nothing emerged from the trees at the familiar call.

Keeping an eye on the edge of the trees, he returned to the front of the little building, calling the dog's name. The wind stung more fiercely the farther he went from the cabin.

Barking erupted from the woods.

*   *   *

There's also timing in being able to keep the flow of the story moving forward. Sentences and thoughts have to move from one to the next smoothly and quickly. This type of timing involves pulling the reader along and progressing the story. An engaged reader will read faster during the action scenes and slower during the love scenes provided they are written that way. Books written with nothing but long sentences full of impressive words that show the authors extended vocabulary will bore the reader. It may also insult the reader if they feel less intelligent or they need a dictionary to get through the book. Obscure words will pull a reader out of a mood immediately.

Which one of these sentences works and which one needs a word doctor?

The throbbing in her temples did nothing to help her concentrate. She mentally pushed the pain down and tried to focus on her work.

Cephalalgia impeded her enthrallment. She exonerated herself of the affliction to pursue responsibilities.

I've been told from readers that they will read my books in just a couple of days because they don't want to stop reading. The story pulls them along. For an author, that's a huge compliment. The reader is engaged and entertained. They keep reading to see what happens next.

Excerpt from *Fate and Destiny*

Heart thudding against her ribs, unable to breathe, she stumbled the few steps to grab the fireplace poker. Wildly scanning the room, she found the only place she could get to quickly.

Dropping to the floor, she squirmed under the bed, ignoring the pains rolling over her body. Forcing deep breaths, exhaling slowly, she concentrated on listening to the noises of the woods surrounding the cabin.

Silence.

In the narrow space, she didn't have room to swing the weapon. Positioning herself to be able to jab the metal iron, her foot met with something cold and hard. Pushing down the pain, she reached around to determine what was under the bed.

Smooth, curved wood and metal. Almost crying with relief, she gripped the rifle, sliding it around in front of her. The fire was dying out, but in the wan light, the gun was the most beautiful thing she had ever seen.

Whispering a prayer that it was loaded, she held it in her grip, slipping her hand over the trigger, the lever action against her fingers. Cocking the gun, hearing a bullet slide into the chamber, she almost laughed.

On her stomach in the narrow space, she fought down claustrophobia. The fireplace poker rested on the floor beside her, replaced by the gun positioned under her arm. The silence was powerful as she strained to hear any noise.

The sick unease in her stomach twisting, she swallowed hard. Mentally repeating the steps in the difficult process of breathing, she controlled the queasiness.

Her mind wandered, seeking solace. A short time before, she had been ready to bash Andrew's brains in with a fireplace poker, not knowing there was a rifle directly under her.

Whispering into the dark, she could not believe her own ignorance.

"Of course he would have a gun you dummy. He's out in the middle of the—"

She forgot how to breathe. Listening for a repeat of what she heard while talking to herself.

Near panic, she trembled.

Wait. The thudding wasn't footsteps.

Her own heart drumming in her ears. The breathing was not the boogeyman, but ragged breaths sucking in and out of her open mouth.

Making herself calm again, she was ready to get out from under the bed to look out the window since she now had a gun to protect her.

She only moved a fraction of an inch. All sounds exploded through the air as the front door opened and Destiny blindly pulled the trigger.

* * *

Do you want to know what happens next? Of course you do.

🦃

Interview with Claire Collins

What are your books about?

Fate & Destiny is a romantic thriller set on a snowy mountaintop. During a blizzard. Andrew's dog, Shadow, finds Destiny, a beautiful woman left for dead, but very much alive. With her, she brings mystery, danger and passion to the little cabin.

Images of Betrayal is the story of Tysan, a teenage girl abandoned by her family. To support herself, she finds works as a waitress in a diner. One cold evening, a beguiling, rugged young man barges into her life. He possesses the remarkable ability to take photographs of events that have not yet happened. Ty narrowly avoids a harrowing death in a disastrous explosion, only to be drawn into a dizzying cascade of conflicts involving a new family that takes her in, Walker—her apparent savior, David—her new admirer and her own family. Kidnapping, betrayal, obsessive love and courageous lovers co-mingle in this romantic thriller.

How long had the idea of your book been developing before you began to write the story?

Most of the time, I may only get a thought or an image or a name, just some tiny detail that I have to write down. I rarely know what it is or what's happening until the characters start to tell me what's happening. I'm just the vessel they use to tell their story. Before I know it, I have a paragraph, a chapter, or half a book.

How much of yourself is hidden in the characters in the book?

Every character, every scene, every conflict and resolution, it all has elements of me or my life in them. Even the parts I don't like. They just appear.

Of all your characters, who are your favorite?

In *Fate & Destiny*, my favorite characters turned out to be the dog and the sheriff. The dog, Shadow, really struck a chord with people and they tend to really love him. I was surprised how he grew as a character in the book when he started out as merely a secondary character. The book wouldn't be the same without him. I also really love the sheriff and his life and his family. I have a sequel for him floating in my head.

For *Images of Betrayal*, I fell madly in love with one of the male leads, but I can't tell you which one. You'd have to read the book to know! The heroines in both books are directly pieces of me, so it's a given that I am one with them.

How long did it take you to write your books?

Fate & Destiny took me over ten years from the first word to the final product. *Images of Betrayal* took three months start to finish.

Did you do any research for your books?

I research anything I don't know as I go along. My work-in-progress, *Seeds of September*, begins in 1956. I researched everything I could about the time period, the region, popular fads, the culture. And then I used very little of it, but at least I had the information in my head if

I needed it.

How do you develop and differentiate your characters?

My characters talk to me. I can see them and hear them and they are all unique to me. I'm always afraid they will seem very flat to others, but they are so alive to me that it somehow comes out the right way for others to see them the way I do.

What is the most difficult part of the whole writing process?

Finding the time to write. I go through periods where all I want to do is write and then there are long periods when I'm so incredibly busy in life that I can't get time to write. For me, writing is the same as a familiar and comfortable friend, always there when I need it.

Do you have mental list or a computer file or a spiral notebook with the ideas for stories that you intend to write one day?

I have a mental list and I have a folder on my hard drive of all of the stories I have in progress. Some are just a sentence or two and some are nearly finished novels.

How many stories do you have swirling around in your head?

So many stories, so little time. I have at least a dozen in various stages.

What advice you would give to an aspiring author?

It's not easy. You can't ever do this thinking you're going to be rich. You can't do this with the mindset that you know everything and no one can make your writing better. You have to write because you have a story to tell and you love the act of writing. You have to write for yourself and to have someone else read your words and really get what you're trying to tell them. You have to be open to other people's opinions. If you can't take a publisher or editor telling you to straighten things up, then how will you take a reader telling you they don't like your work?

What advice would you give other novelists about book promotion?

For me, promotion is the hardest part about writing books. It takes a ton of time that I never seem to have available. The problem is no one else will promote my books and they won't sell if I don't do what I can. I have pride in my work and I tell people about them every chance I get. I do think you get out of it what you put into it and promotion is key to success. A lot of luck helps too!

Have you always wanted to be a writer?

Always. My page on the Second Wind Publishing website (look for me there as Claire Collins) says it well. "Claire Collins began telling stories as soon as she learned to talk, and she hasn't stopped telling stories—or talking—since."

What do you think the most influential change in book publishing will come from?

I think the book publishing world is evolving rapidly. The emergence of the internet, followed by Amazon and then ebooks and ebook readers has vaulted the opportunity for anyone and everyone to be a published writer. Anyone who tweets or blogs thinks they're able to be a successful author. I think readers are inundated with things to read and they will have a harder and harder time finding good quality reading material. I think the standard mass market publishing models are dying and will soon follow the path of the printed newspaper. I don't necessarily think that's a good thing either.

Don't Keep Me Dangling
By
Sherrie Hansen
Author of:
Night and Day, Stormy Weather,
Water Lily, and *Merry Go Round*

🦃

In the little town of Saint Ansgar, Iowa, where I've lived for 20 years, a conscientious Christian has posted a sign on the way into town that announces "The wages of sin is death." Not exactly the greeting you might expect upon first arriving in town.

On the back of the sign, which you can't possibly see until you leave town (unless you can spin your head around and drive at the same time—I can't), is the rest of the story: "But the gift of God is eternal life through Jesus Christ Our Lord."

The Bible verse on the sign (Romans 3:23) is one of my favorites. When read in its entirety, it has a beautiful message. But I hate the way the sign leaves me dangling. What if I don't leave town for several days, two weeks, or a month? What if I leave town by a different route? What if it's dark? I might never get to the good part. I might never know the rest of the story.

If you're one of those people who like to get the bad news over with so you can move on to the good news, you're in luck. But the question is: how long are you willing to wait?

As a reader—of signs and books, I don't like to be kept waiting too long. If the beginning of a book is too depressing or slow-paced, I might not keep reading long enough to get to the good part. If a climax builds too slowly or drags on for too long, I might stop caring before I get there. If a book contains too many cliff hangers, I'm going to be very frustrated, especially if I have to wait a year or two to finally find out what happens next. Even in a series where each book comes to a complete end, with the next installment starting up with a new character or generation of the same family, I don't like to be kept waiting too long. I forget pertinent details, names and relationships and connections between characters.

And what about those books that have multiple story lines about several different characters and so many sub-plots going all at once that by the time you get six chapters down the road and are finally taken back to the main storyline, you can't even remember what was going on? Next time I pick one of them up, I'm going to read Chapters 1, 5, 9, 13, 17 and 21, then go back and hit Chapters 2, 6, 10, 14, 18, and 22... and so on. It'll be much less irritating.

Am I the only one who gets impatient if I'm left dangling too long?

When the third and final book in my Maple Valley Trilogy, *Merry Go Round*, was released, it surprised me how many people bought all three books at once. "We've been waiting until the trilogy was complete", they claimed. "We hate having to wait between books, so we don't even start a series until we can read the whole thing from start to finish."

I wrote as fast as I could when I was working on *Stormy Weather, Water Lily,* and *Merry Go Round*, knowing that those who had started the series were clamoring for the next in line. My publisher worked with me as much as possible to get each subsequent book out quickly. I do understand where those readers were coming from, and am glad I could oblige without leaving anybody waiting for too long.

If the owner of the "Wages of Sin is Death" message is reading this, my advice is to get a second banner and post them like the old-fashioned Burma Shave signs . . . "The wages of sin is death," and then a few yards up the road, a second sign with the hope-filled conclusion, "The gift of God is eternal life..." I don't mind being left hanging for a few yards, but I don't like to be left waiting for too terribly long, or the point is lost on me.

A little suspense is great, but don't keep me on the edge of my seat forever. A nice, slow build up to a tender love scene is very sensual, but don't dash my hopes or put off the inevitable too many times or I may not even enjoy the happy ending when it comes. As a reader and a writer, my opinion is that once you have the momentum going, it's best to keep on climbing at as brisk a pace as you can manage.

Pacing is a constant challenge for a writer. The issue is complicated by the fact that reader expectations have changed dramatically in the last ten years. We belong to a generation that microwaves their food for 2 minutes and it's hot and ready to eat. We grow impatient if we have to wait for things to bake for thirty minutes - roast beef that has to slow cook for 2 or 3 hours? When was the last time you took the time to make it? We want our food done fast – right now! Thanks to high speed computers, we can take a test, and find out how we've done immediately. Letters and information transfers that used to ride a slow boat to China are delivered almost instantaneously via e-mail and fax. As readers, sadly, we've also grown more impatient. When we pick up a book, we want the action to begin on page one, and never stop. We want the answers now.

I like a book that takes a few paragraphs or pages to set the scene and acquaint me with the characters before something dire, life altering, or earth-shattering occurs. When I'm unwittingly thrust into a book that begins with a crisis, I feel emotionally distant from what is going on because I don't know and haven't had a chance to bond with the characters who are involved. Why should I care what is happening to them? Let me get to know the characters and what's at stake before you ramp up the conflict and what happens next will be much more meaningful. But there are many who would disagree with me, who hate slow, arty descriptions and mood setting, who want to be thrown into the action immediately.

A good tease can be absolutely wonderful, but there's a fine line between slow seduction and boredom. Lately I've read some books where the author's timing seemed to be off, where the tease becomes too much, or drags on for too long. I want resolution in due time, which obviously has different definitions for each of us.

One of my favorite series is *Star Trek, Next Generation*, which I watched in its entirety as re-runs aired at 10:30 p.m., Monday through Friday nights back in 1992 and 1993. I loved getting to watch the show every night— the plots seemed far more intense and I got very involved with the characters. If I had had to wait a week between episodes, with large gaps between seasons, my love of the show might never have flourished the way it did.

How can we pace our storylines to capture and keep the imagination of such a wide variety of readers?

1. Avoid lengthy chunks of sitting and thinking. Weave inner thoughts, short descriptions and prosaic musings lightly into scenes that are heavy on action and dialog.
2. Set the scene quickly with prose that is so tight and rich that your readers can get to know and bond with your characters in only a few words.
3. Show, don't tell. Don't tell us your characters are nice, mean, whatever. Illustrate their characteristics by having them do something that shows us what kind of people they are.
4. Cut / chop / slice / dice. Get rid of anything that doesn't progress the story and deepen the conflict.
5. Tease, entice, and then, deliver what you've promised in a timely manner.
6. Make your climaxes so intense and delightful that your reader won't mind waiting for them. Earn the readers trust and consistently respect the confidence they've placed in you.
7. Escalate the level of trouble your character is facing with each subsequent scene, so that his or her problems continue to get worse and worse. Once the black moment has occurred and things can't get any direr, reward the reader's patience with a pleasing resolution.
8. If a scene is slow or lacks luster, identify your protagonist, their goal, and the antagonist, or person who is keeping them from their goal. If there is no specific conflict, ask yourself if there is a value change in the scene. Is something different or has something significant changed as a result of what happens in the scene? If the scene has no conflict and no value change, see suggestion number 4.

I hope these suggestions help you to find the right pace for you story so you don't keep your reader dangling too long. And as for my neighbor, if you're going to tell me the bad news, you'd better not wait too long to find a way to share the good news or I may be long gone and on to the next town by the time you do – and miss the point entirely. Share your story in a way that not only grabs my attention, but satisfies and rewards me with a timely and delightful conclusion.

It's hard to choose a single scene that works as an example of good pacing, when the art generally applies to something that happens over the course of the entire book. But I have chosen a scene from "Merry Go Round", the third and final book in my Maple Valley Trilogy, that I hope will illustrate some of what I've been talking about.

When I was doing my final edits on *Merry Go Round* (cutting, chopping and tightening), I realized that there was no scene when Tracy verbally admitted to her sisters that her marriage was in trouble. It was not known in one scene, then alluded to in the next as though a confession had taken place. But it had not. So I added this scene. I think it shows the tensions that exist between the oldest sister, Rae, and the youngest, Tracy, and that Michelle is caught in the middle, in the role of peacemaker. It has a clear protagonist— Tracy, whose goal is to respect Michelle's wishes by being at the gathering with her sisters, but to get in and out without "saying anything". The antagonist is Rae, who eggs Tracy on and ruffles her feathers by both word and innuendo.

The scene is fairly short and sweet and primarily relies on dialog to move the action along. When the scene opens, the reader knows that Tracy's marriage to Trevor is in trouble, so the suspense lies in the fact that Tracy is keeping the truth from her sisters. The tension escalates as the scene moves on, and the scene delivers at the end when Tracy blurts out her secret… or part of it. (I won't reveal the rest of what's troubling Tracy in case you decide to read the book.)

So when the scene comes to an end, part of the slow tease continues, but the reader is also rewarded when they get to see Rae and Michelle's reaction to the information that Tracy does reveal.

Once you've read the scene, think about this: Tracy did not have to divulge her secret in this scene. She could have strung her sisters—and I, the readers—along a little longer. But in this case, revealing "the rest of the story" gives the scene a satisfactory ending. In addition, it both prolongs the slow, seductive build-up and ratchets up the tension. Will Tracy keep her secret or will she tell them? What will they think and say when they find out? How will they respond? Will it change their opinion of Tracy? Will they keep her secret or tell her parents and gossip to the people who go to Tracy and Trevor's church?

Now that Rae and Michelle know that Tracy's life and marriage are not what they have always appeared to be, they are left to wonder what else Tracy is keeping from them. And the story goes on . . .

Excerpt from *Merry Go Round*

The next morning, Tracy pulled up in front of the Painted Lady and parked her car under a maple tree that was frosted in red. Michelle had called her just as she was leaving Blooming Prairie to tell her about a last minute meeting with Rae. Michelle wanted to show them a quilt their great-aunt Thelma had left to the three of them, and Rae evidently had some sort of announcement to make.

It had already occurred to her that if Rae had wanted her there, she would have called her herself, but Michelle had adamantly insisted that they all needed to be there to decide what to do with Aunt Thelma's quilt, and that Rae would certainly want Tracy to hear whatever news she wanted to share.

She locked the car and started up the cobblestone walkway to the house. She imagined the water lilies would be going inside for the winter before long. The Farmer's Almanac was predicting an early frost followed by a blustery winter.

Michelle met her at the door and shooed her inside. Rae was seated at a table, looking ecstatically happy—until she saw Tracy.

Tracy watched as an irritated look—not really a scowl, but almost—flashed across her oldest sister's face.

"Um, good to see you Rae," Tracy said, wishing she hadn't listened to Michelle.

"You, too." Rae cleared her throat. She looked at Michelle, her eyes shining with fondness once again. "I got my test results back from my twelve month check-up. I'm cancer free."

"Oh, Rae!" Michelle leaped up from her chair and hugged Rae while Tracy looked on.

"That's wonderful!" Tracy said.

Michelle motioned to Madeleine, the head cook. "We're going to celebrate with three pieces of Red Wine Truffle Cake with Dark

Chocolate. It's healthy and decadent all at the same time."

"Sounds great!" Tracy said, feeling happy for Rae and horribly out of place.

Rae kept looking at Michelle, directing her comments to Michelle, smiling at Michelle.

"Mac must be so relieved." Tracy interjected.

"We all are," Rae said condescendingly, making it clear that "we" didn't include her.

She felt like an idiot. So she hadn't called Rae every other day after she'd gotten her diagnosis. So she hadn't sat and held Rae's hand during her chemo treatments. It had gone without saying that Rae wouldn't have wanted her to.

"Be nice, Rae," Michelle said, obviously aware of the tension that was mounting.

This was so unfair. She'd prayed for Rae morning and night when she'd had cancer. She'd put her on the prayer list at Fellowship. She'd bought daffodils and donated money to the American Cancer Society in her name. Theodora had donated her hair to Locks of Love. They'd even bought and lit a luminaria for Rae at the Steele County Walk for Life.

"Don't worry about it," Rae said, her implication very clearly being that Tracy had done something wrong.

"What?" Tracy said, the stress of the past few weeks finally getting the best of her. She didn't want to pick a fight, but she'd bitten her tongue for a whole year because Rae had cancer. Well, she didn't have to anymore. It was time to tell the insufferable prig just what she thought.

"I assume this is because I didn't have my head shaved when you got cancer like Michelle did," Tracy said.

"I never expected you to," Rae said. "I wouldn't have wanted you to."

"So it goes back even further? What, you're still holding a grudge about Mac?" Tracy said.

"It goes back much further than that, sweetheart," Rae countered.

"Stop it right now," Michelle said. "This is supposed to be a celebration."

Rae clicked her tongue. "It's a little hard to feel happy when I've got Miss 'My Life is Perfect in Every Way, and So Would Yours Be

If You Had Only Tried A Little Harder To Find God's Perfect Will For Your Life Like I Did' sitting across the table."

Tracy felt her face blanch. "Of all the..."

"Rachael MacKenzie," Michelle said. "You're supposed to be surrounding yourself with positive energy."

The split second of silence that followed was as cold and dark as a black hole in deep space.

"Just say it," Tracy said. Silence. "Fine, then I will."

Michelle glared at Rae. Rae looked at Michelle.

"Positive energy?" Tracy said. "Then what's she doing here?"

She wanted Michelle to defend her. She wanted Rae to apologize. She wanted them to gush over her, to say how wrong she was—to tell her how much they loved her.

No one said a word. When she realized they weren't going to, she burst into tears.

"I told you," Rae said to Michelle, as though Tracy wasn't even in the room. "This is why I don't invite her to parties. Because it doesn't matter what the celebration's about. Tracy always finds a way to make it about her. It's always about her."

"So you're going to pay her back for all the times she's hurt you and sat in judgment of you by doing the same thing to her?" Michelle said to Rae.

Ouch. That hurt. She knew she hadn't always been kind to her sisters, especially when they'd been single. But she'd really been trying these last couple of years. Rae hadn't even given her a chance when she'd moved back to Iowa. After awhile, she'd stopped trying.

"I'm not sitting in judgment of anyone!" she said in a hushed whisper, resisting the urge to scream. "And my life is not perfect."

"Not according to Mom," Rae said.

"Mom doesn't know the half of it," Tracy said, finally getting angry. Being held accountable for her own misdeeds was fine. She deserved that. But being taken to task for whatever it was that their mother said about her was another matter altogether. Her blood started to boil.

"You think Mom knows what's going on in my life? You think Mom knows anything about me? You honestly think that I confide my hopes and dreams and disappointments and failings with MOM?"

Madeleine whisked into the room and pulled the pocket doors

between she and them closed without saying a word.

"She's right, you know," Michelle said. "I think a lot of the bad blood between you two is Mom's fault."

"Why can't you be more like Tracy?" Rae said, perfectly imitating their mother's voice.

"Tracy never gives me this kind of problem," Michelle said, a close second.

"I'm getting a divorce," Tracy said.

Rae laughed, still on the subject of their mother, not even registering what she'd said. Michelle seemed not to have heard her either.

"Trevor and I are getting a divorce," she said again, this time a little louder.

"What?" Michelle said, a dazed look crossing her face.

"Trevor and I are getting a divorce," she said slowly and succinctly.

"You're kidding," Michelle said.

"You lie," Rae said.

"Nobody knows," Tracy whispered. "Not the kids, not the church. And you can't tell Mom and Dad."

"I don't believe you," Rae said, looking stunned.

"She wouldn't tease about something like this," Michelle said.

"What did you do?" Rae asked point blank. "I mean, we all know Trevor's perfect, so—"

Tracy stood. "Michelle, if you don't mind, I'd like to get started on the Alexander house before it gets any later."

She saw the look that passed between Rae and Michelle, but didn't comment.

"Um, sure. Give me a minute to talk to Madeleine and I'll be over to unlock the door," Michelle said, looking as shocked as Tracy had when Trevor first said the word. "I suppose now's not a good time to talk about the quilt."

"Maybe another time," Tracy said. "Rae, I really am happy that you've been cancer free for a year. Congratulations. Michelle, thanks for including me in the celebration."

"She is kidding, isn't she?" Rae was saying as Tracy fled the room.

Interview with Sherrie Hansen

What is your book about?

Merry Go Round is about Tracy Jones Tomlinson, the youngest of three sisters in my Maple Valley trilogy. Tracy married her childhood sweetheart, is a minister's wife, and has three lovely children. In the first two books, Rachael and Michelle's mother brags about how perfect Tracy and her husband are. "Why can't you be more like Tracy? Tracy never gives me this kind of trouble…" When *Merry Go Round* opens, it quickly becomes apparent that Tracy's supposedly perfect life is anything but. When her husband leaves her for another man and she's faced with moving out of the parsonage, she has nowhere to turn for help but to her older sisters. Rachael, her oldest sister, from Stormy Weather, is none too eager to help, and frankly, feels that it's about time that Tracy gets hers. Tenderhearted Michelle, from Water Lily, wants to help however she can and offers Tracy a job painting and wallpapering the home of Barclay Alexander III, the owner of the house she's decorating. Between Barclay's critical parents, Tracy's three kids, and a town full of people who are depending on Barclay to keep Elk Creek Woolen Mill open despite his father's insistence that the factory be closed, there are all kinds of ups and downs in this story. The extreme changes occurring in Tracy's life make her feel like things are spinning out of control and that all she can do is hang on for dear life.

What inspired you to write this particular story?

I guess on some level, I'm like Rachael, Tracy's oldest sister—I thought it was time for Tracy to "get hers", to have to deal with her pride issues and becomes a real person instead of a perfect, plastic, Barbie doll character. People who have been humbled a little are so much more loveable.

How long had the idea of your book been developing before you began to write the story?

I think I wrote the book very shortly after the idea first came to me.

How much of yourself is hidden in the characters in the book?

In a long ago life in a different place and time, I loved a man who turned out to be gay. I remember how it felt, and how hard it was to move on after I found out. I do need to add a disclaimer at this point, however. Like Trevor, Tracy's husband, who is gay, my husband of seven years is a pastor. He is definitely not gay! The first draft of this book was written before I even met Mark and became a pastor's wife. I think of all the sisters in my Maple Valley trilogy, I am least like Tracy. Maybe that's why she was so fun to write!

Tell us a little about your main characters. Who was your favorite? Why?

I love this book because it has several scenes that involve all three sisters from the Maple Valley trilogy, together in the same room, duking it out. I loved writing Rachael in this book because she gets to say things to her sisters that I never would. She's very gutsy, and totally justified. I love it!

Who is your most unusual/most likeable character?

Barclay (Clay) Alexander III is very unlike my other heroes in that he is wealthy, and has a very distinctive plot line and character arc of his own. He's trying to do the right thing by several different people, and try as he might, he can't please everyone... anyone, or so it seems for a time. Clay is falling in love with the wrong woman, but she is so right for him that it is painful. He has the weight of the whole town of Maple Valley on his shoulders. When he finally gives in to his feelings for Tracy and lets himself indulge in a bit of selfish pleasure, the results are devastating. I have a lot of respect for Barclay and hope my readers feel the same although he is a much more complicated hero than most.

135

How long did it take you to write your book?

I wrote the rough draft of Merry Go Round several years ago in about six months time, tabled the project for years, and then spent the last year re-writing and editing the book.

How much of a story do you have in mind before you start writing it?

I always have a specific framework in mind, but the characters and plot details evolve and grow as the book progresses.

Did you do any research for the book? If so, how did you do it? (searching internet, magazines, other books, etc.)

I interview people when needed and look up details about places on the internet, visiting in person when I can.

How do you develop and differentiate your characters?

I think my characters have very distinctive personalities, and in Merry Go Round, the differences in the sisters is very apparent when they're all in the same scene, interacting with one another. I try to get into their heads and consistently think and act like they would.

Do you have specific techniques you use to develop the plot and stay on track?

I pick my husband's brain occasionally and I constantly ask the question, "What if…?"

What is your goal for the book, ie: what do you want people to take with them after they finish reading the story?

A song we used to sing in my adult Sunday school class in Colorado Springs comes to mind… "Humble thyself in the sight of the Lord, and He shall lift you up…" I think when we are prideful, and refuse to let people see our imperfections and idiosyncrasies, we make it very hard for people to know and love us. It's our humanness that makes us loveable. When Tracy finally lets down her defenses, drops her perfect life facade, and lets people glimpse a little of what she'd been going through, she is lifted up and at long last, truly loved for exactly who she is.

Is there a message in your writing you want readers to grasp?

The subject of homosexuality and the church, nature or nurture, sin or not sin, etc., is a touchy issue for many right now. I tried very hard *not* to let this book become a forum for my beliefs and thoughts on the issue, but to accurately reflect the feelings, emotions and conflicts my characters go through as they struggle through the implications of Trevor admitting he is gay, and dealing with the ramifications to his children, extended family and church. I have been told by my advance readers, whose opinions on the subject probably vary from mine, that I was successful — that they finished the book not knowing what I, the author, thought about the subject. I took that as high praise and hope other readers agree.

What challenges did you face as you wrote this book?

The only struggle I seem to face with my writing these days is finding enough hours in the day to sit down and write. I own and operate a bed and breakfast and tea house and am a pastor's wife. I maintain four houses. It's a good, but very busy life, and when the day is done, I am often too exhausted to think.

Do you think writing this book changed your life? How so?

I think each book that I've written has changed my life. I remember an episode of *Star Trek, Next Generation*, when Jean Luc Picard was swept away to live out his life on another planet. He eventually fell in love, married, had children, and learned to play a musical instrument. When his new world came to an end, he learned that he had never left the Enterprise, and that the whole alternate life experience had occurred only in his mind, in a few days time. I feel like that every time I finish a book. It's like I've visited some alternate reality and lived the life of my character from start to finish, feeling what they feel and experiencing what they experience, when in reality, I've just been sitting at my desk, typing away. In a very real way, I think each book makes me a richer, more multi-faceted, more understanding person because when I've walked a mile (or a hundred) in my character's shoes.

What has changed for you personally since you wrote your first book?

When I first started writing, I was single and had been for almost 20 years. My life changed dramatically when I met my husband and remarried (in a good way, but still... it was a big adjustment!)

How has your background influenced your writing? How does your environment/upbringing color your writing?

I was raised in a very conservative Christian home. My upbringing and personal beliefs color everything I do and think. I have lived in many parts of the world, known many people and experienced many things. My writing is filtered through each of the things that have made me the person I am. Although my books do not fit into the Inspirational Fiction category because they contain some adult scenes, they definitely have a Christian world view which includes characters honestly struggling through issues of faith. The mistakes I've made and life lessons I've learned over the years have become fodder for many interesting characters and scenarios in my books.

Sex SCENES Not SEX Scenes
By
Pat Bertram
Author of:
More Deaths Than One, Daughter A I
A Spark of Heavenly Fire, Light Bringer, **and**
Grief: The Great Yearning

❦

Many new writers (and even some published authors) have a difficult time writing sex scenes. They worry about how their friends and family will deal with idea that their son/brother/daughter/mother knows about sex. They worry about when and where to insert a sex scene, and they worry about how graphic to get. One thing writers don't seem to worry about is the purpose of their sex scene, and that is something they *should* worry about.

Some romance genres require a lot of hot sex, other genres, like science fiction, don't put much emphasis on sex, so be sure to find out the expectations of your genre. Even when titillation is the goal, the scene should also fulfill a story need, should respond to the demands of the story.

An effective scene—sex or not—serves multiple objectives. Scenes advance the story, show us more about the characters, show us how the action changed the hero or show a change in the relationship between the participants. Scenes are always about change, about action and about reaction.

Once you know the objective, you can write a fitting action/reaction sequence (which is the basic building block of a scene). If comfort is the objective, you can show the couple together at the beginning, close the door during the action, and show them cuddling afterward. If tenderness is the objective, you can show a bit of the action in addition to the before and after. And of course, if

139

their desperation for each other is the objective, you will need to leave the door open during the scene.

As with all resonating scenes, when it is over there must be some reaction, some change to the character or the direction of the story. And the objective dictates that reaction. If the scene is about bringing comfort to the characters, we need to know whether they found comfort or failed to find it, and we need to know the characters' emotional response to the success or failure of that objective. This reaction, in turn will help set up the next scene.

A good use of a sex scene would be to show the ebb and flow of human connection. For example, you could have three scenes spread throughout the story. In the first scene, perhaps, the man climaxes, feeling connected to the woman. When he immediately goes to sleep, she feels disconnected. In the second scene, he can't get it up, leaving him feeling disconnected, but since he tries to make it up to her by cuddling her, she feels connected. In the third scene, they climax together, perhaps cuddle afterward, so they both feel connected.

In addition to the sex, then, you show a pattern of connection and disconnection between the couple (in other words, conflict), you show a new perspective of the characters, and you show a change in their relationship. You also end up with a subplot that adds to the overall richness of the story. In other words, you end up with a series of sex *scenes*, not just *sex* scenes.

Scenes help show who the characters are, and where better to do this than when the characters are at their most vulnerable. One of my favorite scenes in *A Spark of Heavenly Fire* is when Jeremy King, a world famous actor, has sex with Pippi O'Brien, a woman he just met in a bar.

The sound of weeping woke Jeremy. He turned his head toward his companion and saw one trembling shoulder and a tangle of gleaming hair.

He stretched luxuriously. The red hair hadn't lied. The girl had been all fire, kindling a passion in him he hadn't felt in years. The memory of it made him hard.

He reached over and pulled the girl into his arms. He smoothed

*back her hair and kissed away her tears, murmuring, "Honey," and
"Sweetheart," and "Dear."*

"I'm such a terrible person," she said, sobbing.

"Shh. Shh," he whispered between tiny kisses.

*Her arms stole around his neck, and her lips sought his. In a
surprisingly short time she bucked beneath him, calling out his
name.*

*You've still got it, King, he thought exultantly. Then, after one
final thrust, he tumbled into oblivion.*

That scene might not be very graphic, but it did what I wanted it
to—define the characters, Jeremy especially. Pippi called out his
name, but he didn't care enough about her to think of her by name.
He cared only about himself and his performance. It shouldn't come
as any surprise that, during other times of vulnerability in the story,
he also thought only of himself.

A sex scene is a good time to show a character confronting her
essence, to play on her self-concept (the treasured idea the character
has of herself). What if a character were making love to a person
other than a spouse? Would this lovemaking enhance his or her self-
concept, or would it go against it? If the scene enhanced the
character's self-concept, we would learn much about the character.
Perhaps she sees herself as a great lover, in which case nothing
mattered except the lovemaking—not her marriage vows, not her
husband, not her children—and so we would learn kind of character
she is. If the scene went against the character's self-concept, then we
have a character with inner conflicts. Perhaps the character sees
herself as a faithful, till-death-do-us-part wife. In which case, no
matter how exciting or tender the scene, it leaves her in turmoil.

In the previously quoted scene from *A Spark of Heavenly Fire*,
Pippi is obviously experiencing turmoil. She had been in the bar to
meet her boyfriend, Greg Pullman, to accept his marriage proposal,
and instead she ran off with Jeremy. She'd been dazzled by the
actor's star power and hadn't given poor Greg a single thought, but
in the night, after her passion diminished, she confronted her truth.

The most explicit sex scenes I've written are in my first novel,
More Deaths Than One. My character, Bob Stark, is stark in

everything he does, but the more one learns about the character, the more extraordinary he seems. His first sex scene is with a stranger. Her manner seemed to be that of a person who had decided on a course of action and now wanted to get it over with as quickly as possible, but Bob turned out to be something of a pro at satisfying women. Since the skill seemed so out of character, I explained it with a flashback, though I do not advocate flashbacks during a sex scene. Of all scenes in a book, sex scenes are the most immediate, and should be done in the present, but in this case I followed an even more important rule: everything in service to the story.

He moved in her, slowly, steadily. He caught the scent of frangipani in her perfume. All at once sixteen years disappeared, and he was back in Thailand, the first time he'd gone to Madame Butterfly's.

The sex scene that followed is graphic, too graphic to add here, but the point is the perfume. Smelling the frangipani catapulted him into a reverie, where the woman beneath him became unimportant, but later in the book when he makes love with a significant woman in his life, the scent has a completely different effect on Bob.

Twining her arms around his neck, she brought his mouth to hers. The kiss was hard and short, but immediately her lips sought his again.

He gathered her closer. Their kiss deepened.

All at once she pulled away and hopped out of bed. "Omigosh!"

"What?"

"I forgot. I have a present for you." She flashed an impish smile and darted into the bathroom. She emerged a few minutes later wearing a dark rose cheongsam that accented the swell of her breasts and the taper of her waist. "I bought it in Chinatown. What do you think?"

He couldn't speak, couldn't breathe. She looked flushed, radiant, beautiful.

She jutted out a hip. The side slit parted, giving him a glimpse of shapely leg.

He felt a shock that started in his groin and radiated upward.

From the glint in her eyes, he knew she was aware of the effect she had on him.

He slid off the bed and moved toward her, stepping slowly and carefully as if he were in danger of falling off a precipice. As he neared her, he smelled her new perfume—frangipani. From now on, he knew, whenever he caught a whiff of that scent, it would remind him of this moment, of her, of the teasing look in her eyes.

Each book I write has less sex in it than the last. In *Light Bringer,* my fourth novel, the characters didn't have sex at all. But what can you expect from aliens? Still, it never occurred to me that I had left off any mention of sex until a reader pointed it out to me, because my characters connected in a way that served the story, as the following voyeuristic scene shows.

Teodora went still. The moment she'd been waiting for had finally arrived. Ninety-nine and a half percent of the subjects' DNA tested as human, but the remaining half percent remained unidentified. Now, perhaps, she would see that unidentifiable half percent in action.

On the other side of the one-way window, the female cocked her head, and her face took on a rapt expression as if listening to a distant melody. When the male entered, her incandescent smile seemed to brighten the room.

The two subjects moved toward each other. The light became more radiant. They stopped an arm's length apart. For a second Teodora thought she saw a rainbow between them, then they were in each other's arms. An auroral glow drifted and whirled around them.

Something as delicate as a spray of perfume touched Teodora. Her skin drew tight, and she felt an immense thirst. She fixed the feelings in her mind so she could take them out and analyze them later, then she set them aside and concentrated all her attention on the subjects.

Hearing a faint thread of music, she held her breath. The music seemed to swell into a heart-breaking song of joy. The colors dancing around the subjects grew in intensity, colors she had never seen before. A distillation of rubies. A blue moon shimmering on

143

restless waters. A green so pure it might have come out of the earth itself.

In the spaces where the colors overlapped, Teodora knew she was seeing the color of love, the color of total harmony and acceptance.

The colors echoed in Teodora's emptiness, and she felt herself crying deep within her soul. This was something she wanted, but could not have. Maybe no human could.

Later, Teodora discusses the episode with her boss, the head of International Institute of Scientific Advancement.

"It was not like watching humans," Teodora told Berhard Petri after reporting what she had learned about the subjects.

His eyebrows shot up, and she realized he'd caught the unusual touch of animation in her voice.

She modulated her tone. "It was like watching a higher form of life."

"It hasn't been established that they're a higher form," Petri said. "They could be a devolution."

"You did not see. Theirs was an interaction on a higher plane, not about individual parts, but harmony of the whole. With humans, it is all about the body parts, the physical attributes. They do the act, but there is no resonance, no color, no song. It is as if humans have an ancestral memory of seeing the gods in love, and now they are trying to have what they had once seen, but only managing the visceral part. Like the ancient Egyptians trying to emulate the pyramid builders from an earlier age, they cannot get it right."

Sex scenes don't need to be deeply meaningful to be effective. Sex scenes can simply bring the couple together or show the intensity of a relationship. Sex scenes can create a change of pace, either as a diversionary tactic or as a quiet time between hectic scenes. A sex scene can be a fast-paced action sequence to get the reader's blood roiling. A sex scene can even be playful or humorous. What it cannot be is a scene thrown in there just because you thought it was time for a sex scene. Such scenes need to be as germane and as necessary to the story as a plot twist or a revelation. If the scene can be removed from the book without leaving a hole, it should be removed or rewritten—unless of course you are writing erotica or another genre that demands lots of titillating sex. In which case, you are probably making a fortune and have no need for these tips.

Film as Literary Influence on the Novel:
How to Approach Scenes Within Novel Chapters
By
Eric Wasserman
Author of:
Celluloid Strangers

🐓

The movie is better than the book.

There, I said it; I broke the sacred oath of all book-lovers. But in some cases it's actually true and there are very good reasons as to why. And novelists can learn from movies a great deal.

This past fall this very issue came up countless times in the undergraduate Film & Literature course I teach at The University of Akron. And perhaps the strongest example we explored was *The Godfather*. Francis Ford Coppola's 1972 masterpiece adaptation of Mario Puzo's novel not only took home the Oscar for Best Picture but is widely regarded by critics to be among the finest American movies of the twentieth century. And although Coppola and Puzo co-wrote the screenplay, it is clear from the first frame what the filmmaker brought to presenting the story on screen that the novelist could have used in his original one on the printed page.

There are valid arguments about film's negative influences on fiction. I can attest to this because it is obvious to me that the majority of young writers I see in my fiction writing workshops have clearly seen more movies than have read novels. However, all good storytelling, especially novel chapters, is comprised of scenes. Effective scenes that operate together as a working unit is what long narrative hinges one, and filmmakers are instinctively aware of this. Great filmmakers know exactly what they want to accomplish in a scene and even more importantly know when to leave a scene and not linger one second longer than is necessary to provide the audience what it needs from it. I, stupidly, did not adhere to this during the original drafting of my own novel, *Celluloid Strangers*, which ironically pays homage to the movies.

The opening of the film adaptation of *The Godfather* is among the most perfectly executed scenes in movie history. But it is not how Puzo originally opens his novel. The novel begins with Puzo utilizing a classic Russian literature technique of having the reader first encounter a supporting character—in this case the undertaker Bonasera who sits in a courtroom and watches a judge suspend the sentence of two men who have beaten his only daughter like an animal—so that when the domineering figure of the story is presented—Don Corleone—he needs little introduction.

In contrast, the film does open with Bonasera, but instead it is a forward shot of him retelling this experience to the don as he sits in Corleone's home office. The camera rests over Don Corleone's shoulder and by hearing his voice and the filmmaker withholding a visualization of him until the moment Bonasera asks for the don to murder the two men, the audience must *imagine*. Here Coppola is demonstrating the first of the two key ingredients to constructing a successful scene: knowing what you *don't* need to show. By not showing the don at first, and only hearing Marlon Brando's chilling guttural voice, the audience instinctively accepts that Bonasera is speaking to a figure of immense authority that warrants great respect. After this, the second ingredient is achieved: incorporating everything the scene demands in as little space as possible and getting out of it pronto and onto the next one.

When writing my own novel, *Celluloid Strangers*, I truly wish I had recognized this early on but I unfortunately did not. I am not joking when I say that at one point the manuscript almost reached 1,000 double-spaced pages. Yes, there were plenty of chapters that never made it even close to the final cut. But the majority of the real trimming was done on a scene-to-scene level. I had too often fallen in love with my scenes and lingered in them long after I had accomplished what their purposes were. This is of course humorous in retrospect. Because near the beginning of my novel I tell the back-story of how a B-movie filmmaker, Barry Lords, is beside himself when he discovers that a very important scene he has shot for his movie is destroyed when the celluloid is developed.

Lords asks the novel's central character, Simon Gandelman, "How do I finish a thriller without the murder scene?" That night Simon has a dream. He is in his hometown, but he is also reliving WWII. There are no people or soldiers to be seen, but he knows the fight is near. He can hear the war, but he cannot see it. And that is what has always scared him the most: knowing that death might be in front of him but not being able to pinpoint just where. At the moment Simon knows he will be able to see the enemy, he wakes up from his sleep, chilled and terrified. The next day he restructures the scene in Lords' thriller for which they are missing footage so as to never show the actual murder, arranging it around the fear and suspense of never seeing what the audience suspects has happened, forcing the viewer to imagine how gruesome a murder can be without witnessing it as the screen fades to black.

I should have been listening to my own characters because when drafting *Celluloid Strangers* I had not yet learned that, just like a filmmaker, a writer does not always need to show everything in his narrative. Watching good movies is a goldmine of inspiration for doing this in fiction. Likewise, it is often what doesn't need to be in a scene, especially in a novel chapter, that, when removed, tightens the narrative so that you keep the reader in the scene only as long as necessary.

In my novel I withhold a very important piece of the personal history about Simon's love interest, May Park. She is a complicated character who was a joy to write for because, out of all of my characters in the book, I had the hardest time understanding where she was coming from. Before meeting Simon, she had been raped as a teenager. After a lot of consideration I felt I needed to show that life-changing evening of her young life so readers could better understand her and, more importantly, empathize with her worldview. The chapter itself came easier than I expected but in draft after draft I could not bring myself to create the actual moment of horror on the page. I simply kept "[RAPE]" typed in white space as a placeholder. I couldn't write that part of the scene because just *imagining* such a horrible act of violation disgusted me. It still does.

In the end, that was what I wanted readers to feel as well. I decided to write the scene right up to the boys overtaking May after she puts up a strong struggle. I then cut to white space and picked up the scene directly following the incident after the boys have left her in the place of the terrible act. She is alone and I have not shown what happened, but by describing her emotional and physical condition following it I feel readers are given an even more chilling experience because they have to *imagine* it. And the movies taught this to me more than any work of fiction could. I don't have to see Bonasera's daughter being beaten like an animal in *The Godfather* nor do I need to see him watch the judge suspend the culprits' sentences. His devastated emotional state over just knowing of his only daughter's torment lets me know everything. It lets me know that I don't need to show my own character being violated to achieve the reaction I desire from readers.

Knowing what is necessary to show readers and what isn't in the specific scenes of novel chapters does not come easily to most fiction writers. Scenes that involve sensitive material are often the most difficult to navigate regarding this. When depicting sex scenes, the late Oakley Hall advised his writing students to "cut it off at the fireplace," so to speak. But I think that approach gives fiction writers rigid boundaries. There are times when sex or violence must be presented in a story and there are times when it is not necessary. It's something with which all writers need to be cautious. But a healthy dose of good movies is a great place for all novelists to start from when considering the tricky balance.

What Eric's Characters Were Trying to Teach Him: An Excerpt from *Celluloid Strangers*

The first time Simon ever heard a person scream at Sunrise was during post-production for his first screenplay: *Shelter in the Dark*. He and Jack Thallman co-wrote the script in five weeks and it was budgeted for a tight eighteen-day shoot. Even Simon knew it was nothing special. He caught on to how the studio worked quickly enough. The first draft was looked over by Marty, who said, "This isn't advanced mathematics. Millions of people go to the pictures every week, give them what we know keeps those seats filled." The draft had been tossed back as if it was a melon that wasn't ripe enough. "Chop the background crap. It doesn't matter what happened when the killer was a teenager that turned him into what he is. And pump up the love story. Assume the audience is dumb."

The screaming came from the print development department. Barry Lords had been assigned to direct *Shelter in the Dark*. Lords was known for having no sense of style whatsoever, but Simon really liked him. Lords was the only director who ever turned to Simon after a scene-take to say, "It's not working, any ideas?" Then again, the next take was usually the last. But for all his faults, Lords really enjoyed going to the pictures, even the bad ones. Simon had never once heard the man criticize a film. When asked what he thought of a picture, Lords would usually say, "It was good."

Barry Lords was a real gentleman. And maybe that's why he never made it far, why he was considered washed up at forty-five. He actually gave compliments without expecting anything in return. And he was lucky. He had been discovered eleven years before by a studio scout who saw a weekend production of *Much Ado About Nothing* Lords directed at the San Diego Community Playhouse. The next day Lords was offered more money than he ever made selling life insurance.

Lords did not complicate things. He positioned the camera at the same angle for every shot and told his cinematographer to roll. One take: sometimes two. No coverage. If that first take did not work he would politely say to an actor, "One more try." That was it. He always followed a request with, "thank you." He was the only person in Hollywood Simon met who did not owe money to anyone: not a bookie, mortgage, nothing. Lords also might have been the only director who was still married to his first and only wife. His kids even attended public schools.

When Simon heard Lords scream in the print development department it was obvious that this cheap picture was the man's last chance at keeping his job. Walter Alston, the print manager, had said, "We have a problem."

"What do you got for me, Walt?" Lords had asked in a pleasant voice. It amazed Simon. Lords' wife could tell him she was having an affair and he would probably say, "How can we mend this?" But Alston's news was different.

The developer had over-exposed an entire can of film. He tried to re-soak it in solution, which occasionally worked for exterior scenes shot with too much light. Unfortunately, the can contained an interior scene filmed with low light. The celluloid had been burnt blood red. Normally Lords would shrug and say, "That's Hollywood," because these incidents typically occurred with second unit filler material. Simon and Thallman could not believe what came out of Lords' mouth, because the man had difficulty even hearing God's name taken in vain.

"You little fuck!" Lords screamed. When the room went silent, Lords' face was moist. His voice broke. "How do I finish a thriller without the murder scene?"

"Relax," Alston said. "We'll develop it again, just give me the negative."

There was no negative.

Lords had been kept under contract for eleven years for one reason: He brought in every picture he directed under budget. Thus he remained employed making films that the studio used to showcase new talent and that the critics never ceased to pan. Anybody could direct them, but not as cheaply as Lords.

How did he make them so cheaply? He took scripts that were period pieces and revised them into contemporary stories; sometimes did away with second unit shots or assumed the audience would not notice him using the same stock footage three or four times. But more than anything, Lords minimized post-production costs by going directly to final print out of the can. He had not developed a negative in eight years.

Lords' fingers shook as he sipped whiskey at the Pacific Bar on Tangerine Street, three blocks from the lot. Simon drank a club soda. Thallman had wanted nothing to do with the problem.

"I'm finished," Lords had said. "This time next month I'll be going door to door trying to convince people I'm selling them a piece of mind. Do you know what life insurance is, Gandelman? You're betting against yourself. The way it pays off is if you die."

The only solution Lords could conceive of was to ask the studio for more money, go back and re-shoot the scene. That was, if the actors were still available and if Katz did not replace him with another director. Sunrise would spend the money, but Katz would see that Lords had lost his cheap man's touch and would cut him loose. Simon convinced him to take a day to think it over.

That night Simon had a dream. He was in Dorchester, but he was also in a war, only the battle was now on Kenstook Street. There were no people or soldiers to be seen, but he knew the fight was there. He could hear the war, but he could not see it. And that was what had always frightened him the most: knowing that death might be in front of him but not being able to know just where it was. And at the moment Simon knew he would be able to see the enemy, he awoke, chilled, terrified. The smell of gasoline and gunpowder consumed his nostrils. He threw off the sheets and went to his typewriter.

The next morning Simon found Lords and insisted they edit what they had already shot according to his new restructuring. Lords said, "Do whatever you want."

Rather than complicate matters by going to producer Cal Drankin's office, Simon dragged Lords to Alston's bungalow and did not let him leave. If anyone saw Lords' face it was over. Lords sat nearly comatose sipping whiskey in the corner while Simon dictated the new edit of the picture, complete with voiceover narration of his own speech, altered to an octave lower by chain-smoking and speaking through a handkerchief. Thallman's only comment was an emotionless "Hmm?"

When Lords handed the studio the final cut they had no idea what to make of it. This was not the film they had assigned him to direct. Word spread around the lot like giggles in a high school cafeteria. "You won't believe it, Barry Lords now thinks he's Hemingway or something." Lords left the studio without being asked. Simon had to call him in San Diego two months later to share the good news.

By never showing the actual murder, by restructuring the picture around the fear and suspense of never seeing what the audience suspected had happened, by forcing the viewer to imagine how gruesome a murder could be without witnessing it as the screen faded to black, *Shelter in the Dark* put Simon and Thallman on the map as the hottest young writers in town and provided Lords with his first complimentary reviews. Simon read from the *Herald* over the telephone:

LOS ANGELES — Barry Lords' bare-bones, single-positioned camera angles and the simplicity of what he has pioneered as the "anti-style" approach, force even this critic to question if all along we have not watched this genius' pictures with the release of expectations he demands. "Shelter in the Dark" is not only the best structured of Lords' films, but is also the most emotionally involving. Lords arrives as a mature artist backed with a brilliant screenplay by newcomers Simon Gandelman and Jack Thallman. After seeing this picture it is now clear that the world would be a better place if it was directed by Barry Lords.

Lords laughed. "They make it sound like I had fans all these years."

"Get back here," Simon told him over the telephone. "You're career's saved."

Lords breathed heavily. "I know this will take you guys places. But I think it's a nice way for me to bow out. I'm not a real cineaste like you, Gandelman. Watch your back, kid. And more important, remember that there's a life beyond pictures. For god's sake, go see a baseball game. That's real. All this, it's just celluloid."

Two years later, just before the war, Simon ran into Lords in San Diego when scouting locations. Lords was in the restaurant at the Hotel Del Coronado, sitting with his wife, who was what Simon had expected—a soft-faced, heavy-waisted woman who lovingly stirred sugar cubes into her husband's coffee. Lords mostly talked about his kids. Simon was happy that the man was content living the life he never wanted for himself.

Lords was back selling life insurance, but was also directing Chekhov's *The Cherry Orchard* at the San Diego Community Playhouse. "Just for fun. It runs the next two weekends." Simon returned to San Diego the next weekend. After the show he found Lords in the lobby and did what Hollywood had taught him best: he lied and said, "I really enjoyed it."

Lords had smiled and said, "Thank you." He then pulled Simon aside and said, "You're changing; I can see it. But don't let them change your destiny. Don't allow them to let you direct a picture— ever. Directors are businessmen, expendable managers. You're a writer. If you direct you'll never write true again, not as you're destined to." He then gave Simon a hug. It was more affection than his own father had ever shown.

153

❦

Interview with Eric Wasserman

How long had the idea of your novel been developing before you began to write the story and how long did it take you to write it in general?

If I were to literally start at the beginning when the very first seeds for my novel, *Celluloid Strangers*, were planted, it was fourteen years in the making. Naturally, during that time I was doing other things; going to graduate school, completing my first book, *The Temporary Life*, which was a collection of short stories, working on another novel I abandoned, getting married. But this project literally began well over a decade ago. I just didn't know it at the time.

In the fall of 1997 a college friend of mine thought it might be fun for us to go see a screening of a new documentary called *Red Hollywood* at the Northwest Film Center in Portland, Oregon that would be followed by a discussion with the film's director, Thom Andersen. My friend was a history major; I was a film buff. It seemed like a nice evening could come from it. The documentary was not my first exposure to the Hollywood Blacklist and the HUAC hearings, but I was completely engrossed by it and this led to a hobby of reading up on the era and devouring the films of the time. It really all started off as an innocent personal interest. It was also around this time that I began having a fascination with my family's history in Los Angeles since we've been residents of the City of Angels in some capacity since the 1920s, if I am correct.

In the fall of 2001 I was earning my MFA in creative writing at Emerson College in Boston. I was still a movie junkie and my usual companion to the theater was John Zamparelli, who remains one of my dearest friends and is among the very few people whose critical eye I trust when it comes to my writing. I had acquired a bootleg VHS copy of the film *Murder Incorporated*, which is actually now available on DVD. It's a classic 1960 noir with Peter Falk and its opening scene is actually paid tribute to in *Godfather II*. Jewish gangsters; you can't beat it. Anyway, that night John told me this haunting story about his father, who was the son of Italian immigrants. John's father essentially had a very similar experience to that depicted in the opening chapter of *Celluloid Strangers* where Benny comes to Mori's house and insists that he quit the crime commission or face dire consequences. At the time I was having trouble with another novel I was trying to write that I knew was falling apart. I thought taking a break to write a short story would be fun so I asked John if I could use that story about his father as a loose plot and he told me it was mine to take. I moved the situation from Boston to Los Angeles, changed it from the 1950s to the 1940s, made the characters Jewish instead of Italian, and so forth. I wrote very rough drafts of the first three chapter over a few weeks and then put them away. But the idea for the novel was securely in place. I knew I wanted to write about these characters, I knew I wanted to explore postwar Los Angeles in the late 1940s, and I knew I wanted to have the HUAC hearings and the Old Hollywood Blacklist play a part.

I wrote and published my short story collection, finished a draft of that other novel, then from about 2005 until 2010 I dedicated myself to realizing *Celluloid Strangers*. In the past year I did a very strong edit on my own and my editor, Mike Simpson, then provided the suggestive polish points to bring it home to what the public now sees.

What inspired you to write this particular story? What do you want people to take with them after they finish reading it?

I try to tell my aspiring fiction writing students that the reason you begin writing a story and the reasons you see it through to the end may very well change over the course of the writing process, especially when it comes to writing a novel, which can often take years to get right. The initial reasons I had are arbitrary at this point, especially that movies have always been America's unspoken national religion, although I think an element of that remains in the narrative. What I do know is that I hope *Celluloid Strangers* is a novel that shows that Los Angeles is a real place where real people live and work. Yes, there is, I like to believe, an exciting story of crime and Old Hollywood intrigue and political history that we should never forget. But the story is in the end about a family, about siblings. I hope it shows that good people often fall in love with terrible ideas, in this case communism. I hope people come away from reading it with the view that the Blacklist and the HUAC hearings were complicated and not entirely black and white. And I really hope postwar California comes off the page as a real place, maybe not one that exists any longer but one worth remembering nonetheless.

How much of yourself is hidden in the characters in the book?

I used to be pretty dogmatic that I am the writer and the characters are the characters and that there is a clear separation between us. As I get older I've come to realize that that was a youthful defense as a young writer to deflect the accusation of crafting autobiographical fiction. None of the characters in *Celluloid Strangers* are representational of me. But they are all emotionally autobiographical in some capacity. All four of the Gandelman brothers have a bit of me in them. I can identify with Joe's deep sense of responsibility, Mori's aspiration to change his destiny only to have it compromised, Benny's unflinching loyalty, and Simon's failings as the result of initial good intentions. What's so funny is that Simon, who is a writer and the central figure of the novel, is probably the least like me.

Even a character like Doris has a bit of emotional autobiography. I understand what it's like to achieve a morsel of your dreams and not reach the finish line in the end. If I can't emotionally understand a character the writing is typically flat. I don't have to relate to what the character is going through on a factual or literal level. I've never killed another man to save one of my brothers' lives, as Mori does in the book, but I have felt incredible regret in my life. Haven't we all? I'd like to think that if I am emotionally autobiographical with the characters, such as infusing a character with great regret, readers will also feel that closeness because everyone regrets something. That's just one example of course, but I stick to it.

Who was your favorite character in the novel to write for?

Every time I got to a section with May Park, Simon's love interest in the novel, I was completely in my element. "Wounded Birds" is one of the most horrific chapters in the novel but it was one of the easiest to put to the page. So many of my important readers who saw early drafts of the manuscript found May to be an unsympathetic character and completely unlikable. Those views are fair but we'll see what the general readership thinks of her. She is not based on any real person, but she was somewhat inspired by two people I have known in my life. Both of those people were very angry at the times I knew them. However, they were also wonderfully thoughtful and caring people. I never particularly asked these people what had happened in their lives to make them so angry at the world but I am certain they each had their reasons. I do provide May a reason for her anger, something in her background that I think even the most hardened reader can have empathy for. I truly see my job as the writer being to never pass judgment on my characters. My job is to present them, admirable attributes and flaws combined. After all, we are not all angels nor are we all demons. We're combinations because we're human and I want my characters to be that way. I do not judge their decisions and actions. To do so is to disrespect my reader. If the reader chooses to not care for May I have no problem with that, but when I was writing for her I had so much joy because she was and remains the hardest character for me to figure out.

How much of a story do you have in mind before you start writing it?

I always start with situation. I've been at this a long time now and I've just accepted that that's how my process begins as a writer, whether it's a short story or a novel. As I said before, with *Celluloid Strangers* my friend John told me about a situation his father found himself in decades before and that was the spark. I know a lot of writers who begin with character or environment but I land on a situation and then start thinking about what kind of person we might find in that situation. That said, Los Angeles in the late 1940s was a goldmine for setting.

I am cursed with always having two projects going at the same time. I am not necessarily simultaneously working on them but they are both in mind. When I was dedicated to completing my short story collection I was always scribbling notes or collecting items of interest for when I would be able to dive head first into *Celluloid Strangers*. When I was writing *Celluloid Strangers* I was taking notes and outlining for the novel I am currently involved in. Right now I am working on that novel but have already begun a folder for the project after that which has recently started to germinate.

Did you do any research for the book? If so, how did you do it?

Is water wet? Yeah, research was a huge part of the process of writing *Celluloid Strangers*. And incorporating research into a fictional narrative is something I have actually written about and have lectured on. For the novel, the research took on a variety of endeavors. My generation was the last to enter college before the Internet, so those old fashioned academic skills are ingrained in me. I love libraries; I love getting out in the field. Yeah, I probably watched as many movies as I read books, particularly because I wanted the dialogue in *Celluloid Strangers* to often have that terse tit-for-tat rhythm of the films of the era. But I was also living in Los Angeles when the first complete drafts of the novel were written. When I was getting stuck with the story my future wife encouraged us to go about the city and visit some of the locations in the book. We took hikes up to the Hollywood sign; we went to the Silent Movie Theatre on Fairfax; we went to Angels Flight. Heck, Taylor's Steak House was the inspiration for The Copeland Club where Benny and the Moskowitz crime organization are based in the novel. I was combing through old editions of the *Los Angeles Times* and finding out just how conservative that newspaper was back then. I was looking through old fashion magazines to decide what Morris' wife, Helen, would wear. I was listening to the music of the time as well. Anything to get me into that world I was creating. You name it. But to be honest, old family photographs were the best help because, again, I wanted to portray Los Angeles as a place where real people lived. Old photographs have those little details I was looking for.

I want to be clear that I fully admit that the HUAC elements of the novel are portrayed with a leftist leaning. However, I don't believe I am preaching a political agenda. The characters simply warrant that angle. I made sure to really examine both sides of the concern about potential communist subversion in Hollywood at the time and really encourage others to do the same. You can read a great book like Paul Buhle and Dave Wagner's *A Very Dangerous Citizen: Abraham Lincoln Polonsky and the Hollywood Left* and get a lot out of it. But you can also read a book like Kenneth Lloyd Billingsley's *Hollywood Party: How Communism Seduced the American Film Industry in the 1930s and 1940s* and get just as much.

I know this sounds crazy, but at one point the manuscript for *Celluloid Strangers* almost reached 1,000 pages. The published version is a few pages over 400. While I did eliminate subplots I liked that did not exactly advance the story, junked some of the testimony chapters and eliminated three-fourths of the original interview sections, I can tell you that a lot of what I had to get rid of was related to my research. In certain places of the original manuscript I was clearly either so fascinated with my research that I made the mistake of thinking readers would be too instead of keeping in mind that they come to a novel first and foremost for a great story, or I was simply showing off everything I was learning.

Research is often necessary, especially when working in the historical literary novel realm, but it can also get you bogged down. In my first book I have a short story in which a young man needs a bone marrow transplant. After immersing myself into the science of that process I realized that I only needed a few strong details to establish story logic believability and my credibility as the author, that the reader could trust me. I'd say about only twenty percent of my overall research found its way into the final version of *Celluloid Strangers* you have in your hands. And that's how it should be. Serve the story first is always the rule to go by when researching as a fiction writer.

Finally, it should also be warned that falling in love with researching is often an excuse not to get down to the serious work of crafting the story itself. I have seen research used as an excuse to not actually write on more than one occasion, present company absolutely included.

How do you develop and differentiate your characters and is that connected to how you develop the plot and stay on track?

I work with an outline but I don't really stick to it entirely. It's typically very loose, general stuff. Occasionally I know what I am specifically going to do in a chapter as I initially set it down, but usually not. Again, I begin with situation. My characters develop as an outcome of those situations. There are four brothers in *Celluloid Strangers*. I am the third of four brothers in my own life but that's about it. I never developed one of the Gandelman brothers thinking I wanted him to represent one of my own brothers.

I differentiate characters the same way I go about writing in general. I think it's dangerous to go about writing something as laborious as a novel prematurely declaring what you are championing. If you already know what you want the novel to be, you are killing the joy of discovery in the writing process and are putting up walls for yourself as a creative force. When writing *Celluloid Strangers* I knew a few things I did *not* want the book to be but never declared what I wanted. I went about developing the characters in a similar way. I knew I did *not* want Benny and Mori to have the same speech patterns. I knew I did *not* want to completely destroy Meyer Moskowitz, the Jewish gangster, nor Louis B. Katz, the film studio mogul, at the end of the book. I did *not* want to reward Simon with what he thought he wanted in life but instead I wanted to reward him with what he needed. I knew I did *not* want the novel to end in Los Angeles for a variety of reasons. And I absolutely knew I did *not* want the union issues raised in the novel to be solely political, that they had to be about real working people. Had I decided what I *wanted* the novel probably never would have been written.

That said, capturing the voice of even a relatively serviceable and supporting character like Remy Dirsk is very important to me as a writer. I often spend hours just scribbling by hand fictitious letters a

160

particular character might write to another character just to get a hold on the beats and rhythms of his or her voice. I especially did this a lot when working on Benny's character, which is so ironic because Benny is the least likely letter writer in the novel.

What has changed for you personally since you wrote your first book?

My first book, *The Temporary Life*, was a collection of short stories that was released in 2005 and was reissued with a new foreword and reading group guide in early 2010. I could talk for hours about how my life has changed since then. When my first book came out I was living in a tiny one-bedroom apartment in Los Angeles with no job security and no health insurance. The economy was still doing well but I was struggling. But don't get me wrong, I was very happy and in some ways miss those times, especially living in Los Angeles, the city that allowed me to truly discover who I am and who I am not, which is why I partially dedicate *Celluloid Strangers* to the city itself.

Today I'm an Assistant Professor of English at the University of Akron where I serve as the campus coordinator for the NEOMFA, our graduate program in creative writing. I'm now a homeowner restoring a ninety-year-old house room-by-room. I have health insurance. The economy is struggling but I have job security for the first time in my life. And most importantly I finally quit smoking cigarettes for good, exercise at the Jewish Community Center gym regularly, and married the woman I am going to share the rest of my life with and grow old with. I live a quieter life than the one when my first book was released, but it's also one that is far more fulfilling and gratifying. And I think I'm a better writer as a result of it. I think *Celluloid Strangers* became a better novel because of it.

I'm proud of my first book but I am no longer the man who wrote those short stories. There will always be a wonderful feeling I have about that book. But I can't tell you how excited I am that *Celluloid Strangers* is about to enter the world. It's the book I want people to pick up. It's the book that truly represents me as a writer at this time in my life and I'd like to think the writer my readers will come to know for a long time to come.

What's your writing schedule like?

When I was younger I was a total night owl. I lived for all night writing sessions concluded by making coffee as the sun rose. Those days are pretty much over. I do my best work by starting when the sun rises these days instead of when the moon is out. Part of that is related to now being a college professor and having teaching responsibilities as well as advising, administration and committee work. But my writing schedule generally depends on what part of the writing process I am in. I like to write every day but that doesn't always happen. Life intrudes. Sometimes it's a family emergency. Sometimes it's as simple as my St. Bernard mix putting his head on my lap and looking up at me with those big sad eyes and me being unable to resist taking him on a dog walk for an hour even though I was going to write. I used to be much more aggressive about closing myself off from the world and writing forever. I am still incredibly disciplined. But I now don't feel bad if I take a few days off. My younger brother came to visit me from Seattle last weekend. It was a great time. We went to a baseball game, worked out at the gym together, barbequed in the evening, and watched movies at night. I didn't write at all while he was here and I was fine with that. In my twenties I would have felt so guilty for that. But not now.

I would like to say that just because I am not sitting with a manuscript does not mean I am not writing. I am constantly thinking about whatever project I have underway. If I am in the car on the way to work and I am working out a sticky problem I am having with my current story in my head, that's still writing to me. I find that people with the true creative impulse are all like that. Just remember that even when he was almost completely deaf Beethoven was said to be walking around humming to himself. He was writing music even if he wasn't actually setting ink to the sheet.

That said, I do try to write in the mornings and try to set aside evenings for reading.

162

What are you working on right now?

Grading midterm papers. But once that's done, it's back to my next novel. I don't like to give too much away, but it is influenced by Jewish folklore. I enjoy having a question to ponder when working on a story. I don't set out to answer that question but it gives me something to think about. Again, for *Celluloid Strangers* I was wondering what happens when good people fall in love with bad ideas; hence Simon and May's romantic inclination towards Marxism. For the new novel I am working on now I keep asking myself what would drive relatively grounded people to commit reckless acts. It's a far more ambitious undertaking than *Celluloid Strangers* in many ways. Right now it's pretty messy. However, the prologue, which is a self-contained short story, is going to be featured in the next issue of *Confrontation Magazine*. It's a retelling of Abraham being instructed by God to sacrifice his son, Isaac; only I tell it in first person from Isaac's perspective. But that really isn't the focus of the novel itself. To find out about that you'll have to stay tuned.

What is the most difficult part of the whole writing process? What is the easiest part of the writing process?

I absolutely struggle with first drafts. They come so slow. I know other fiction writers who say that's the most joyful part of the process but I detest it. I literally can't do anything until I have a complete first draft on the page and printed out, no matter how bad it is. I wouldn't say editing is the easiest part of the process but it is what I live for. I am sort of old fashioned. I do work on a computer but I always edit by hand on a printed manuscript. In the case of *Celluloid Strangers*, I always had a printed draft of the manuscript in a monstrous three-ring binder I could work with. Editing on a computer just doesn't work for me. Besides, when I go back to the master file on the computer to make the changes I have scribbled on the printed manuscript it becomes almost an additional edit, making the story stronger. I work especially hard as a line editor near a story's completion. I can't tell you how many times I have had a graduate student in our creative writing program mention frustration and I've suggested they do not edit on a computer. Editing by hand on a printed manuscript is working a totally different part of the creative part of your brain. It might not be for every writer but it's essential for me. Granted, I began writing fiction before every household had a computer, but I stand by my process.

What do you like to read?

I have a wide, eclectic range of taste and interest. It really depends on what I am in the mood for or feel a need to explore. For a very long time I had not been reading short stories but I have recently gotten back into them and just finished Josh Rolnick's debut's collection, *Pulp and Paper*, and was simply blown away by the workmanship quality of those stories. Matthew Guenette's new collection of poetry, *American Busboy*, is also just fantastic. I actually read a lot of poetry when I am having trouble with the language of a story I am working on. I know it sounds strange, but this past summer I decided to reread everything I could get my hands on that Franz Kafka ever wrote. It wasn't as much of a trial as I thought it would be.

I need to say that, whatever it is I am reading, I do not generally do so to have my worldview, values or sensibility reaffirmed. I read to be challenged. I love authors who take me by the throat, shake me, and force me to think really hard about the world we live in. I'd like to think that even though *Celluloid Strangers* is set in the past it makes readers pause and consider what the story might also be saying about the times we live in.

What, in your opinion, are the essential qualities of a good story?

Stories are important. They enter our lives early on in life. There's a reason parents still tell their children the story of the boy who cried wolf. Stories inform us right from the start. Contrary to what some of my students might assume, or even readers, I am not a snob. I want stories that make me think and feel long after they end. I've read beautifully written stories that make me think and feel absolutely nothing. It may sound strange, but I am absolutely willing to forgive a poorly written or clumsily constructed story if it makes me think and feel something profound. I am not joking when I say that I choke up every time I see the near-ending scene of the movie *Star Trek II: The Wrath Kahn* when Spock is dying and Captain Kirk is saying good-bye to him. That story is saying something far more profound about the nature of friendship and selfless sacrifice than many of the prize-winning and critically acclaimed literary novels I have read. It's making me think and feel something. Those are the most essential qualities of a good story. Yes, a good story should also be entertaining, hopefully well-crafted and also, in a perfect world, sincere. But if I am not thinking or feeling anything I don't care much for it. And keep in mind that some of the funniest stories ever given to the world are the ones that also do just that; they go beyond entertaining humor in masterful ways.

Who gave you the best writing advice you ever received and what was it? What advice would you give to an aspiring author?

Frederick Reiken, whose newest novel *Day For Night* was an L.A. Times Book Prize finalist alongside Pulitzer Prize-winner Jennifer Egan and National Book Award-winner Jonathan Franzen, was instrumental in my early development as a fiction writer. His literature course on the short story was my very first graduate school class. The very first thing he said to all of us was, "If you're not willing to submerge yourself in the world of reading fiction, give up now on being a serious writer of fiction." I wrote this down the moment he said it, went back to my dingy Boston studio apartment that evening, and taped it across the screen of my TV. I literally made the decision that evening that I was going to be reading fiction whenever I was not writing it—every chance I got. And that's really how I remember my mid to late twenties. I was an avid reader before that but I just embraced books, especially fiction, in a new way that has stuck with me ever since.

I'd give the same advice to any aspiring author. It just amazes me how many people I meet who say they want to write but don't like to read. It's the same as when a student tells me he or she wants to be an English teacher but doesn't like to read. I just don't get it. So, as

Stephen King advises in his wonderful memoir, *On Writing*, "Read a lot; write a lot." But I would also add that writing, for me, is really about embracing the editing process. If you are unwilling to often not just clean up your spelling and grammar but completely re-approach how you are telling a story you know isn't working, you aren't going to get far as a writer. The best fiction writers I know are the ones who are not afraid of editing—they thrive on it. I would also advise aspiring writers who are considering earning an MFA that you better be absolutely sure you want the writing life if you attend a graduate program that might force you to take out thousands of dollars in student loans.

In the end, I could give all the advice in the world to aspiring writers, but I can't help somebody really want it, and I mean *really* want it. I can't force you to spend long hours alone in a room falling into an imagined world. Writing is not a team sport, although many a great editor has left his or her loving mark on a book. If you are an uber-social creature you might consider a different form of artistic expression such as joining a band or something.

How Much Narrative is Too Much?

By
J. Conrad Guest
Author of:

One Hot January, January's Thaw, and
Backstop: A Baseball Love Story in Nine Innings

❦

Finding the right balance between narrative and dialogue in a novel is critical. Too much dialogue—too much "he said," "she said"—tires the reader and reads like a stage or screenplay. Too much narrative (thanks to our television/internet/cell phone society, which provides instant gratification while destroying attention span) bogs down the reader.

Still, narrative, whether an action sequence, a description of place or character, or the introspective thought process of a character, is essential to a novel. On a movie or television screen, everything appears before the viewer. It's a visual medium and so very little imagination is required. But in novel writing, it's up to the author to create those images in the minds of the reader through narrative. Or as Samuel R. Delany, one of my favorite novelists growing up, said in an interview: "Above all things, the story, the poem, the text is—and is only—what its words make happen in the reader's mind."

So what's the right mix?

That's difficult to say and often is personal preference. It should be noted that genre novels, such as romance, generally rely more on dialogue than do mainstream novels.

Detroit area novelist Elmore Leonard (*Get Shorty*, *Out of Sight*, *Hombre*, and *Rum Punch*, which was filmed as *Jackie Brown*) claims he leaves out of his novels anything that he believes the reader will skip over. He also criticizes narrative as the author's attempt to butt into the story. His way is right for him; but it's not the only way.

My early novels were very heavy on narrative, close to seventy percent or more, which is the upper limit most experts advise. Several of my novels are written in first person, with a lot of introspection. Like Raymond Chandler, that style lends itself to narrative.

Chandler is considered one of the great stylists of all time. Consider this gem, from *The Big Sleep*:

Then she lowered her lashes until they almost cuddled her cheeks and slowly raised them again, like a theater curtain. I was to get to know that trick. That was supposed to make me roll over on my back with all four paws in the air.

Three simple sentences rife with imagery—consider the lashes cuddling the woman's cheeks, before rising like a theatre curtain. What does this passage imply about the woman? It's all a show. She's manipulating Marlowe. That she expected him to roll over with paws in the air indicates she's had previous success with this tactic. And Marlowe's description shows he's on to her!

This visual is ever so evocative and plays beautifully on the movie screen of one's imagination, and yet many creative writing courses would have you write: She batted her eyes at him.

A writer's job is to engage the reader and what better way to engage than with narrative?

Our children are taught to "see Dick and Jane;" but as adults, we want to see what Dick and Jane look like, the jewelry Jane wears, how each dresses—how low-cut Jane's blouse is and how short her skirt may well give us an indication as to whether Dick may bring Jane home to meet his parents—the body language they display toward each other—is Dick on the prowl and Jane merely a tease?— maybe the smoky nightclub setting in which they find themselves on their first date; we want to hear the music playing on the juke box— is it playing Jane's favorite song and if so, what does this tell us about her?—the background hum of the other patrons lost in their own conversations, the occasional male guffaw and female titter as other couples continue their own mating ritual, the clinking of cocktail glasses …

It's been said that dialogue drives a storyline, and that's true. But the narrative that accompanies dialogue helps propel the dialogue.

Think of your own everyday conversations with colleagues at work, your spouse or children. Facial expressions, gestures, almost always accompany an exchange of words. A well-placed grin or a raised eyebrow, a hand gesture or a sip from a drink rather than a dialogue tag can say a lot about what a character is thinking without having to spell it out for the reader.

Yet sometimes less is more. Consider all that is left unsaid, and how telling it is, in this brief excerpt from my novel, *January's Thaw*:

I recalled the vision of a few minutes ago: A woman undressing in shadows—mottled light from between window blinds set to motion by a gasp of early summer night air, slashes of luminosity split rounded breast, hip's parabola. My own gasp whispered to the darkness as my desire responded to hers.

Descriptive narrative can go a long way toward defining setting as well as period, as in this excerpt from *One Hot January*:

* * *

The man jerked and twitched—an epileptic in seizure. His right foot stomped in rhythmic time; shoulders bunched as fingers flew in a frenzied attack on black and white ivory. Sweat poured from beneath the stocking that was a cap and ran in torrents down his face. A brief respite from his self-perpetuated paroxysm, and he mopped from his face what moisture he could with the stained handkerchief that lay beside him, before giving way to another fit of spasms.

Whether the demented cacophony that spewed from the piano he assailed with a vengeance was a result of the convulsions he initiated or the notes themselves responsible for the musician's spastic throes, I only wondered. For all the split notes, all the crazy chromatic chord changes, for all the irregular intervals and rhythms that made his music unique, Thelonious Sphere Monk, the expectant father of modern jazz, would be scorned by critics, his music laughed at, misunderstood and unappreciated by the uninitiated for years. Until his death in 1982, when with the advent of the compact disk much of his music would be reissued and embraced by a new generation, proving that all great artists enjoy their greatest success posthumously.

I sat and watched, amused, as Monk now stood and danced in a tiny circle, lost in a world of eccentricity as profound as his music, his arms swinging in time as tenor saxman Don Byas blew notes that rivaled Monk's own in their dissonance ...

*   *   *

Giving characters some "stage business" instead of just a "he said" or "she said" tag makes for more engaging dialogue. This excerpt is also from *One Hot January*. See if you agree that the accompanying narrative adds to the character sketches:

*   *   *

"I was afraid to confide in you, because of the magnitude of the implications. I didn't think you would—or could—believe me. I didn't think you'd help me."

"I still may not," I said, "and not because of what happened at Minton's five-and-a-half years ago. Miss MacIntyre, I value honesty above all things. In my personal life as well as from my clients—*especially* from my clients."

"I know you do, Mr. January," Melissa said, bravely meeting my glare. "I'm impressed by your integrity. Why else do you think I looked you up again after all this time? It was because I knew I could trust you."

"Just not enough to trust with me all the facts."

Melissa looked down again, but try as she might, she just couldn't hide her shame in the glass she couldn't help but turn round and round in her hands.

"I'm sure she has a good reason, Joe."

I nearly blurted, *Any reason would be reason enough for you, Lance,* but bit back the rebuke. To Melissa, I prodded, "What about it, Miss?"

Melissa continued to toy with her glass, seemingly oblivious to my question, before, some weighty decision reached, she set the glass down with purpose, the tablecloth robbing the finality of the gesture of its effect. Whether her newfound courage was a result of that simple act or merely an act, I couldn't be certain. She looked me

170

square in the eye, as if to challenge me to dispute the validity of what she was about to disclose.

"Mr. January, I didn't even know my brother was missing until last Friday."

"Yet you let me assume he flew off in search of your father a couple of days ago."

"My brother is often away on business, so I had no reason to question his whereabouts. But then last Friday ..."

"Go on, Miss MacIntyre. What happened last Friday?"

Melissa looked at me, and something in her look told me that whatever information she was about to impart would be the truth—or at least some twisted part of the truth—and that she knew how much of that truth I believed would be paramount in achieving the business arrangement she so greatly desired.

* * *

Note the mix of traded dialogue lines with no identifier tags or action with the other pieces of business—Melissa toying with her glass displays her uncertainty; January's distrust of Melissa, her sincerity a façade to cover up her devious intent; even the rebuke of Lance that January bites back serves the purpose of showing that January is well aware Lance is sweet on Melissa and is far too trusting of her.

There are five people in the room; but if each one has strong "voice" or manner of speaking, or they use the name of the person they are addressing, you need not add an identifier tag on the end of each line of dialogue.

Check out this brief descriptive passage, also from *One Hot January*, and the dialogue that follows, with expressions, actions, the game-playing between January and his adversary, humor, and even the introspective thoughts carefully placed. Does the variety distract you, slow you down, or does it add to the scene?

* * *

I stepped one leg out, then the other, landing lightly on the Packard's bumper. From there I bounded down onto the brick that was Broadway and made my way around to the driver's side of the Packard. Flinging open its door, I reached in, grabbed the still startled driver by the lapels of his cheap tweed suit, and shook him violently several times. The last of the repetitions partially dislodged the pince-nez from the bridge of the nose it spanned. The blue eyes, now just inches from my own, swam beneath water that wasn't tears. One eye, the left, focused its terror on me while the other, due to a weakness of its tendon an optometrist would diagnose as strabismus, seemed to focus furtively on some distant object behind and to my left. I resisted the urge to turn around to see what it was that held that other eye's interest.

"Now that I have your attention," I rasped, "maybe you'd like to tell me just what it is you're doing tailing us."

The great eyes blinked; yet the pools of water still threatened to spill over their levees.

"I haff no idea vat you are talking a-bout." The man spoke, his high tenor surprising me, in a carefully metered pace that betrayed an uncertainty of the English language and I felt my stomach sink. We had yet to leave New York and already my worst fears were confirmed.

The man's a Nazi! I concluded.

"Shit!" I said. An image of the man whose lapels I still firmly held dressed in the black of the German Gestapo flashed before my eyes.

And to think I was concerned over the likelihood that he was an agent of our own government. Damn!

"You always make a point of enjoying a cup of coffee while reading *The Wall Street* in front of my office on 59th before following me uptown?"

"I haff no idea—"

"Yeah, yeah," I broke in, giving him another violent shaking. The action provided a release for my slightly trembling hands, the result of my surging adrenaline. "I've already heard that."

I snorted aloud and a new strategy began to take shape. I released my grip and fussed over the rumpled lapels.

"Obviously you're a tourist," I said, righting the glasses that still teetered precariously near the end of his nose.

"Ja, a tourist," the German answered with a slow nod.

I watched the conspiratorial gaze that had been residing in the right eye make its way none too stealthily to the good eye. In the vacancy left behind, I thought I detected a certain nonchalance that surely was intended to disarm me.

"Ja," I mimicked. "Well, being a local maybe I can help you find whatever landmark it is you're looking for, Herr Tourist."

"Land-mark?" the big German enunciated carefully. Neither eye looked like it comprehended what I was talking about.

"Ja," I repeated. "You know … sightseeing." I watched the light come on in the cerulean of the left eye and the thin lips parted in a good-natured smile to reveal a good-sized gap between the two front teeth.

"Ja, sight-seeing," the stranger acknowledged with a nod, and his smile broadened.

"Ja," I repeated a third time with a nod of my own. "What would you like to see?" The smile inverted itself. Neither eye met my penetrating gaze. "The Statue of Liberty?"

Silence.

I nodded. "I see. Been there already. Well how about the Empire State Building, then?" Like all native New Yorkers, I slurred into one syllable the second and third words of the proper name that identifies New York's most famous landmark. The stranger brought one eye to bear on me while the other stared off into the distance. I wondered if any object it might focus on would register an image for the German. "No? Well what about Columbia College? You seen that yet, Herr Pal?"

"Co-lum-bia Col-lege?" The German enunciated each syllable carefully, uncertainly.

"Great!" I said, allowing my own manufactured smile to break out. "I know just where Columbia College is. Why don't you slide on over and I'll have you there in no time."

* * *

Keep in mind that dialogue between characters is only a part of the story. An important part, yes, but other parts—description, action, introspection (or internal dialogue)—play important roles, too.

There is no right or wrong way to approach a novel—not if a writer has the right tools in their toolbox, they know and understand the rules of good writing. Sure, it's a good idea to know your audience, but, as Delany says, "All readers are not the same." So a writer should write, first and foremost, for their own pleasure—what they're moved to write.

Writers are advised to find the story that only they can write; but remember, there are only a half-dozen or so ideas—ideals like love and loss and death—that make up fiction. Beyond that, it's in the telling of the story that gives it any semblance of originality.

The truth is, you're never going to be able to please every reader. You think Hemingway didn't have his detractors? Guess again. While *The Old Man and the Sea* became a book-of-the month selection in 1951, *Across the River and Into the Trees* received negative reviews in 1950. Hemingway, by the way, wrote novels that relied heavily on dialogue; but he is an exception to the rule.

Excerpt from
Backstop: A Baseball Love Story in Nine Innings

I wait for Higgins to dig in and think of my father, whether, wherever he is, he is proud of my accomplishments in baseball, or whether he is merely ashamed of what I did to Darlene. I want to forgive him for so much—as I want desperately for Darlene to forgive me—especially for handicapping me in so many ways. But in order to forgive him, I somehow feel I must elevate myself into a position of judge, and that's something I find I just can't do. I accepted long ago that I am who I am, the good and the bad, as a result of this man about whom I know so little and who left me before I could prove myself to him. If I could only resolve to stop staring at my past looking for answers, or to assign blame, I might finally be able to consign him to a less prominent place in my life, into a favorite corner to which I can go from time to time if only to dust off the cobwebs.

Somehow I found the courage to risk my dreams, even when they seemed to exceed my grasp, despite Dad's inability to succor me. Still, in failing Darlene, I failed to become the man I always wanted to become. The sin rests entirely with me. Yet in the aftermath of that sin I fought for Darlene. As I continue to fight for us. But it's a battle I can't win alone.

In my youth I once considered that my father, due to my mother's unhappiness, should not have married and, in my own unhappiness with my father, that he should not have fathered children. But what did that say of me, my self-image, my self-value? Indeed, what does Darlene's unwillingness to fight for what we once had say of me? Yet I'm unwilling to concede defeat—perhaps the result of the ballplayer in me—although my resolve, like my knees, weakens day by day.

🦃

Interview with J. Conrad Guest

What is your latest book about?

January's Thaw is the sequel to *One Hot January*. In *One Hot January*, Joe January, a private investigator circa 1947, grudgingly helps a pretty young woman find her father, a professor of archeology at Columbia College in New York who's been missing for six years. When January finally tracks him down, Professor MacIntyre spins a wild yarn of time travel and alternate realities. All January knows for sure is that two nefarious individuals are hot on his trail. Only at the end, when January is transported a century into the future, does he come to believe in the validity of MacIntyre's claims.

In *January's Thaw*, January must come to terms with his misplaced past, which includes losing the woman he loved but never told, while trying to survive in a world that has, in his eyes, gone mad: "Pornography, prostitution, pollution, government corruption, global warming, terrorism, and for all your purported connectivity through the internet and cell phones, your society is more disconnected than ever. On top of that, the war between men and women is no closer to a cease fire than it was from when I come."

Written in January's own first person narrative, it's a convoluted story that ends where it begins. If that makes little sense, well, don't expect me to explain. You'll just have to read both books for yourself! Trust me, when all is said and done, it'll be crystal clear.

Tell us a little about your main character.

Joe January was fashioned after Philip Marlowe, Raymond Chandler's character in many great novels from the 1940s and 50s. Chandler did so much to shape the hard-boiled detective genre that others, like Mickey Spillane, John D. MacDonald, Robert B. Parker, Sara Paretsky, Sue Grafton, and, yes, even Elmore Leonard, have pushed to new heights.

January is my tribute to Chandler. Think Marlowe working against a science fiction backdrop of time travel and an alternate reality in which Germany has won World War II.

How (or when) do you decide that you are finished writing a story?

The answer to that is twofold. I usually have the end of the story in mind before I sit down to write the first word; I also have in mind an approximate word count. Therefore it's simply a matter of writing to that end while I allow the characters to tell their story through me. I make a number of discoveries as we go, taking digressions and detours, all the while keeping track of the word count. Just because I hit that word count doesn't mean I just end the story. I give myself permission to go over if the story requires it. Subsequent drafts usually add to the word count.

The second part of my answer is that I'm never truly finished writing a story until I approve the final proof. Frankly, I could make revisions indefinitely. Each time I read a novel of mine I'm capable of tweaking this or that, adding narrative or an exchange of dialogue. I'm a perfectionist that way. Jack Kerouac would accuse me of self-censorship, but I can't help myself: I'm constantly looking to improve something I've written. But once it's published, it's done and I won't revisit them.

January's Paradigm, my first novel, has been available for more than a decade and I haven't looked at it since. What would be the purpose? I'm sure I'd find ways to improve it; however, that's where I was, both as a person and as a writer. Why would I wish to change it to reflect who and where I am today?

Someone recently told me they thought *January's Paradigm* is my best novel. I have to say I felt somewhat insulted. If I'm not writing better today than I was twenty years ago, then what have I learned about the art of writing? I think what they meant is that they connected to that story more than they have to my other work.

Is there a message in your writing you want readers to grasp?

The January books are composed of a number of messages. In *January's Paradigm* the reader learns that there are people in the world—men and women alike—who are not very nice, and that men don't have a corner on the mean market. Men, too, can be hurt through a woman's infidelity. *One Hot January* shows that no government is benign and that we must care about a world we will not see. While *January's Thaw* is largely about redemption, that it's never too late to close the door on the past and to live in the moment, for tomorrow.

Do you think writing this book changed your life? How so?

I think every story I've ever written has changed my life in some way.

The January trilogy took ten years to write. During those years I lost both my parents. I struggled with the creative process as I struggled through my grief; but I also struggled because I was so caught up in publication and the rejection letters I received. It was like playing the dating game. I constantly questioned why I was doing it—putting myself through the agony of looking for approval of my work through publication. I questioned my talent and ability—ignoring the reality that the book industry is a business concerned with bottom line and that acquisition of a manuscript is, like wading through profiles at an online dating site, largely subjective—and I often talked myself out of a writing session, procrastinating to another day because I doubted the value of my work. It was only as I neared completion of *January's Thaw* that I finally learned to enjoy the process of creation. At that point I knew I was a writer.

Coincidentally, success came when I stopped focusing on trying to manifest it. Just like dating: when you stop looking, someone usually comes into your life when you least expect.

What are you working on right now?

I just completed my seventh novel, *500 Miles to Go*. Set in the 1950s and 1960s, the story centers on Alex Król and his drive to win the Indianapolis 500. A sports/romance novel in the vein of *Backstop: A Baseball Love Story in Nine Innings*, *500 Miles to Go* is largely about the importance of, and the risks associated with, pursuit of dreams.

I'm presently in the process of making revisions to *A Retrospect in Death*, my sixth novel, and I'm nurturing the seed for my next major project, which was given to me by a beautiful and creative woman I met on Facebook.

What is the most difficult part of the whole writing process?

Revisions are the most difficult process for me; yet it's a process I enjoy immensely. I constantly seek ways to improve my work—even before I finish my first draft. First draft is really a misnomer, because I edit as I go. I sometimes think my first draft is really the equivalent of a third or fourth draft because of all the changes I make as I go.

But it's difficult, too, to cut something you really love but know you must because it contributes little to the overall piece.

What is the easiest part of the writing process?

Putting on a Sunday morning pot of coffee, going to the humidor to select the right cigar, unwrapping it, snipping its head, inhaling the fragrance of the wrapper, lighting it, and watching the smoke permeate my den. Then I put on a Beatles CD and crank up the Bose speakers. The Beatles were turned down by Decca Records because some suit didn't like their sound and also thought that guitar-driven music was on its way out. The Beatles inspire me to one day create my own White Album (which, at present, might be *500 Miles to Go*).

Honestly, that's all a part of my routine, and writing, for me, is all about routine. While I've heard other writers talk about waiting for their muse to show up, I find that, with a cup of coffee and a good cigar, my creativity gets a jump start and pretty soon the muse shows up, out of curiosity, to peek over my shoulder to see what the tapping is all about.

Does writing come easy for you?

It comes a heck of a lot easier today than it did when I first started. It's like anything you do with regularity—like a workout routine. The first few times you hit the gym, your muscles rebel. But after a time, your body craves that workout; miss a few days and your body complains. For me, a day without writing is like a day without sunshine. And a day without sunshine is like … night.

But does it come easy? No. Nor should it. I've gotten better at arranging words on a blank screen. I'm more efficient about it. I rarely struggle for thirty minutes or more over the construction of a simple seven-word sentence like I did early in my career.

I don't write formula, or even in a specific genre. I find that easier than writing to a particular audience. The January books combine science fiction with the hard-boiled detective and mix in more than a dram of romance—just not the bodice-ripping romance novels that sport Fabio on the cover. *Backstop* and *500 Miles* are both sports-themed novels with romance; while *A Retrospect in Death* deals with searching for love and never finding it. *The Cobb Legacy* is a mystery-romance with subplots of infidelity, divorce, and a son trying to connect with his dying father.

Always in my novels you'll find something decidedly different. If you're tired of regency romance because of the formula, why not try one of my novels? Another Facebook friend of mine says I write gritty love stories ... what she calls "romance for the non-romantic." I like that, although that in no way reflects on me as being non-romantic. I may be curmudgeonly and smoke cigars and drink scotch, but I know how to romance the right woman. The trouble is it's been a while since I dated a woman who I thought was the right woman. I suspect that's about to change.

But enough about my love life.

I suppose writing would come easier if I chose to write following the formula many creative writing courses teach; but then I'd see myself as a mercenary, writing for a paycheck to appeal to the masses. I still write largely to amuse myself and hope my audience one day will find me.

I like the challenge of writing a good story—outside the confines of genre—creating characters with whom readers can relate, and writing engaging dialogue. If it was too easy, I'd grow bored and find something else to challenge me.

Wow. What was the question and did I answer it?

How did you learn to write?

Is there really a right way to write, to write right? We all have our quirks, idiosyncrasies, rituals, even superstitions. It's whatever works for us, right?

Honestly, I've been asked so many times over the years I've lost track—how do I do what I do?

Trust me when I tell you I'm not trying to be flippant when I say I really have no idea. It's like Ted Williams trying to explain to a novice the art of hitting .400. By the way, I was a pretty good ballplayer in my youth, but when it came time to play organized ball, well, my parents had other ideas, and so I never got the chance to see if I could learn to hit a curveball. Who knows, maybe it saved my life, too. For every kid who makes it to the major leagues there are hundreds who fall short of their dream. Perhaps even a few whose careers are cut short, maybe even have their lives cut short, when they take a fastball to the noggin. That, by the way, was one of the arguments my parents gave for not letting me play in high school: "They throw hard and they don't always know where the ball is going."

My point is I could listen to Ted Williams (if he were alive) talk all day about hitting—about sweet spots and keeping my hands back and my head down, rotating my hips out of the way—and about patience at the plate and how pitchers are the dumbest SOBs in the world and how, if I'm patient enough, they'll make a mistake and that's when I make them pay.

I'd sit there, take it all in and nod, and it might all make sense. But it doesn't mean that I'm going to be a .400 hitter because, while you can teach a kid how to throw and hit a baseball, great hitters like Williams are born.

One thing I've learned in my life is never say never.

Ring Lardner wrote of Ty Cobb: "It defies human capability for anyone to average almost .400 in the past five seasons." Yet that's precisely what Cobb did, and at one point in his career he won nine consecutive batting titles. Nine! Cobb hit a mere .367 lifetime, over twenty-four seasons, twenty-two with Detroit.

They said Ruth's single season record of sixty homeruns was unassailable. Roger Maris topped that mark—long before steroids. So maybe one day we'll see someone hit .400 for a full season. I just don't imagine it'll be in my lifetime.

So how does all this talk of baseball relate to writing?

Well, a lot of people I meet tell me they have a novel in them. But when I ask them when they intend to start writing, they stammer something about not knowing where to begin. To which I usually reply, "How about at the beginning?" Yeah, Mom always said I could be a smart-ass.

The truth is, when I started writing my first novel, *January's Paradigm*, in 1992, I didn't have a clue what I was doing. I'd written the first and last sentences in my head and then, for several weeks, put off sitting down to write that first sentence because I had no idea how I was going to fill the four hundred or so pages that connected the two sentences.

But guess what? I learned. Not from an online correspondence course. Not by taking a creative writing class at a community college. I learned simply by doing it. Line by line, sentence by sentence, paragraph by paragraph, page by page, I strung the story together.

I've since written six more novels, a novella, a host of short stories, and a variety of articles and memoirs, and I'm a much better writer today than I was nearly twenty years ago when I started writing *January's Paradigm*. And I *still* haven't taken a creative writing course. It's certainly not because I know it all—I learn something about the craft of writing each time I sit down to write something.

The reason I haven't taken a creative writing class is because I'm afraid someone will try to teach me that what I've been doing the last twenty years is wrong. For instance, would a course teach you to write the ending of a novel before you got there? That's precisely what I did in *A Retrospect in Death*. I was maybe two-thirds of the way finished when the ending just came to me out of nowhere and, rather than risk losing it, I devoted my next writing session to getting it all down on paper.

Understand that most correspondence courses are designed to help the writer become published, and the best way to achieve that end is to teach a formula—keep sentences short, stay away from words longer than two syllables, any word that ends in "ly" is bad, so never use an adverb. In short, write to a sixth-grade level.

I won't deny there is a market for formula fiction; however, as the publishing industry continues to lose money at an alarming rate, I suggest they take a look at the product they continue to peddle.

Looking back at *January's Paradigm*, I can say that, if I was writing it today, I'd do a lot of things differently. But I'm still proud of it. It's representative of where I was—both as a writer as well as in my life. In retrospect, I'm surprised by how much I knew *before* I commenced that project. Somehow I'd learned, probably through a voracious appetite for reading in my youth, not only the basics of grammar and sentence structure, but also of storytelling.

Do you have any advice for an aspiring writer?

As a writer, it's up to you to decide what you wish to be: a mercenary who turns out word count for remuneration, or an artiste who creates for love of the word in hope that one day his audience will find him.

What words would you like to leave the world when you are gone?

In the words of former Spinal Tap keyboardist, Viv Savage: "Have a good time all the time."

No, seriously. Don't let the novel die. Wherever the technology takes the novel, there's something about words—whether on a page or an e-reader—and what they make happen inside a reader's head that can never translate to the small or big screens. It's been said that all change begins with a thought. And what is a thought but words that ultimately compose an idea.

If the novel is dying, what's that say about imagination? Watching a movie requires little imagination—it's all done for you. A picture may be worth a thousand words; but never underestimate the power and value of a thousand words and what those words, in the hands of a skillful writer, can do to inflame a mind. Words can inspire support for a cause; they can stir the oppressed to rebellion; they can bring understanding to two sides at odds; or they can bring two lonely hearts together for a lifetime.

So many people today in our immediate gratification society don't have the patience for reading. I find that sad because, like stopping to smell the roses—which requires disconnecting from technology—getting lost in a good book is truly one of the most gratifying, and rewarding, indulgences.

Where can people learn more about your books?

You can find out more about me and my literary world, which includes all my novels and works in progress, events, cigars, and a link to my blog, at http://jconradguest.com/ I'm also on Facebook.

A Jerk's Guide to Comedy Writing
By
Noah Baird
Author of:
Donations to Clarity

🐦

Analyzing humor is like dissecting a frog. Few people are interested and the frog dies of it. — E.B. White.

Comedy is an outlaw in that it doesn't have to follow any rules except one: be funny. Comedy, like love and fear (the other two outlaws), is personal and defies explanation. Just as someone prefers one mate over another, or fears snakes and not heights, what is funny to one person is not funny to someone else. This is one of the hurdles a comedy writer has to overcome. I know what I think is funny, but it's harder to understand what the audience thinks.

Psychologists have described humor as the sudden release of tension. On a physical level, laughter is our body's response to the surprise of an unforeseen stimulus. One of the tools a comedian uses to create tension is to discuss something uncomfortable; enter the sex, fart, and poop jokes. Pushing the audience into an uncomfortable area raises their tension levels. The punch line is the release valve to bleed off that tension. If you think about it, comedy writing is the art of forcing a biological response to the written word. Stories may tug at the reader's heartstrings or make them melancholy. Erotica may—well, we know what erotica will do to us. However, comedy is the only writing that has as its focus the creation of a physical response.

Do an internet search on comedy and you will find dozens of articles on comedy writing. Nearly all the articles cover mechanics and structure. What they don't tell you is how to be funny. I can't tell you how to be funny either. There's no secret Mel Brooks gland; you're either funny or you're not. My advice is to go ahead and write your book. If you're funny, then it will come out. If you aren't; then you still wrote a book.

So, you still want to write comedy? Here's the part you don't want to know: comedy is work. Stop laughing, it's true. You have to train yourself to see the humor in things. You may have been a quick-witted class clown, but how is that going to help you write comedy? It won't. Aping *Saturday Night Live* skits is not the same thing as being funny.

I need to warn you: the training will make you a jerk. Once you've learned to make a joke out of anything, you won't be able to quit. You'll become the smart-ass. On the other hand, your partner won't try to drag you into too many let's-talk-about-how-you-feel conversations anymore. So, you've got that going for you.

Part of that training requires reading; a lot of reading. This includes the news. There are a few reasons why you need to read the news everyday:

•People are stranger than you think. If your zany characters are eclipsed by the news, then you aren't pushing hard enough. As soon as you think you've developed a character that is going to be your comedic vehicle to drive your jokes, someone will do something even crazier. Herman Cain quoted a Pokemon movie in his farewell address. If I wrote that scene a year earlier, you would've thought I was insane. Now, writing anything less would be tame.

•You have to remain current. Humor has a relatively short shelf life. The edgiest material is what is happening right now.

•You need cultural anchors. What I mean by cultural anchors is your references have to be widely understood. Prior to 2009, the tea party had a different meaning than it does now. Before the tea party movement, we weren't debating the merits of the Boston Tea Party (maybe historians were, but nobody listens to them). Today, the tea party has had a polarizing effect in our culture. Your humor has to consider that. Dennis Miller gets away with dropping obscure cultural references mixed with a robust vocabulary; you can't. I love Dennis Miller. I think he's a brilliant comedian, but you need a

dictionary and an encyclopedia to follow along with him.
•Language trends change every few years and the news typically reflects it. Remember a few years ago when the media merged celebrity couple names to make one name? Now every political incident is a something-gate. In the '90s, there was a period when we dropped Jewish words into normal conversation. The good news is, keeping up with language trends doesn't require any effort. Just by reading you will pick up the trends organically.

There are a couple of ways I tend to write jokes. I don't know if these are the best ways or if this is what other writers do, but it works for me. Usually, I start off with an idea for a joke. I know what the punch line is, or what I think it is. I then write the chapter as a delivery for the joke while also maintaining the plot. I usually tend to write this type of joke for what I call 'transition scenes'. In your plot, you have to move your characters from A to B, or you have to give the characters a piece of information they need later in the plot. I punch up these transition scenes by essentially writing a joke inside the transition.

I also love to use jokes during character development. This method tells the reader something about the character, whether it be an eccentric view of the world or how they react to a funny situation. I tend to write over-the-top characters which allow me to repeatedly use them as a vehicle for certain jokes.

Another method I use is to punch up a chapter for humor. One way to do this is to look at the words you use. Some words are funnier than others. One belief is words with a 'k' sound funnier (Don't ask me why, 'kay?). If a character offers another character a cup of coffee, make it a macchiato. Both words have the hard 'k' sound, but macchiato sounds funnier. If a character is offered a beer, have them offered an appletini. It's just more fun to say.

You can also go back through your chapter and look at the dialogue. Find a place where you can put in a humorous comment while still keeping your character's personality. An example I like to use is Harrison Ford's character, Han Solo, in The Empire Strikes Back. Think of the scene when Han Solo is going to be frozen in carbonite. The scene was set up beautifully; the audience's tension was built up to the point of popping. Carrie Fisher's character,

Princess Leia, confessed her love to Han Solo, and Han Solo replied, "I know". Now, that wasn't how the scene was written. The script had Solo saying he loved Princess Leia too. Harrison Ford inserted the funny response during filming and it stayed. It made a classic scene better. More importantly, it fit the character. It took a dramatic scene and released the pressure valve while remaining consistent with the character's personality.

As a comedic writer, most of your jokes will be dialogue driven; characters talking to other characters. There are other styles you'll use, such as situational and environmental. You could even write physical comedy (slapstick). Here's my advice for dialogue: Go to your neighborhood bar; not a nightclub or meat market, unless you are specifically seeking something from that element. I mean a nice Irish pub: blue-collar, middle class. Hit it at happy hour for a couple of weeks and just watch. You'll begin to see trends. There's a group of regulars. They usually get there as soon as the place opens, and they stay after the happy hour crowd leaves. Some times they go home to eat, and then come back to the bar. These are your tickets. They are golden fountains of verbal diarrhea. Get to know them. They will tell you the funniest and strangest stories you've ever heard. My idea for the weight of the human turd conversation in my book stemmed from one of these conversations.

When I first started writing my novel, *Donations to Clarity*, I fully intended to write a book for guys. I'd read an article which described how women read much more than men. Besides being alarmed for my gender, I was slightly insulted. I read far more than most women I know (except for my mother, who devours books). It occurred to me most books for men were the lone-Navy-SEAL-hunting-the-missing-nuclear-submarine-against-all-odds type of books. I wouldn't read many books either if I thought that was all I had to choose from. I wanted to write a book for men that wasn't anything like those books. I also wanted to write a comedic novel aimed at a male audience, and I didn't care if women liked it or not. I was wrong. What I learned was: women appreciate typical male humor just as much as men. That is not a sexist statement, nor do I think women don't have a sense of humor. I am referring to style. I underestimated how much women would appreciate masculine humor.

A question I get from aspiring comedic writers is: How do you know if you've gone too far? You don't. The concept is subjective because what is funny is personal. It's the same argument as what is pornography and what is art. In my novel I wrote several chapters with questionable content. I wrote a character who was a homophobe and a character who impersonated a homosexual. These are two subject areas I needed to be careful of. In the '80s, comedians could beat up homosexuals all day long. Eddie Murphy made a career out of roasting homosexuals and Richard Simmons. That doesn't fly in 2011. You can still make fun of Richard Simmons, but not because he's gay. The hair and the striped shorts are still free game.

One of my rules for comedy writing is to not to insult anyone-directly. Offended? I don't care if they're offended, and you shouldn't either. You don't want to insult. In this case, making homosexuals feel like I'm picking on them. It's not about gay rights or embracing everyone. To me, comedy is about enjoyment. My goal is to take the audience out of their lives for a small time, and give them something to laugh about. That does not include abusing a subset of the population. Along with this, I was worried about how I portrayed women. I'd never written women before, and I was concerned I was too degrading to them.

I could get away with writing a book without the homophobe and the homosexual impersonator. I couldn't really write a book without any women in it. Because I chose to write the characters anyway, I did a couple of things to protect myself:

•I wrote the homophobe and the homosexual impersonator as idiots. In the case of the homophobe, the way I developed the character, it made sense for him to dislike gays. It would have been incongruous if I'd written him any other way.

•I asked a few homosexual friends and women read the chapters. I explained what my concerns were and asked for their honest opinions. A funny thing happened: not only did I get their blessings, but they gave me insight to develop the characters better.

Now that doesn't mean I was completely protected from criticism. I recently had a female reader email me claiming I degraded women. If you read my book, you know I made the guys idiots and the women were the only sane characters. Normally I don't respond to these emails, or I send a quick note with several suggestion of what they can do with their opinion. This particular woman hit a sensitive button for me; I wanted to know why she felt the way she did. And wow, did she! I got a page and a half on how I degraded women because I had a female character pee a little when Bigfoot scared her.

Which brings me to my next point: if you're going to write comedy, you'd better have a thick skin. You need a thick skin to be a writer. It needs to be thicker for comedy because you are going to piss someone off. Comedy isn't pretty. No matter how careful you are, you are going to offend someone. And they will write you and tell you all about it. The good news is they're just giving you a new character to put in the next book. It's the circle of life.

Another piece of advice I want to leave you with is to stop using punctuation to force the joke's timing. You, as the writer, may have a concrete idea of how the dialogue of a joke should be projected. Your instinct may be to add dashes or commas to interrupt the flow of the joke at just the right moment to make it funnier. Stop it. The readers are not actors waiting for their cue, and you aren't a stage director. You have no control over how the reader perceives the joke. If the reader doesn't get the joke because they didn't get the timing right, then let it go. Sometimes the joke will be even funnier because of the reader's internal timing. Bill Murray is famous for altering a joke's timing, making the joke funnier than intended. You put the joke out there, now let it go.

This leads us to losing joke. You will write several jokes which will be hit or miss with the reader. I've written several jokes I thought we were really clever, but fall flat with the audience. You are at a disadvantage as a comedic writer. When you see a comedian doing stand-up, especially on TV, their routine has been practiced until it was perfect. Those jokes you are hearing have been through more comedy clubs than chlamydia. As a writer, you aren't going to have that kind of opportunity. Also, resist the impulse to explain the joke. If you have to explain a joke, then it isn't a joke. Go with you gut, and put it out there.

One of the last things I want to talk to you about comedic writing is style development. By style development, I am referring to how you portray and relate your humor. Some comedians are snarky (Please don't do snarky. We have enough). Others are observational (Have you ever noticed . . . ?). I believe my particular style is irreverence. I've always been fascinated by the duality of human nature. By duality, I mean literal duality. We often have two thoughts going through our heads for most situations. One is the public thought. This is the thought we express out loud. It is usually non-offensive and doesn't ruffle any feathers. The other thought, the private one, is what you really think. This the thought we all think, but don't say. In those private thoughts is a piece of the truth. Truth, in my opinion, is the core of all humor. For me, expressing those pieces of truth which we collectively withhold, is my style. Find the truth in any situation, and you will find the humor. Whether your style is observation, satire, or simple storytelling; the truth is your punchline.

My last piece of advice is a little more nebulous. Have fun while you are writing. Don't try to write comedy when you are in a bad mood or frustrated. A foul mood will sour your writing, and you'll come off catty and malicious. Get yourself into the right place in your head. People read comedies to forget about their own lives. Look at it as a gift you are giving the reader. It's gratifying to hear your writing made some laugh so hard they dropped their book, or were kicked out of bed because their laughing woke their spouse. I had one reader tell she wasn't able to read my book in public because she laughed out loud like a maniac. Your goal should be to make the reader laugh, and forget about their troubles. But don't forget it's a gift for you too. Enjoy yourself. Laugh at your own jokes. This may sound hokey, but I believe when the writer laughs and has fun, it comes off on the page.

Excerpt from *Donations to Clarity*

"How much do you think the average human turd weighs?" Earl

asked as he sat down at the table, pulling the plastic lawn chair up behind him and reaching across the table to dig into Harry's basket of buffalo wings.

"Are you serious? Why?" asked Harry.

"Well, answer me this: how much does an order of wings weigh?"

"Regular or jumbo?"

"Jumbo" Earl mumbled with a mouth full of meat, spraying Three Mile Island sauce across the table. Droplets of orange-tinged spit peppered the table. Earl snatched a paper towel off the roll sitting on the table and wiped the table once, leaving an arc of smeared wing sauce across the table.

"Dude! Say it, don't spray it!" Harry yelped, holding his beer out of the mist with one hand, while trying to cover a baskets of wings and celery sticks with the other hand.

"You know: my usual. How much do you think that weighs? The parts I eat?" Earl said, craning his neck around looking for a waitress. Harry could hear the frustration in Earl's voice. Earl hadn't sat down with a beer, and he didn't usually like going for very long without one. Especially in The Beaver, not because the wings were too hot, but because Earl swore Yuengling tasted better from The Beaver's taps. Everyone else in the village thought The Brown Beaver's draft beers tasted skunky because the staff never cleaned the lines. "That's bullshit!" Earl would bellow to anyone who would listen. Earl had the proud distinction of having been in two fist fights and arrested once for defending The Brown Beaver's honor. The second fight (and arrest) was with The Brown Beaver's owner, Seamus, who refused to give Earl any more alcohol one night.

"I don't know. Why?" Harry said, responding to the back of Earl's head.

"I'm just trying to figure out how much I'm eating, is all." Earl said, holding up one finger to the waitress.

"What? Can't shop in the Miss's section anymore, Meatball?"

"Screw you! I'm serious!"

"Okay, okay. I'm sorry. Good for you! I'll support you on your diet. I hear they can be tough." Harry was switching gears, downshifting into sincerity drive, and hoping he sounded convincing or at least supportive.

"I'm not going a diet! I'm trying to figure out, in pounds, how much food I eat."

"Here you go, Earl" interrupted Cindi, placing his beer on the table.

"Well, thanks, darlin', and keep 'em coming." Earl cooed after taking a long drink. He gave Cindi his biggest smile, like a proud little boy showing his mama he ate all of his dinner.

"I sure will, honey." Cindi cooed back. She was a good waitress. She played along with the customers' little games, and ignored the slurred speech and rude pick up lines. She had wide hips and full breasts, her body was often described as good breeding stock by the old ranchers and lumberjacks sitting at the bar without their wives. She usually wore T-shirts with a low v-cut neckline when the weather was warm because she got better tips when she did.

"Cindi, how much does a jumbo order of wings weigh, not including the bones?" Earl probed, trying to sound intelligent in front of Cindi while still pumping out the charm.

"Uh, I don't know," Cindi responded sheepishly. Why do customers always think of strange things to ask me?

"No idea? Can you ask the cook how much an order of wings weighs without the bone? Do they weigh differently depending on the sauce?"

"Uh, sure," was all she could reply as she backed away from the table. Why can't Earl do like Harry does and just stare at my tits instead of asking weirdo questions?

"What's this have to do with turds?" Harry asked, watching Cindi's ass walk away.

"I'm trying to achieve neutral buoyancy within a human vessel." Earl deadpanned, also watching Cindi's ass walk away.

"Huh?"

"I said I was 'trying to achieve neutral buoyancy within a human vessel,' that is, me." Earl repeated with what he thought should be the impatient air of an academic.

"You see, Harry," Earl continued after taking a long pull from his beer, "I don't like taking shits." Earl stated, pausing for effect. Harry raised his eyebrows. Earl mistook the raised eyebrows as a signal to continue. "I'm tired of taking shits. It is the most despicable of all bodily functions," Earl continued, gaining speed. "Either through design or evolution, our waste disposal system is lacking. Our scatological process needs to be revamped. It's disgusting. It smells. It can be embarrassing. Leaves you feeling uncomfortable. I'm tired of it. I've done some research, and the average adult turd weighs between half of a pound to about a pound and a half."

"Really? That's it? I've had some whoppers I thought must've been heavier than that" replied Harry, his curiosity peaked, wrinkling his brow as he pondered Earl's latest bit of trivia. Another part of Harry's brain was simultaneously wondering why he was entertaining this conversation.

"I know. I thought the exact same thing" replied Earl, pleased Harry was showing some interest. "Anyway, I figure the weight of turds must equal the weight of excess food we consume. Food our body doesn't need." Earl was now punctuating the air with the fat end of a buffalo wing as he spoke. "So, I figure, if I reduce the amount of food I eat by the weight of my bowel movements, my body won't need to crap anymore. I will consume exactly what my body needs. So no waste. No more taking the Browns to the Super Bowl, or dropping the kids off at the pool! Close and seal the hatch. My crapping days are over."

Harry sat in amazement by the range of subjects Earl could pull out of his ass and discuss, without fear or embarrassment, in a public place. Maybe sealing the hatch would be best? "So, how's it going so far?" asked Harry, unconvinced.

"I'm still working on the ratio."

🐓

Interview with Noah Baird

How long had the idea of your book been developing before you began to write the story?

I worked on the idea for *Donations to Clarity* for about two or three years. My original intention was to write a very different book which included more mythical creatures, such as the Loch Ness Monster, but when I sat down to write the book, the Bigfoot story took over. Instead of resisting the idea, I just went with where the characters took me

What inspired you to write this particular story?

This is an interesting question because I'm really not sure. I was fascinated with Bigfoot when I was younger. The town I grew up in had several Bigfoot sightings, so I think those stories fueled my curiosity at a young age. Part of the Bigfoot legend has always been the idea it was a hoax. Some of the evidence is obviously hoaxed. I'm not sure about all of it, but there are certainly Bigfoot hoaxers out there. It was the hoaxing which really drew my attention – who would do something like that and why? Then I wondered: if Bigfoot exists, what does it think of these people hoaxing Bigfoot? The novel grew from that question.

How much of yourself is hidden in the characters in the book?

I'm not really sure. I suppose there are bits and pieces of me in all of the characters.

Who was your favorite character?

Bigfoot was really fun to write. It took a long time for me to decide on what type of character he should be. I wanted to stay away from the typical scary-creature-in-the-woods Bigfoot. I also thought Bigfoot would be a great vehicle for looking at our world through different eyes. The interesting thing that happened when I started writing him was this misogynist pig came out. I went back through what I wrote, and I thought it was really funny. It was great to be able to shut off the filters and write from the reptile side of the brain.

How much of a story do you have in mind before you start writing it?

Very little – I start with an idea and go. I read somewhere Tom Robbins purposely writes himself into a plot corner just to see if he can get himself out of it. I found the idea – that writing didn't have to have a regimented approach, but could be a game for the writer – really attractive. So, I sat down with the idea 'What would Bigfoot think if he saw a Bigfoot hoaxer?', and I went from there.

What challenges did you face as you wrote this book?

I didn't have people around who supported my writing. They weren't taking it as seriously as I was. As an unpublished writer, it was difficult to convince them this was something I needed to do. It was also hard to know if the writing or the story was good. It takes a great deal of faith in yourself and the story to see it all of the way through.

What was the first story you remember writing?

I didn't start off writing stories, but jokes. I really wanted to be a stand-up comedian. I studied comedy extensively, and trained myself to see the joke in everyday things. I was a horrible stand-up comedian. I didn't like speaking in front of a crowd, but my joke writing wasn't bad. It occurred to me I could write some very funny jokes – I just couldn't tell them. In some ways, jokes are micro-novels; they follow similar trajectories, timing, etc. Some of the chapters in the book follow the framework of joke writing.

What writer influenced you the most?

I picked up *Still Life with Woodpecker* by Tom Robbins when I was about 21. It was the book which really spoke to me. I'd always enjoyed reading, but it was the first book I felt like it was written to me. I loved Steinbeck, Twain, etc, but they were from another generation. Woodpecker was the literary equivalent of hearing Nirvana's "Smells Like Teen Spirit" or Don McLean's "American Pie" for the first time. I felt like someone else out there saw the world like I did. Christopher Moore, Tim Dorsey, and Carl Hiaasen are larger influences on me now, but Tom Robbins was the first to knock me down the rabbit hole.

Did you do any research for the book? If so, how did you do it?

I read probably a dozen books on Bigfoot and hoaxing Bigfoot. I don't think I ended up using anything from the research. I tend to b.s. my way through with just enough facts to make it seem plausible.

Is there a message in your writing you want readers to grasp?

Absolutely not. I write sitcom literature. It's mental fast food. I just wanted to write an enjoyable story.

Do you think writing this book changed your life? How so?

I think people thought I was pretty weird before the book. They still think I'm weird, but I think I get a pass now because I'm a writer.

What one book, written by someone else, do you wish you'd written yourself?

Mark Twain's The Diaries of Adam and Eve. It is the funniest, most honest analysis of the complicated relationships between men and women I've ever read.

Where can we go to learn more about Donations to Clarity?

You can find out more about me and Donations to Clarity on my author page at Second Wind Publishing, LLC

The Challenges and Joys of Writing a Novel Series
By
Christine Husom
Author of:
Murder in Winnebago County, Buried in Wolf Lake, and *An Altar by the River*

🦃

I have enjoyed reading a number of series novels over the years, but never planned to write one of myself. The first book of the series, *Murder in Winnebago County* was inspired by tragic event. It started with a phone call after midnight, the one nobody wants to answer. The caller's voice was trembling. "Your father is dead. . . . He drowned in the hospital pool." *Hospital pool?*

It was late July and my father was being treated for pneumonia. He had been given a sleeping aid, one, it was later discovered, sometimes caused sleepwalking. Dad went missing between one nurses' round and the next. We will never know exactly what, why, or how it happened, but he got out of bed, around his bed rail, ripped out his IV needle—and evidenced by the blood trail—walked directly to the emergency exit, and pushed open the door. The recently installed alarm did not sound. But when tested multiple times the next day, it worked fine.

Dad went out into the pouring rain, made his way down a fairly steep hill, fell into a pond at the bottom, and drowned. The doctors determined he had suffered an episode of "sundowning," a condition where an elderly person wakes up, sees he or she is not home, and feel compelled to get to the familiar. My father had no dementia. He wasn't depressed. Was it sundowning, or was it the drug he'd been given that caused such a bizarre scenario?

I obsessed about the whys for a year, then one day it occurred to me, *What if it wasn't an accident? What if someone deliberately hurt him?* My father was a retired district judge, and had been widely respected as firm, yet compassionate and fair. But he had received threats over the years, nonetheless. Would a person bent on revenge seize an opportunity to hurt him? Who would that person be? What would be his or her motivation?

My imagination gave birth to a number of characters who lived in the fictional Winnebago County in central Minnesota. As a former Wright County Sheriff's Department officer, the semi-rural county was a natural setting for the story.

After writing about half of *Murder in Winnebago County*, I knew I wouldn't be able to retire the characters after only one case. They had become people I thought about almost as much as the live ones I was closest to. Dramatic incidents from my days with the sheriff's department came to mind, and I formulated basic plots for the next two books.

I learned from research and experience that the key elements for success in a story or book series are: creating realistic characters who continue to evolve with each book; writing an ending that leaves the reader wanting more; and letting the reader know what happened in a previous book without getting bogged down in lengthy descriptions.

1. Create characters readers want to follow and/or have a relationship with.

Write a background for each of your main characters as a base for their motivations, their beliefs, their morals. Much of who they are is based on their life experiences. Not all aspects of their past lives need to be included in the story, but may come to light in a subsequent novel.

How do they feel? What do they look like? Do they have a pet? What are their strengths, their talents, their fears, their strengths, their vulnerabilities? How are they connected to the other characters? What role do they play in the story?

Create characters who become living, breathing, thinking, talking people who are interacting with other characters, going to jobs, falling in love, committing crimes, etcetera, for your readers. People want to see how your characters react under pressure, what they do when they get knocked down, how they handle compliments. Vince Flynn has Mitch Rapp, a counterterrorism operative. John Sandford has Lucas Davenport, a Minneapolis Police Department Detective. William Kent Krueger has Corcoran O'Connor, former Chicago cop and current part-time investigator in northern Minnesota. Patricia Cornwell has Kay Scarpetta, Chief Medical Examiner for the state of Virginia. Millions of people know the names of those characters as well as they know the names of real-life famous people.

The protagonist and main character in the Winnebago County Mystery Thriller series is Sergeant Corinne "Corky" Aleckson, a young sergeant with the sheriff's department. Corky is dedicated to her work and loyal to her family and friends. Her longtime challenge has been pursuing her dream career without causing undo worry for her over-protective mother.

Corky has great instincts, but recognizes every day on the job is a learning experience. She gets called to task by the sheriff from time to time. She works closely with her friend and mentor, Detective Elton "Smoke" Dawes. They have a mostly comfortable, sometimes uncomfortable, relationship. A mutual attraction, which they push beneath the surface, occasionally rises.

While Corky is closely involved with family and friends, Smoke is more of a loner, a self-protective device he put into place following a failed long-term relationship. Although he sees his brothers and their children fairly regularly, he spends the majority of his free time fishing on his private lake, strumming his guitar, and playing with his dog.

As an insight into their relationship, here is an exchange between Corky and Smoke after Corky is injured and lands in the hospital.

Excerpt from *Buried in Wolf Lake*

I woke up on Monday aware of the fading late afternoon sun on my face and a hand resting on my arm.

"Hello, little lady," the familiar, melodious voice crooned.

My eyes blinked closed. "Detective Dawes."

"How are you doing? Tired of sleeping, yet?"

"Isn't that like an oxymoron, tired of sleeping?" A smile tugged at my face.

He snickered. "Could be. I finally convinced your mother to go home for a while, told her I'd sit with you. She said they're weaning you off the sedatives, so you'll be awake more."

"Good, although I haven't minded the break from thinking and processing everything that happened." A brief retreat from reality.

I felt his breath near my ear. "Are you feeling any better?"

"My head hurts—no surprise there. But, I gotta say, since I actually lived through the very worst day of my life, I am mostly feeling just plain grateful." That was it.

His hand was heavy on my shoulder. "Corky, truth be told, I have to say it was the worst day of my life, too." He made a 'humph' sound. "I expect my hair to turn completely gray by Friday."

A man accustomed to stress. "You didn't think you'd get me in time, did you?"

"Oh, no, I knew we would." I saw him cross his fingers to cover his lie. "But you should consider less dramatic ways to capture criminals."

"Really? You think being threatened in my own home with a gun and getting knocked over the head and thrown in a trunk and driven away is dramatic?"

"A little over the top, yes."

"I will strive for less drama." The image of my captor's wild, hate-filled eyes came to mind. "Tell me about Parker."

"He is our monster, all right, but you should heal some more before you get all the gory particulars."

"I've got a lot of the 'gory particulars' on this case already." I pushed on his chest. "I need to know."

Smoke didn't answer right away. "Parker's locked up in the Hennepin County Jail, in segregation, mainly for medical reasons, but also for keeping an eye on his mental status. You were right when you thought you cracked his rib—you cracked two of 'em. You should've cracked his skull like he cracked yours. Justifiable use of deadly force, in my book. Sergeant, you were badly injured, in danger of passing out again. Definitely justifiable to use deadly force."

Easy to say, after the fact. "I guess. If he hadn't gone down with that back strike, I would have gone for a spine or head strike. I was relying solely on my training—my brain was pretty rattled at the time."

"My god, Corky, when we moved in to make the arrest, I was so overwhelmed with the need to shoot that depraved you-know-what, I had to holster my gun because I was convinced I would kill him if I didn't."

I squeezed his hand.

* * *

2. Write an ending that leaves the reader wanting more.

The plot of novels, in general, and mysteries, in particular, start with a problem or situation that needs to be resolved. Each plot points builds on the next until the story reaches its highest point—the climax—which is near the end of the book.

Readers need to be satisfied the book has ended, so tie up, or at least address, loose ends. (I usually do a one or two page summary, answering questions that were raised during the course of the story.) But don't tie up all the ends. Leave personal or professional issues unresolved, introduce your next case, or introduce a new, intriguing character who will play a key role in your next book.

In *Murder in Winnebago County,* Corky began dating Nicholas Bradshaw, the hospital administrator. At the end of the book, readers were left wondering who Corky would choose—Nick or Smoke. They hoped they would get an answer in of *Buried in Wolf Lake*, an answer is given at the end of the book, but is it final?

Excerpt from *Buried in Wolf Lake*

Smoke was sitting on his dock. The moon was full overhead and a kerosene lantern rested on one of the dock's poles.

"Why are you out here in the cold?" I asked as I approached him.

"Cold? It's close to fifty degrees."

"After the warm Indian summer day we had, it feels nippy," I said.

I sat on the bench next to Smoke and watched him cast and reel in his line.

He gave me a side-ways glance. "I thought you had a date tonight?"

"I did until I got dumped."

He turned toward me. "Dumped? As in, Nick broke up with you?"

I couldn't speak so I nodded.

"What happened?"

I swallowed, hoping the lump in my throat would go down. "He . . . couldn't . . . take . . .it . . .me . . .being . . .a . . ."

"Cop?"

"He . . .made . . .me . . .choose." Tears spilled out of my eyes.

"Come here." Smoke locked his arm around my shoulder and pulled me close. "You're shivering." He bought his other arm around the front of me and rubbed to warm me up. "Let's go inside."

"It's . . . fine."

"You sure?"

I nodded.

We sat in silence for a time before Smoke spoke again. "You know, not that Nick's right, but I can understand how he might feel. You've had some pretty close calls over the last few months. Probably didn't know what he was signing up for, dating a cop."

I shrugged.

"You want to talk about it?"

My tears had stopped and I shook my head. "Not tonight."

"You going to get through this?"

I nodded.

"Got any plans of what to do next?"

"There is something I've been thinking about for a while."

"What's that?"

"I'm going to get a dog. A big watchdog that likes to go on long runs."

He squeezed a little tighter. "Mighty fine plan."

"Will you help me find a good one? One like Rex?"

I felt Smoke nod. "I think I can handle that. We'll get on it, a-sap."

*   *   *

3. Letting the reader know what happened in a previous book without getting bogged down in lengthy descriptions.

This is the most challenging of the three elements. Each book in a series needs to written as a stand-alone book, yet fit in the series. Background information on the characters, laid out in the first book, needs to be shortened to a sentence or two in subsequent books.

In the second and third books of my Winnebago County series, Alvie Eisner, the antagonist from the first book reappears. In the fourth book, to be published in 2012, Alvie Eisner is mentioned and the antagonist from the second book reappears.

The two ways I address past issues and introduce characters from a previous story are through conversations between the characters and tapping into Corky's thoughts about the situations or the people.

In the following example, Corky is meeting with her psychologist. They discuss two past cases, Corky's relationship concerns, her grandparents, father, mother and her brother's marriage problems.

Excerpt from *An Altar by the River*

Dr. Kearns was standing by his desk when I entered his azure blue office. I had chosen, subconsciously or not, a polo shirt the same shade when I dressed that morning. The color of serenity. The state of being I longed for and strived toward.

Dr. Kearns and I shared our customary handshake. Since the first time we met, I tried to duplicate his grasp when I shook others' hands. His hands were warm and dry, but not too dry. He had a way of gently sliding his fingers slowly in until his thumb was in place. That's when he squeezed firmly and quickly, passing on the assurance that he was there, confident and competent to help.

"And how are you today, Corinne?" Although most people called me Corky, I seldom corrected the people who didn't. As a child, I thought my given name was embarrassing, but the older I got, the better I liked it.

"I'm feeling well, more like my old self all the time."

"Glad to hear it."

"Thanks to you."

Dr. Kearns smiled, a fairly rare occurrence. He wasn't exactly stingy with his smiles. He kept all facial expressions to a minimum. "You know this a team effort. Sit down and bring me up to speed."

I settled into a cordovan colored, stuffed leather chair. Dr. Kearns lifted a notebook from his desk, then sat down across from me in another.

My eyes closed for a moment as I sorted my thoughts. "I was lying in bed last night, thinking about a case I'm working on, a case involving children who suffered horrific abuse, and for some reason, it put what I had been through in a whole different perspective."

"Oh?"

"Alvie Eisner tried to kill me because I was hampering her criminal intentions. Langley Parker abducted me, apparently because I fit the profile of the women he liked to torture, kill and dismember."

"Yes."

"Of course those experiences traumatized me, but everything you've been telling me these last few months finally sunk in. I am strong. I love my job, and can't let two crazy . . . sorry . . . people dictate my life. Or my thoughts. Or my feelings. After both of those incidents, I remembered feeling so grateful to be alive, that I had survived. I kept thinking I was fine. Okay, I wasn't so fine, but I was grateful. That's it. I feel I'm on earth for a reason, and Eisner and Parker are not going to interfere with that."

Dr. Kearns nodded, then changed the subject. "How about your personal relationships? Nick? Smoke?"

An equally difficult topic. "I've had to accept that I don't have much control there. I was falling in love with Nick, and he made me choose between him, and my career, after only a few months of dating. A part of me will always love him, and his daughter."

Dr. Kearns took notes, his head bobbing slightly here and there.

I took a quick breath. "Smoke? He's put too many obstacles in the way, and he's probably right. He's a lot older, we work together, he was my father's best friend. All good reasons not to get involved personally."

"You mentioned at an earlier session that you wondered if you were looking for a father figure in Smoke."

I mulled that over for a second. "You know, growing up, the important men in my life were my grandfathers. Mother didn't date. I don't necessarily feel like I'm looking for a father figure. Because I had my grandpas. It could be, since they were forty and fifty years older than me, a man twenty years older than me doesn't seem that old. I don't know. Obviously I'm still confused about men. I sometimes wonder if I'd even know how to have a lasting relationship."

"Your grandparents' marriages provided you with good examples."

"True, but we didn't live with them. Could that be at the heart of John Carl's marriage problems? He didn't have our father as a role model of how to be a husband. According to Emily, and I think it's true, all he does is work."

"Of course I don't have answer about John Carl's marriage. But, you've talked about how your mother works so much. He may be modeling his work ethic after hers."

Very possible. Likely.

* * *

Although I never planned to write a novel series, the Winnebago County Mystery Thrillers have given me great satisfaction and joy. Each book presents its own set of challenges, but also reunites me with characters I love, and appreciate, and who constantly surprise me. I also get to know characters who are spiteful and frightful. They are not easy to be around, but they give my Winnebago County Sheriff's Department officers job security with one more case to solve.

🦃

Interview with Christine Husom

What are your books about?

Murder in Winnebago County centers on a woman bent on revenge. She blames the criminal justice system and holds its officials

206

responsible, following her son's death while he was incarcerated. She begins a killing spree, staging the deaths to look like suicides so the victims' families will suffer as she has. Sergeant Corinne "Corky" Aleckson takes the initial call on the first death and works closely with her mentor, Detective "Smoke" Dawes to solve the strange cases.

About halfway through writing the book, I knew I couldn't retire the Winnebago County characters. They had become too much a part of my life. Dramatic incidents from my days with the sheriff's department came to mind and I knew what the next two books would be based on. *Buried in Wolf Lake* follows a psychopath who is obsessed with power, and commits the ultimate crimes on two victims (that we know of). *An Altar by the River* addresses a cult subculture, ritual abuse, and a long-standing sheriff's department cover-up.

The Winnebago County Mystery Thrillers are slightly more action-driven than character-driven, but the characters are the heart and soul of the stories. They are serious and—at times—chilling stories I felt needed to be told. But I interject humor, everyday events, and romance into the books for a little levity, and, well, romance.

How long does it take you to write your books?

It takes me about six months to write a book, but for *Murder in Winnebago County* there was five years between writing the first half of the book and the second.

Did you do any research for your books?

For *Murder in Winnebago County* I needed some detailed information on a classic GTO car and went to the library for a book on old cars. With new information available on the internet every day, I am accessing that more and more. And I double check the accuracy

For *Buried in Wolf Lake* I did fairly extensive research on the difference between a psychopath and a sociopath, and on dismemberment cases for about a month before I started writing.

I studied a wide variety of materials on cults and Dissociative Identity Disorder for three months before I started *An Altar by the River*. I also interviewed a professional who worked with victims of satanic ritual abuse. I continue to research while I'm writing because questions arise and I want to be certain what I write is as error-free as possible. In *An Altar by the River*, I wrote that a doctor had graduated Summa Cum Laude. My sister, a medical doctor, told me it was Alpha Omega Alpha. Oops.

Learning as much as I can about the topics in my books makes the stories and characters come alive for me.

How much of yourself is hidden in the characters in the book?

Many people think I am the main character, Sergeant Corinne Aleckson, probably because she tells the bulk of the story. Perhaps they hear my voice. Corky shares my core values, and also likes to go on runs to relieve stress and process her thoughts, as well as stay in shape. I'm more like Corky's mother, Kristen. She is something of a worrywart, protective of her children, and over-extended. The rest of the characters aren't much like me, but my sense of humor and sick jokes come out of their mouths from time to time.

Do you have specific techniques you use to develop the plot and stay on track?

I formulate some main plot points and build on them, but I don't feel bound to follow a pre-set course. I've tried, and failed, to do outlines. Another technique I've tried with some success is to do a storyboard. You make twelve boxes (more or less) on a sheet of paper. In the first box you write the question your story asks. In the last box you write the answer to that question. The other ten boxes are the main events, or plot points, in your book. It's a nice visual aid for me.

What's been the most surprising part of being a writer?

The way my characters take over the story I'm supposed to be writing.

How has your background influenced your writing?

I learned to appreciate law and justice from my father and creativity from my mother. I have a very broad range of interests, but when I served, first as a corrections officer, then a deputy, I realized criminal justice was in my blood, right along with the red and white cells. Writing mystery thrillers set in my home county is a natural fit.

What are you working on right now?

I'm writing *The Noding Field Mystery,* the fourth book in the Winnebago County Series. It differentiates from the first two books because the perpetrator(s) of the crime is not identified until near the end. It begins with the discovery of a man's body in a soybean field. His hands and feet bound to stakes. The cause of death is not evident, nor is the manner.

Have you ever had difficulty "killing off" a character in your story because she or he was so intriguing and full of possibility for you, his or her creator?

Yes. My second intended victim in *Murder in Winnebago County* is still alive and well, mainly because I liked her too much to kill her. More accurately, I liked her best friend too much, and didn't want to put Corky through the tragedy of losing her.

Do you have mental list or a computer file or a spiral notebook with the ideas for or outlines of stories that you have not written but intend to one day?

I have a small suitcase full of ideas and storylines and uncompleted manuscripts. I'm pretty sure that's what's keeping me alive—I need to finish them before I die.

Creating a Believable Science-Fiction Environment
By
Dellani Oakes
Author of:
Lone Wolf and *Indian Summer*

🦃

It's easy to create a believable environment when you're Earth bound. You pick a spot you're familiar with and write away. Creating a believable setting for a science fiction environment is more problematic. Granted it's a lot more fun, but it presents its own difficulties.

My science fiction novel, *Lone Wolf*, has a variety of settings, none of them on Earth. First, the main characters are on a mining station in deep space, impersonal, metallic, cramped. The station is a large ship, utilitarian in nature. It has room for the essentials only. Luxury is a thing you get on planets.

I have a picture in my mind. I see a ship with a control room, lots of cargo space, almost prison sized quarters for crew and multiple points to attach the miner's vessels. These are also small, compact ships which house the miner when he's on planet. Clumsy, clunky and not very pretty, they are strong and durable. They also are high powered in case the miner has to evacuate in a hurry.

My second environment is a planet called Aolani. It's in a well settled portion of space. Aolani is a beautiful planet. Because of its position in relationship to its sun, most of it is a tropical paradise. Visualize Hawaii on a global scale. Aolani is a pleasure planet. It's also the home planet of the Galactic Mining Guild. Though it has many major cities, there is a great deal of undeveloped land.

Here again, I don't go into all the detail about the actual size and scope of the planet. That isn't necessary. All the reader needs to know is that it has beautiful beaches, crystal clear waters, sultry breezes and fabulous waves.

They could see Aolani beneath them. Her golden beaches and clear blue water enticed them from space. The Mining Guild headquarters were located on the mainland in the southern hemisphere. And: *The restaurant was perched on the end of a pier, dotted with pink and white striped umbrellas. They sat at a table with a panoramic view of the azure surf.*

Like any planet or city, Aolani has its seedier elements. Not all of the people live in the lap of luxury. One of the major scenes of the novel is set in this section of town. The setting is much more important here, so I go into more detail with the description. I wanted it obvious that it was old, decrepit and laced with decay.

He reluctantly followed her to the porch of an old house on a back street. Debris and filth filled the empty lots around it. An old sign hung above the doorway, squeaking and thumping in the wind that had suddenly sprung up. The door opened quietly inward, the hinges smooth and soundless.

A dry, raspy voice emanated from a back room behind the faded curtain of cheap green beads. "You are expected, children. Come in and be quick!"

The room was Spartan with a single round table top sitting on crates. Though it was freshly swept, the small room smelled of decay and mold. A timeworn ceiling fan moved the thick, moist air with very little effect. Four dented, old, metal chairs surrounded the table; three on one side, the fourth facing them on the side near the curtain. The beads jangled aside, moved by a gnarled, age spotted hand, more like a crustaceous claw than a human appendage. An old woman stepped through.

Space ships are decidedly more difficult than land based environments. A ship isn't going to be as large as a planet, but it has very distinctive parts that must be considered. For example, you won't have the noisy engineering section near the quarters of the higher ranking officers or dignitaries. It wouldn't make sense to have the majority of the crew there either for safety reasons. Conversely, the chief engineer shouldn't be far away in case there's a problem.

Because of shows like Star Trek, in all its permutations, people have very distinct ideas of how a spaceship looks. Admittedly, it influenced my thinking as well. In a way, that's helpful. I don't have to go into great detail describing the environment because my readers already have a pretty clear idea what I'm talking about. I can concentrate on my story rather than the setting. The main thing to remember is that not everything is on one level. I must have in mind where things are on the ship so I know which direction my characters are going. I may not map it out for my readers, but I have to have a firm idea of where things are in order to describe it accurately. Action can take place in any portion of the ship, so I must have clear directions and layout in my mind.

For example, the bridge and Captain's ready room are near the top of the ship. Engineering and the Tech Repair are lower. The middle, more protected part of the ship, is devoted to crew quarters, the medical section and other areas common to the support crew. The bottom and outer aspects of the lower hull are devoted to the miners and their equipment.

I think of my mining vessel as being more or less spherical, like the Death Star, though not nearly as large. Since they are built for durability, not speed, they tend to be cumbersome. The military vessels, on the other hand, are made to be fast and maneuverable. *Flotilla* is a cryoship, so is even slower and more ungainly. However, the interior is nearly sterile in its cleanliness.

The rooms housing the engineering equipment were so clean, they could have been used for an operating theater. White walls sparkled, the metal fittings glittered, everything looked as if it had been scrubbed, polished, swept and wiped until not even a microscopic particle of dust could possibly exist.

Not all the areas will have the same amount of space. Medical, for example, is airy, open and well ventilated. The Robotics Lab, on the other hand . . .

They got to the transport tube and hit the button for the robotics lab. It whisked them along, stopping with a sigh. The door opened on the bot doc's lair. It was as clean and sterile looking as the medical lab.

They went into a unisex dressing area that offered no privacy. There was no extra room to set aside for modesty.

The cryo-hopper, *Flotilla*, is their home and environment for a large portion of the book. It isn't until later novels in the series that I introduce my readers to three new planets and a heavily populated asteroid. For the purposes of this article, I will include excerpts from those novels as well.

Although it's brought briefly into *Lone Wolf*, it's in Book Two, *Shakazhan* (*Sha*-kaz-ahn), we come to our first truly alien planet. Aolani, while not Earth, is still very much a human environment. Iyundo (eye-*yoon*-do) is not. It's a hostile, seemingly dead world. Life on Iyundo is silicon based, not carbon based Earth dwellers. Below is the excerpt from *Lone Wolf* where the planet is first described:

Riley landed, wondering what he could possibly do now. The planet was devoid of anything recognizable as sentient life. Putting on his stasuit and helmet, he did a scan of the outside climate. The temperature was a little on the hot side of comfortable. There was an atmosphere, though quite thin. He'd supplement with oxygen, but if need arose, he could breathe.

The landscape went far beyond desolation. No air moved. No animals scurried about. Vegetation, such as it was, eked out a meager life here. Half of what he saw was dead or dying. He didn't even see bugs around. Maybe there was life below the surface.

They approached the long abandoned ruins warily, unsure where to find Riley. The remnants of a magnificent fountain formed the centerpiece. Slimy, green water gurgled lethargically in a noxious smelling stream.

It was narrow, dark, dank and littered with ancient bones. The bones fell to dust as they passed, holding their shape all these centuries merely from habit.

When introducing a new planet, the author needs to keep several things in mind:

What's the scale?
Is it bigger than Earth?
Smaller than Mercury?

What is the climate like?
Temperature, rainfall, etc.
What sort of atmosphere has it got?
Will they need survival suits, oxygen, etc?
Is it a verdant, lovely place, hot and dry or cold and unrelenting?

How many moons or suns?

Distance from the sun?

Is it capable of sustaining human life?

Is it completely hostile to humans?

What is the indigenous population like?
Are they sentient?
Deadly?
Welcoming?
Ignorant of outer space?
Are they humanoid?
Do they look like giant cats, bugs or leeches?
What is their home environment?
Can they vocalize or are they telepathic?

How do your characters get from Point A to Point B?
What sort of vehicles are there?
Do they have to travel by horse (or planet's equivalent)?
Must they walk?
Are there well maintained roads?
Do the vehicles need roads?
What's the terrain like?

What is your level of technology? Not all futuristic worlds are the same. One need only watch TV shows or movies to see the vast differences in approach.
Is yours a post apocalyptic world (*Resident Evil, Book of Eli, Planet of the Apes*)?
Are machines in charge (*Terminator*)?

Is it a more utopian society (*Star Trek*)?
Is it highly technical or more rustic (*Firefly, Farscape*)?
Are the characters at war (*Battlestar Galactica*)?

Social strata:
Is there slavery?
Are all inhabitants given equal rights?
How does the indigenous population regard humans?
Are there classes or casts? Is it possible to advance?
Is it a monarchy? Democracy? Dictatorship? Communist
society? Anarchy? Religious fanatic? Autocracy? Something
completely different and unique to them?

Not all of these characteristics need to be mentioned in your
story to make it believable. The author must know what kind of
environment the characters are in. How they react to their
environment or how it acts upon them can make a huge difference in
a story. Characters will not behave the same way in a jungle that they
will in the frozen wasteland. If the space is confined, that makes a
difference too.

Place rules and adhere to them. If you say the sky is purple, the
grass is blue and water is pink, then don't violate that later. If you're
going to get this off kilter, though, have a ready explanation for it.
Some readers will question when the setting is too bizarre. Your
readers must be willing to suspend their disbelief and embrace their
new environment. Don't make the mistake of creating a setting so
odd that it makes the readers focus on that instead of the action.

Rather than making a really peculiar environment on Shakazhan,
the major planet in my series, I opted for keeping it normal. The
events move the story forward, not the setting. When the characters
initially arrive, they find a planet torn by an intergalactic war. What
they see is nothing short of terrifying. Below is an excerpt from
Shakazhan.

The bridge crew gazed at the screen, seeing Shakazhan for the
first time. Who knew the last time human eyes had beheld her, eons
perhaps.

This side was pristine and perfect, the beauty from Wil's vision,
but stark and lifeless, frozen in time. They approached the far side of

the planet, as it turned toward the dawn. Where the first side had been ethereal and lovely, this side was utter annihilation. Nothing was left, not even the land. Huge gaping holes full of melted, twisted metal and shattered, liquefied stone covered the landscape as far as they could see.

The transition was immediate—one side was the Garden of Eden, the other Hell.

The view changed slightly and they were looking at what was apparently the epicenter of the eradication, a lifeless, blackened hole so deep, the bottom could not be seen.

I go into a great deal of descriptive narrative in this scene in order to set the stage for the coming action. Eventually, the planet undergoes a fantastic terraforming project, but not until Book Three, *The Maker.* It is transformed from a desolate wasteland back to a beautiful paradise. Still deadly on the inside, the outside has been converted to an environment suitable for human life forms. The people from the ships set up their base camp, eventually building more permanent structures.

This planet is roughly the size of Earth's sun. It dwarfs anything in Earth's solar system. Therefore, the fact that the Kahlea (evil aliens) were able to damage the planet to the extent they did, makes their technological level virtually unattainable by the humans. It's at this point that the characters realize what a formidable foe the Kahlea are.

A second planet I introduce later in the series, is Bankaywan. It's a very different environment from Shakazhan. Where Shakazhan is devastated by a war and hardly livable, Bankaywan has become a truly utopian society. Their unique system of government has a lot to do with it. Instead of their court cases being argued by lawyers, they have the duelists guild.

Duelists are a select group of fighters who are hired to settle disputes. They fight, sometimes to the death, and the winner determines who wins the case and who is punished. Fights to the death are only for very serious crimes. While a death match is hard on the duelists, they and their guild are well paid for their work.

The monetary system is also unusual. Instead of money, they use fame. When criminals are convicted, they can lose some or all of their fame, depending upon the severity of the crime. To lose all ones fame is to be outcast by society. Small differences like this make an environment unique and fun. Only one or two small changes and the society now seems quite alien in nature.

Bankaywan is unique in another aspect. All the creatures we consider to be fantasy; fairies, elves, gnomes, unicorns, minotaurs, nymphs and pixies all live here. If it exists in a fairytale, it's on Bankaywan.

🦃

Interview with Dellani Oakes

What is your book about?

Lone Wolf is set in the year 3032 when humans have conquered long range space flight and have settled into many parts of this and other galaxies. Hovering in space far from civilization, members of the Mining Guild, Marc Slatterly & Matilda Dulac, wait for their miners to return from the planet they've been working. Unbeknownst to them, one of their miners has harvested Trimagnite, a toxic and volatile liquid ore. Exposure to Trimagnite causes madness and death. Their ship isn't prepared to handle this load.

Enter Wilhelm VanLipsig, the Lone Wolf. He is assigned by the Mining Guild Commandant, John Riley, to pick up the ore and carry it back to the Mining Guild home planet. He and Marc have a history, apparently one ending in violence. Despite this, the two men agree to work together with Matilda in order to track down the villainous Commandant Riley before he can wreak havoc on the galaxy.

How long had the idea of your book been developing before you began to write the story?

The characters were in my mind many years ago. The idea for the three main characters of Marc, Wil and Matilda came from a role playing game my husband and I played. I had originally set out with the idea of recording their adventures in game, but that changed almost immediately. The characters took on a life of their own and insisted on telling a different story. What they came up with is far better than what I had initially had in mind.

What inspired you to write this particular story?

As I mentioned above, the idea came from a "Traveler" game we played back in 1982. However, the characters apparently thought that scenario rather lame and came at me with other ideas. I like theirs better.

How much of yourself is hidden in the characters in the book?

Matilda is a lot like me in some respects. Her fierce devotion and the way she takes up for those she loves is totally me. Oddly enough, some of the aspects of Wil's personality come from me as well. Mostly, he and Marc mirror aspects of my husband's personality.

Tell us a little about your main characters. Who was your favorite? Why?

Of the three main characters in *Lone Wolf*, I love Wil the most. I'm very fond of Marc and Matilda, but Wil stole my heart the minute he walked through the airlock. He's smart, sexy, handsome, wicked and not scared of anything. He always has a contingency plan and he's easily the most paranoid character I've ever created. His paranoia keeps him alive and one step ahead of his enemies. As long as he's lived, that's quite a feat.

Who is your most unusual/most likeable character?

I think that Caprilla Mayeese, the enormous Fellician warrior is the most unusual and likeable. Fellicians are giant cat people who speak and walk upright. They are almost all mercenaries and fight like no others in the galaxy. Caprilla is the leader of a small group of mercenaries, all Fellicians. He's about eight feet tall, with sleek black fur and penetrating blue eyes. He's got a quick wit and a wonderful sense of humor. He's also loyal to the death and will gladly kill anyone who gets in his way or threatens his friends.

How long did it take you to write your book?

Lone Wolf took a few months to write, but far longer to edit and perfect. It was one of my earliest novels and it took me awhile to get my style down. I didn't really figure out what I was doing until the fourth book in the series, so each of them requires a lot of perfecting. Now, I can sit down and write a book that's close to finished with the first draft.

How much of a story do you have in mind before you start writing it?

I had quite a lot in mind when I started to write, but the characters took me in a totally different direction. I can honestly say that absolutely nothing in *Lone Wolf* was in my mind except for the three main characters. What's on the page came from Wil, Matilda, Marc and the others telling their story in their own way.

Did you do any research for the book? If so, how did you do it? (searching internet, magazines, other books, etc.)

It's hard to research something set so far in the future. Since I created my own worlds and locations, I didn't have to study maps or anything like that. However, in order to get the Mining Guild and Galactic Marine ranks correct, I had to do some research into military rank. Most of my research is done on-line as it's the most easily available. Thank God for the internet!

How do you develop and differentiate your characters?

The characters delineate themselves. I come up with a body for the slot, give it a name and it develops its own personality and characteristics. Even minor characters speak loudly wanting a name and an occupation. Some of these seemingly unimportant people later become major players in the series. One character in particular that comes to mind is introduced in book two, *Shakazhan*. I thought Dr. Stanley Savolopis was unimportant, merely a cog in the corporate wheel. By book three, *The Maker*, he's a main mover and shaker.

Does writing come easy for you?

Writing comes very easily for me. The ideas come faster than I can get them down, which is why I have so many unfinished stories. I've learned to work on one until the 'muse' grows silent, and move on. I come back and work on each story a little at a time until it's done.

Other stories come to me all at once and I write until I'm finished. One in particular I can think of—I'd finished my NaNoWriMo (*National Novel Writing Month*) project early and got the idea for an entirely different book. I started it Thanksgiving afternoon and finished four days later.

Have you ever had difficulty "killing off" a character in your story because she or he was so intriguing and full of possibility for you, his or her creator?

I greatly dislike killing a character and avoid it if I can. However, there are times when a character must die to advance the plot. The one who upset me the most was a guy named Murdock Pickford. He's in a prequel to my sci-fi series. Murdock is a nice guy. He's kind, capable, loving and forgiving. He's engaged to a woman who's pregnant with another man's baby & he agrees to raise her as his own. He's thrilled about the baby, excited about getting married and he has to die—horribly, brutally—for the book to move forward. I'm not ashamed to admit that I cried when I had to kill him off.

Do you have mental list or a computer file or a spiral notebook with the ideas for or outlines of stories that you have not written but intend to one day?

I've got a list in the back of one of my notebooks with story ideas that one day I might get to. Let me finish the 54 novels and short stories I've got pending before I take them on. (Gosh, didn't realize it was so many. Kinda sorry I counted them up.)

How many stories do you currently have swirling around in your head?

Apparently 54, because that's how many are unfinished.

Have you written any other books?

I have one other published novel, *Indian Summer*, also available from Second Wind Publishing. *Lone Wolf* is the first in my sci-fi series. I've written six books in the series so far & am working on a 7th. Finished books not in the series—27 and probably 20 short stories.

Where can people learn more about your books?

My novels are available through my publisher, Second Wind Publishing at www.secondwindpublishing.com. *Indian Summer*" and *Lone Wolf* are also available at Amazon.com where they can be purchased in paperback or Kindle format. The books are on Smashwords.com and a variety of other websites.

To find out more about me, check out my blogs:
http://dellanioakes.wordpress.com/
http://writersanctuary.blogspot.com/

Or look for me on Facebook:
http://www.facebook.com/dellanioakes

Write it Right or Yes, Virginia, Mechanics Count
By
Dellani Oakes
Author of:
Lone Wolf and *Indian Summer*

When I was a child, I couldn't spell. I'm still spelling impaired and love spell check above any of the other features of my word processing program. I am glad I have a good background in punctuation, because word processors are woefully inadequate there. Rule of thumb, if *Word* corrects your grammar, it is probably wrong. Second rule of thumb: If you rely on *Word* to correct your grammar, you need a lot of help.

I can remember saying to my mother, "But they know what I mean! Why is it wrong?"

Because it simply is. There are rules and conventions in spelling, grammar and punctuation that we have come to expect. When they aren't used properly, they interfere with the message we are trying to convey. I don't remember my mother's exact words, but that is the essence of what she told me.

As a high school A.P. English teacher, I got a lot of that same attitude. My students could not see the importance of spelling, neatness and punctuation until their essays came back covered in so much red ink they looked like they'd been slaughtered by Attila the Hun. I couldn't seem to stress enough, mechanics matter!

Spelling is one of the most ignored conventions in writing. Of course, with the onset of massive text messaging, we ignore spelling completely and go to how it sounds. Abbreviations, typing it in quickly, getting the message to the other party fast—all this becomes more important than saying it correctly.

Comma Placement

The second most ignored convention is comma placement. Commas crop up in all the wrong spots, but get left out of all the places they belong. Certain commas are expected.

When using direct address, use a comma. "Brad, look at that!" Or "Look at that, Brad!" The comma is there to let the reader know that the comment is addressed to Brad. The speaker is not saying "Look at that brad." He or she wants Brad to look at something.

Another anticipated and neglected comma is the one used to separate items in a list. "The big, black, ugly, smelly, dirty, nasty dog ran over and jumped on me." While on occasion, one may dispense with commas to separate, it's not considered a good idea. If the list is very long, as in the sample sentence, the commas have to be there.

Commas before the word 'and', can be debated until the cows come home. Many will tell you that comma is a must. Others will tell you that it's completely unnecessary and redundant. Choose a method and be consistent. I'm one of the "Leave the Comma Out School".

I realize that sometimes the creative juices flow and the urge to get something down as quickly as possible is very compelling. We all go through manic writing phases. We hammer away at the keys and stay up half the night to get the story written. I understand this well. However, putting aside the mechanics of proper writing for speed is not a good idea. Figuring that you can go back later and neaten it up is fine in theory, but not in practice. It is impossible to read through and get all the errors on your own.

There are some common grammatical errors which will get an author in trouble every time. As an English teacher and editor, I notice them in the work of others. Even some famous authors make these errors. Apparently, their editors didn't know any better either—a fact which chills me.

Lay, Laid, Lie

The first and among the most common, is misuse of *lay, laid, lie*. I could go into all the grammatical reasons as to why you use this form or that, give you an entire, lengthy lesson, but I won't. You don't care, you won't remember and the WHY isn't as important as doing it right. Using some examples from my sci-fi novel, *Lone Wolf*, I'll show you correct usage.

After a shower and a meal, she *lay* down on her bunk, examining the fragment more closely.

In a case like this, it's proper to use *LAY*. The first impulse for many is to use *LAID*. It might be used in spoken language, but it's not appropriate in writing. Below is proper usage of *laid*.

Hiram *laid* the object carefully on a large glass lens under an enormous microscope.

Hiram didn't *LAY* the object carefully. He didn't *LIE* the object, he *LAID* it. I think one reason we avoid the use of *laid* is because of the sexual connotations of the word. Don't be afraid to use it properly.

As it was, he was forced to *lie* here, worrying about his sanity.

Lots of us would say, he was forced to *lay* here. Not only is that grammatically incorrect, you've just changed the verb tense (another common error). The only time you can cut yourself a little slack with *lay, laid, lie* is if you're using it in dialog. Since many people don't speak grammatically, all conventions are set aside. Anything goes in dialog.

With punctuation, there is some leeway as there are differing opinions on what's correct. In the use of *lay, laid, lie*, there is no such wiggle room. It's right or it's wrong. I've seen some authors over correct. This is still wrong. I read in a very famous book by an outrageously rich author, incorrect use of lay vs laid.

Instead of the correct usage, *He **laid** the book on the table.* She used, *He **lay** the book on the table.* She made the same error more than once and her editor didn't catch it, leading me to believe neither of them knew the difference.

A Then and A Then

One of the most overused words in the English language is **then**. Some authors, both experienced and inexperienced, use this word way too often. Generally seen when listing events, **then** rears its ugly head. *For example* (I did not use this in a book):

He ran toward the lift, **then** pulled his weapon from his belt, **then** went up in the lift. He arrived at the cargo bay, **then** lowered his weapon, **then** fired at the alien who had just **then** arrived.

You might think I'm kidding, or exaggerating, I assure you, I'm not! I edited a manuscript that was rife with **then**. I found seven of them on one page—two within the same sentence two words apart! The above sentence can be better written without **then**.

He ran toward the lift, pulled his weapon from his belt and went up in the lift. He arrived at the cargo bay, lowering his weapon before firing at the alien who had just arrived.

Not a **then** in sight! Each of us has habits we need to break. My daughter has been reading my second sci-fi book to help me with editing. She told me I have an obsession with obsidian and ardent. I know what I'll be looking for when I start editing again.

In writing this article, it wasn't my intention to give an entire, conventional grammar lesson. Instead, I've touched on a few common errors that many authors make. If you're unsure of your grammar, please don't rely on Microsoft or some other program to correct your work for you. As good as they are at catching misspelled words, their grammar check isn't worthwhile. Much of what they tell you is wrong, or at the very least, arguable. If you must rely on a program for advice, I strongly urge you to seek out a class, find a good grammar and style guide or hire a tutor. Learning the basics will make your life as an author more fulfilling and a lot more fun.

When That All Important Scene Isn't

I've got a scene in the novel that I'm editing that's always been a favorite. It's fast paced, exciting, well timed, lots of action.... And I have to cut it out. Why? Because it doesn't advance the story.

I love this scene! It came together so well when I wrote it. It has a unique rhythm. I even remember the music I listened too while I wrote it (*Crazy Benny* by Safri Duo). Everything about it clicks! And it doesn't lead anywhere.

Soon it will be part of the trash on the cutting room floor. That makes me a little sad, but I have to toughen myself up and do it.

Below is the scene. Matilda is a human and she is fighting Ariella, a large, sentient cat. Matilda has fashioned extendable claws to mimic Ariella's. They're fighting with swords Fellician (cat people) style.

* * *

They began with the Ritual of Weighing, where each of the competitors chose her weapon. Taking their stance across from one another, a sharp snap of a bongo signaled the start of the match. Matilda attacked quickly and low, going for her opponent's knees. Ariella's reach was longer, but Matilda's comparatively diminutive stature next to hers, made getting under the big cat's guard easy.

Ariella swatted Matilda away with her tail as if she were a gnat. Matilda flew across the stage, landing with a grunt. Shaking her head, she rose, taking her stance again.

The bongo signaled as before, Ariella attacked, moving in on Matilda's exposed left side. Maneuvering rapidly, Matilda jumped for her block, grabbing her dagger as she sped by. She parried Ariella's attack, barely avoiding a blow from her other side. Ariella had grabbed her dagger too. Matilda caught Ariella's knife in her claws, extended for that purpose.

A gasp came from the crowd as Ariella extended her own, grappling with Matilda briefly before the woman moved out the of big cat's range. The two of them slashed, kicked, and danced around the stage, hardly a sound but the bongo accompaniment and the clang of their weapons above their ragged breathing.

Ariella stooped to slash at Matilda's legs. The human woman jumped lightly up and rolled over Ariella's back, landing in a crouch on the other side. Back and forth they dodged and parried, swooping into an opening and back out again to avoid their opponent's blows.

It looked as if Matilda were winning, then Ariella rushed in and got her pinned to one side of the stage, advancing, blade held ready before her, preparing for the killing blow. Calmly taking a deep breath, Matilda ran at Ariella, sprung forward and up, doing a handless cartwheel over the big cat's head, flipped as she landed spinning to face her opponent. Getting her feet under her, Matilda launched herself at the large feline, knocking Ariella down and sitting on her chest, blade ready at the throat, Matilda prepared for the kill.

Striking her blow, she didn't notice Ariella's dagger coming up behind her, deploying the handle blade, until too late. Both blades struck home simultaneously, blood sprayed everywhere.

*　*　*

Sometimes that all important scene—isn't. We as authors may love it, it may be the best thing we've ever written. It might be noteworthy and enough to move our readers to tears, but it has to go. Take a deep breath and delete it. There, the world didn't end, did it?

In our editing phase, authors must often be brutal with their work. This is especially true early on in your career. My first novels lack the spark and sparkle of my more recent work. I was still exploring, still looking for my voice. Once I found it, I geared up and never went back. Looking at my early work, which the current editing project is, I see all the mistakes I made. Now, I have to correct them!

As I explore this novel, the second in my sci-fi series, I realize that more and more of the scenes need to be heavily edited or cut entirely. I call this phase of my editing the slash and burn phase. It ain't pretty. It's brutal, harsh and dirty. Later on, I pretty it up, but right now it's raw with big gaping holes.

Often, in this phase, I also look at the sequencing of the story. With this novel, I had started it in a completely different spot from where the first left off. Instead of doing that, I went back to the end of the first novel and made it the beginning of the second as it literally takes up at the same moment the other left off.

Important thing to keep in mind: *Save your deleted passages!*

I make a file that I call a *cut from <title of novel>* file. I take the scenes, paragraphs and pages that I cut from the story and put it in a special file to save it. I may not want it for that particular book, but I might want to refer to the information or even use some of it in a different novel.

One of my author friends did that with passages he'd cut from different books in a series. He managed to get nearly three more books from those deleted scenes.

As I go back through the novel, I will find places where I need transitional passages to fill in the holes I left with my slash and burn. This second, less primal phase, is where the healing begins.

By the third pass through my novel, I'm looking for the small errors—verb tenses, typos, vague words and any number of other pet peeves we as authors all possess. In this phase, I try to pretty it up even more, laying a heavy coat of cosmetics on it. At this stage, it's often helpful to read the text aloud and/or have someone else read it. A second pair of eyes catches things we miss.

Tips:

1. Print a copy of troublesome spots in your manuscript, read through them aloud and look for errors.

2. If you're having difficulty with pacing, try writing to music. Find something that has the emotion you're trying to convey and listen to it before and during your writing session. The right kind of music can make a world of difference. I had a final fight scene in one of my novels that was too slow. I put in some fast moving instrumental guitar (Joe Satriani and Jimi Hendrix) and rewrote it.

3. Sticky notes are wonderful! Jot notes to yourself on a printed copy of the novel to help you remember what to do on a particular page or remind yourself where you left off.

4. Use bright colored pens when you edit. Select something dark enough to read but will catch your eye on the printed page. As you add the corrections to your computer file, check them off in a different color.

5. When editing on the computer, make comments to yourself as you go. Believe it or not, you will not remember all the things you want to do and handwritten notes can be lost. As you make the corrections, delete the comments.

6. Read through what you wrote in a prior writing session. Not only does this remind you about what you've already written, it's a good editing habit. When you find an error, correct it right away or make an in text comment so you can go back and find it later. Don't expect to remember—trust me, you won't.

7. Don't try to do everything at once. Do the big things, like cutting scenes, first. Why make grammar and spelling corrections to something you're going to cut out later?

Editing is probably the most difficult and frustrating part of writing, but it's also the most necessary. Agents and publishing companies get hundreds of submissions a day. A well written, good looking manuscript will catch their interest more than a badly presented one. When editing costs them money, why would they accept something that needs a lot of work over something that doesn't?

We all get anxious to get our work into the hands of someone who will publish it. No first draft is perfect. Every novel needs editing. Slow down, spend some extra time, and make sure you're sending the best book you possibly can.

What Happened to the Cat?

My husband is a detail oriented person. As a medical professional, he has to be. It amazes me, however, what details his analytical, scientific mind will latch onto when he reads my novels. He'll read the entire story and start demanding clarification. Some of it I've thought of, other things I make up, glad of my improv experience, because I honestly hadn't gone there.

It's not unusual for me to make up some BS answer out of thin air just to get him to quit asking. Sometimes, if the subject really interests him, he'll expand on it to the point where I'd pay real money just to get him to shut up.

Often, these sessions are helpful, clarifying those nebulous ideas that I hadn't fully considered. A typical exchange:

"Have you thought about <*insert random weird concept*>?" He asks me.

"The readers don't need to know that," I reply, somewhat miffed.

"But it's interesting. You could . . . "

"Yes, maybe, but why? It's not the least bit important. Why do you do that?"

"Do what?"

"Ask about the most unimportant elements?"

"I don't do that. Now, what about . . . ?"

He's gradually learning not to ask what I'm working on because ninety percent of the time it's something I haven't told him about. I shuffle projects and might work on a dozen different stories in a week. I love the fact that he's interested, but I don't always want to stop what I'm doing and explain what the book is about.

Once, in a weak moment, I told him about one of my unpublished novels where the psychotic ex-wife of the hero breaks into the heroine's apartment, shaves her cat and duct tapes it to the hood of his car. Yes, it's messed up, but the neighbors find the cat a short time later, call the police and take the cat to the vet. I mention in passing that the cat is at the vet's and he's fine. I read the passage to him, pleased with how well it came together.

"Someone broke into your place, Mandy."

"My—what?"

Pale and shaking, she leaned against Derrick for support. He and Jasper helped her sit on the bench just inside the entry way.

"Why? What did they do in there?"

"They took your cat," Jasper said quietly.

"What? Muse? Where is he? Is he okay?"

"Yeah. He's okay. We sent him to the vet. Someone shaved him and taped him to the hood of Derrick's car."

"My car? Why the hell would they do that?"

"I was hoping you could tell me."

Apparently, there wasn't enough information for my husband. "What happened to the cat?" He asked when I got to the end of my explanation.

"What? Which cat?"

"Amanda's cat, Muse. What happened to him?"

"He's at the vet's. I said that. He's fine."

"But you don't mention him again."

"So? You don't even like cats. Why are you worried about the cat?"

"I was curious."

"Forget the cat. He's fine!"

"Whatever you say, baby." There's a long pause, to the point where I'm busy again and have forgotten about the conversation. "You really need to clear that up."

"Clear what up?"

"The part about the cat...."

The point I'm making is that little details, things we forget about or think are inconsequential, can bother our readers if left unresolved. My husband, who positively loathes cats, was worried about Muse to the point that it detracted from the climax of the story. So I gave him a little more to help satisfy him

When Amanda opened the cat carrier door, Muse came out. He looked hopelessly thin in his shaven state, but rubbed against Derrick as happily as ever. Amanda looked inside the carrier.

"Where's your friend?" She asked Muse.

The cat, as if he understood her, went to his carrier, nosing at the door, mewing softly. An answering mew came from inside the carrier.

"He made a friend at the vet's. They were both traumatized and the little one latched onto Muse. He protected her, wasn't that sweet?"

She reached into the carrier, gently pulling out a small, scrawny white cat with blue eyes.

"She's beautiful, Amanda. What did you name her?"

"Aphrodite. I couldn't resist."

Muse hopped into Derrick's lap as he lounged on the couch with

Amanda snuggled next to him. Aphrodite leaped prettily into her lap, turned three times and settled into a comfortable mound of white fur.

I'm not suggesting that every reader is quite so easily misdirected as my husband, but some are. Those are the people we have to satisfy by tying up the loose ends. Make sure the subplots are resolved. Give enough of an explanation that it sticks with the reader. Keep distractions to a minimum so that the thread of the story isn't lost along the way. A few moments spent on housekeeping will prevent the inevitable question: "What happened to the cat?"

Finding Your Style

A good friend made a comment after having read one of my books. She said, "You have two styles of writing. You write like a writer and like an English professor."

Ouch! Admittedly, I do have a fairly good vocabulary—not that I always use it. I used to teach Advanced Placement English, so I know about antecedents, subject and verb agreement and the correct use of semi-colons. Until she said that, I had no idea that there was such a difference in style until I went back and re-read the first few chapters. What I saw surprised me. The difference was startling, making the text difficult to read.

When I taught high school English, the students had to read *The Scarlet Letter*. What a tough book. I had to sit and read it with a dictionary by my side. My poor students were really suffering! I found some sections in my own writing that were nearly as difficult. Grant you, I was not incorporating words like *physiognomy*, but I did use *ephemeral*, *supererogatory*, and *geosynchronous*.

I think I was trying to make every word count, not use fluff words which mean little to nothing. By incorporating bigger, better words, I hoped to convey my meaning more forcefully. Apparently all I did was cause a mad rush for the Webster's. I never intended my books to be hard work. If I want to make my readers sweat, I'll put in a hot love scene! My novels are purely for entertainment.

A day or two later, my daughter told me, "Mom, your sentences sometimes confuse me. They go on forever, and I lose track of the beginning when I get to the end!"

After a brief moment of remembering William Faulkner's nine page parenthetical sentences, I decided perhaps I should change that too. I found myself going to the other extreme—Ernest Hemingway. His short, choppy sentences always got on my nerves. I don't deal well with it. I don't like it. It annoys me. It worked for him. It does not work for me.

What's my point in all this? Write to your audience, not down to them. Give them a little mental exercise, but don't make them work too hard. Reading is for expanding the mind and titillating the imagination, not making the reader's mind turn to slush.

If I want to be completely confused, I'll read James Joyce! In the meantime, I think I'll continue to search for my place somewhere between "Moby Dick" and "Peter Pan."

To Outline or Not to Outline

I continue to be amazed by people who make outlines of their stories, know where the story line is going and most of all know the ending before even writing the book. Who are these godlike folk and why am I not like them? I am a very off the cuff writer, I don't know where the story is going to go, although I like to have a general idea before I begin. I usually start with an idea or, more often than not, a sentence that seems to resonate in my mind until I get it down on paper. Novels and short stories start the same way, a compelling first sentence.

I read an interview with a famous author, several years ago, with fascination. The gist of his interview was that an author *must* know where the story is going before s/he begins writing. Every detail *must* be chronicled in outline form. Detailed notes are *mandatory* (not simply necessary) before one word gets written.

I read snippets to my husband asking him (like *he* knows), "How can he do that? How can anyone do that?"

Outlines? Those are strictly for formal papers and are always written after the paper is done. The only reason I ever wrote an outline was because my teacher required it. I am the "No Outline Queen".

I rarely know where my stories are going. I don't always know what I'm going to do with a character after I've introduced him, but I know he'd not be there if he weren't important in some way. I adhere to Ray Bradbury's advice: *Find out what your hero wants, then follow him.*

For me, writing is an exploratory process. I can't sit down knowing what will be. I have to let it unfold. To know everything in advance takes some of the fun out of my process. Don't misunderstand, I think it's marvelous that some people can do that. I find it incredible that they are organized enough to work their way through the entire book before actually writing it.

I think the idea of outlines is very intimidating for some writers, especially new ones. I was terribly put off by the above interview, thinking I had to follow the directive because the author was famous. Don't think that anyone one person's word is law when it comes to writing. It is a very individual process. Find what works for you.

Outlining or not is a matter of preference and personality. If your mind works well with outlines, do it. At the very least, make some general notes so you know where you want your story to go. My method of chaos (if such an oxymoron is possible) is to jot notes on sticky pads and keep them in a notebook or stuck to the speakers on my desk. It's not perfect, but it's what works for me. Having tried writing an outline, I can honestly say that doesn't. I got halfway through my first outline and found I was putting in too much detail. I decided if I were going to put that much time into it, I might as well just write the book. The outline hit the trash and I put all that creative energy into the novel instead.

What I think I was trying to say when I started, is this: Don't be intimidated by the idea that you *must* outline. Don't think you can't start the novel you've been dreaming about because you have no clue how it's going to end. Go with what is comfortable for you and find your way. By all means, try outlining because it is a wonderful tool, but don't lock yourself into the thinking that you have to follow it once it's there. Nothing is cast in stone, everything is malleable. When the creative juices flow and the words pound at the inside of your skull demanding to be set free, you can give them the outlet they need, hammering away at your keyboard or pouring from your pen. Whatever you do, just keep writing and let the outlines take care of themselves.

Breaking Writer's Block

Writer's Block—these ominous words send shivers down the spine of any writer. Insidious, it strikes with no warning, clogging the brain, paralyzing fingers, bringing grown writers to their knees. There are many types of writer's block, each with its own pernicious characteristics. Below, I have listed those which plague me the most often.

1) *Mid-Line Crisis*: This is less destructive than its brothers, but still annoying. This is the unfinished sentence, incomplete thought or dialogue left hanging. The tortured . . . of the soul. Though frustrating, it is not insurmountable. Usually a little brainstorming, trial and error and copious use of the delete button get me past this tiresome creature.

2) *Ex Thesaurus*: Also known as "What Word"? This usually runs with mid-line crisis and is fairly easy to circumvent. A visit to Thesaurus.com or a quick flip through the desk copy of *Roget's* can pull a writer past this hurdle.

3) *Post Climactic Stress*: Or "Where Do I Go From Here?" The hero has saved the day, villains vanquished, lovers unite, children dance around May Poles—celebration time! All right, where does the story go now? It's not over, but it needs to be soon. However, these pesky little loose ends suddenly electrify, screaming "Solve Me!" What to do?

Writing the conclusion after the "climax" isn't always easy. The one question a writer fails to answer is the one readers will point to and say, "Hey! What about this?" To avoid the lynch mob, sometimes it's better to eliminate a secondary thread unless it's absolutely necessary to the plot. Otherwise, it's a trip to blockage category # 4.

4) *The Never Ending Story*: As much as we might want our book never to end, it must. Sometimes though, we can't seem to find a stopping place. The book goes on *forever* until we get fed up and stop writing, or force an ending.

I have one book that is 423 double-spaced, typed pages. Not only can I not find an end point, I can't even read all the way through it without getting lost. The problem is too many sub-plots. (Hearken back to Post Climactic Stress.) Everything needs resolution, making the book go on forever. It will require a mighty re-write or splitting into multiple books.

None of these minor blocks are as frustrating as the fifth category. It really needs no introduction because even the most prolific writers have, at one time or another, suffered from it.

5) The Full Monty: Like its name implies, this is full blown, frontal exposure writer's block. Insurmountable, uncompromising, frustrating, infuriating, aggravating, annoying, constipating.... There are no words at our disposal formidable enough to fully describe this condition.

Any writer who has never experienced Full Monty Writer's Block obviously hasn't written long enough. Suddenly, out of nowhere, completely by surprise it strikes! I equate it with being hit by a Volvo station wagon at 90 mph (Hmm, can a Volvo go 90? Maybe an Escalade?).

In any case, *wham*! In the face, hard core, heavy metal writer's block. There's no way to avoid it. Once in awhile the Muse takes a coffee break and so must we. As frustrating as they are, embrace these blocks. They force us to leave the security and sanctity of our homes and participate in life for awhile.

Instead of fighting the block, which only ends in tears, take a break from writing. I read a good book, watch a few movies, participate in mindless video games and otherwise do things to distract myself.

Next, after an unspecified period, ranging from hours to days, I sit down and try to write something. *Anything*! It doesn't have to be connected with the book, usually it's better if it's not. Long or short, good or bad, I write. Sometimes just embarking on the composition process is enough to break the block.

Doing short writing exercises can help. When I taught high school English, one thing I had the students do as a class writing project, was write thank you notes for ridiculous gifts. Each student chose a gift at random drawing a slip from jar.

The rules for this exercise are as follows:
1. Must be sincere.
2. Mention the gift in the first paragraph.
3. Site at least two uses for the gift (or plans of where to put it if it's decorative).
4. Must be at least three paragraphs of two or more sentences each.

Suggested gifts:
Umbrella holder made from an elephant's leg.
Bookends decorated with miniature loaves of bread & shocks of wheat.
An incredibly fuzzy pair of house slippers.
A really ugly sweater.
Something impossible to identify.
A painting with dogs playing poker (I know, some people think this is cute.).
Clothing that is too small (too large, hideous color, wrong gender, etc.).
Music CD that is of a type you abhor.
A movie you hated and never wanted to think of again.

The list can go on forever. Don't only use my list, make your own. Sometimes just generating a list helps get past that pesky creative blockage.

Sample note Thanks for the ?:

Dear Aunt Fanny,

Thank you so much for the really interesting gift you sent! I can't imagine what I've done without it all these years. It will add a great deal to my decor. I can't wait to find a place for it in the living room. I showed your gift to my friends and they were speechless. What an unusual present! They wanted to know where on earth you found it, several of them would like one for themselves.

Again, thank you so much for your incredibly amazing gift! I shall treasure it always and remember you every time I look at it.

Your Loving Niece

A Second Exercise:

I belong to a writing group that meets once a week. Each week we have a writing prompt and try to write something on that subject. Then, after we all share our writing, we hand out a bag of word slips. Each person picks five and tries to put them into a sentence or paragraph.

To help your writer's block, generate a bag of words. Jot down words, type them up, print and cut apart. Keep them in a Ziploc bag and use as needed. You don't have to use just 5. Another group I've attended uses 10.

The simple act of thinking of words helps get your brain kick started. Writing the sentences is fun and provides a creative outlet while not putting pressure on you to *write!*

There is no set cure for writer's block. Sometimes the creative well simply runs dry. The key is to accept it and try to move on. Fighting yourself, screaming and carrying on like a crybaby are pointless, unproductive and unprofessional. Instead, be proactive. Face your block and find your way past it.

Excerpt From *Lone Wolf*

Lights on the computer console flashed, catching her attention. The bridge was dark since only the bots were supposed to be at work. Matilda checked the instruments carefully.

"Rubee, lights," she told the ship's computer.

"Initiating. Welcome, Commander Dulac."

The lights came up slowly, allowing her eyes to adjust. There was a flicker of movement on one of her screens. Why was a mining unit on approach? Curious, she activated the Tri-D viewer, focusing on an incoming ship. None of the miners were due until 0800. Glancing at the chronometer, she saw it was only 0230.

"Mine Unit One, what is your status?"

Getting only static in reply, Matilda zoomed the viewer trying to get a visual on the pilot. The miner ignored the station's auto-hails. Her long fingers flew over the keypad as she tried to figure out what the hell was going on.

"Mine Unit One, do you have an emergency?"

Nothing. Hitting her comlink, she beeped Marc Slatterly's cabin. "Captain!"

"Hmph?" He answered, still naked in the bed where she'd left him twenty minutes ago. "What? Matilda? Where the hell are you?"

He rubbed his face to wake up. Standing groggily, he loomed over the console. His heavily muscled body was cast into stark shadows and highlights by the Tri-D projection of her face.

"The bridge. We've got a problem. Get up here."

"What?" Suddenly all business, he reached for his pants.

"Unit One. Billy's coming in hot and erratic. He's not answering hails."

"You know Guild protocol, Matilda." He struggled into his pants, getting tangled as he tried to put his feet through.

She exhaled slowly, wiping her brow. She knew protocol as well as he, but in the ten years of Mining Guild service she'd never had to use Regulation Seventeen—Destruction of a Manned Vessel. Until now.

"Maybe his comlink is borked."

"Hail him one more time, then initiate protocol."

"Are you coming?"

"On my way." He didn't bother to finish dressing. Grabbing his gun belt, he took off at top speed to the lift.

"Mine Unit One," Matilda continued. "Slow your approach or I will enact Guild Regulation Seventeen. Do you copy?"

More static. She keyed in the coded sequence necessary to transfer the miner's load to the cargo hold. Taking a deep breath, she tried once more.

"Mine Unit One, this is your final warning before I implement your self-destruct." Tapping her comlink, she prayed Marc would answer.

"On my way, baby. I can go only so fast. Damn lift is slow."

"Shit. I used the transporter."

"There went my power. You know the drill, Commander."

"Yes, sir."

She lifted the clear Lucite lid over the red destruct button, hands shaking as she keyed in the final sequence.

"Mine Unit One, Billy? Can you hear me? Slow down!" Still no answer. "You made me do this," she whispered as her finger pressed the button.

The miner's craft imploded, folding on itself like a deflated balloon. Biting her lip, blinking back tears, she turned away. Marc walked onto the bridge a second later, eyes glued to the screen. Taking her in his arms, he held her while she cried.

"You had to do it, Matilda. You had no choice. Look at his trajectory. He'd have come right through us."

"I never had to do it before." She wiped the tears fiercely away. *And to a friend.*

Marc checked the console, securing the destruct button without a word. Taking a life was never easy, but he'd grown used to it over time. Years as a Galactic Marine had hardened him. More as a Mining Guild officer had taken the sting out of senseless killing, but the first one was always the worst.

Taking her shoulders, he turned her to face him. "You did your job, Matilda. Sometimes that's not easy." Puzzled, he paused, looking around. "Why are you up?"

"Something didn't feel right. I came up to check it out." She shrugged, pressing against him as his arms held her.

"You're like me. Your hunches are rarely wrong." He secured the console. "How about we go back to bed?"

"Yeah," she agreed. "I need something to take my mind off..."

Marc slung an arm around her shoulders, kissing the top of her head. "I reckon I can distract you for an hour or two." He chuckled, white teeth flashing through the confines of his dark red beard.

Back in his cabin, they wiled away the next hour. Afterward, though she was tired, she couldn't go back to sleep. Something still felt wrong, like an instrument played off key, making her skin crawl. Now that there was nothing to occupy her mind, she focused on her misgivings. She wanted to wake Marc so she'd have some distraction, but one look at his sleeping face told her that was unlikely. He didn't sleep much, but when it did, it was deep.

Instead, Matilda rose and showered, dressing in a fresh uniform. She intended to go back to her own quarters after kissing him goodnight, but her feet took her to the cargo bay. As she approached, the creeping feeling on her skin grew worse, the hairs on her neck rising. Something wasn't right, but she couldn't determine what. Pulling herself away from the doors, she ran to the bridge, calling up the ship's manifest.

There was a load of Trimagnite ore collected from the destroyed mine unit. In a panic, she buzzed Marc's quarters.

"What the hell? Romance, where are you up to now?"

"Get dressed and get up here now! It's urgent."

"Again? Dammit! Can't I get some sleep?"

"Not if you want to live."

Within five minutes, he joined her. She gave him a cup of joe to clear his befuddlement. Gulping it down, he made a face, but in a few seconds, he was clearheaded as she told him what she'd found, showing him the scan. Trimagnite had a very distinctive pattern.

"Damn! What was he thinking? He didn't have the equipment or storage capability for this. Digging that shit without proper shielding is lethal!"

"So, what do we do? Trimagnite can make us all go nuts! Why didn't he tell us?" Her voice held a note of panic.

"We both know the raw ore is not only toxic, it's a very strong neural stimulant. I'm surprised he lived long enough to get it to the ship. I'm contacting Commandant Riley. We can't carry this, we're only minimally shielded. Even if we'd known ahead of time, we're not prepared to transport it."

His fingers flew over his keypad as he sat at the console, waiting impatiently to connect. Matilda stood nearby, hugging herself. Knowing it was Trimagnite made her feel worse. Everyone in the galaxy knew the damaging effects of the semi-liquid ore: disorientation, hallucinations, madness and death. Once the process started, there was no halting it. They would die—horribly.

The Importance of Formatting
By
Deborah J Ledford
Author of:
Staccato and *Snare*

It is becoming the norm to submit novels and short stories electronically. Now more than ever it is crucial that you format your work by adhering to current industry standards. Agents, editors and publishers look for any excuse to reject your work, so don't give them an excuse due to being unaware of how your story or novel should appear on the page.

Below you will find step-by-step instructions for setting up your stories and manuscripts in order to present a professionally formatted file.

To set up your **TEMPLATE** for each story you will write:

Open a Blank Page
Click on FILE
PAGE SETUP:
MARGIN Tab:
TOP: 1"   BOTTOM: 1"
LEFT: 1"   RIGHT: 1"
GUTTER – 0   GUTTER POSITION: Left
GUTTER POSITION: Left
ORIENTATION: PORTRAIT
MULTIPLE PAGES: NORMAL
APPLY TO: WHOLE DOCUMENT
CLICK: OK

Novel Writing Tips and Techniques

SETTING TABS, SPACING

Open a Blank Page.
Click on Format, then Paragraph
Indents and Spacing Tab will come up.
Within the box:
Alignment: LeftOutline Level: Body Text
Indentation:

| | Left: | 0 | Special: | By: |
| | Right: | 0 | First Line | 0.3" (this is your first tab) |

Spacing:

| | Before | 0 | Line Spacing: |
| | After | 0 | Double |

Click: OK

FOR EXISTING FILE - SETTING TABS, SPACING:

OPEN THE MASTER FILE
HIGHLIGHT ENTIRE FILE (Control A)
Then, FORMAT, PARAGRAPH
Follow instructions above.

WIDOWS AND ORPHANS OFF:

(tab behind Indents and Spacing Tab)
Same thing—Format, Paragraph, but then change the tab to: LINE &
PAGE BREAKS
Click OFF ALL ARROWS
Then, OK

HEADERS AND PAGE NUMBERS:

Open your file.
At the top: Click on VIEW
Then HEADER/FOOTER
A dashed box will appear.
Hit ENTER once.
Type: Last name/TITLE (in caps)

Then:
At the top: INSERT
Click on PAGE NUMBERS
ALIGNMENT: RIGHT
If you implement your contact information, Do NOT check the
SHOW ON FIRST PAGE box for page # to appear.
If you merely want to print out pages, CHECK the box for SHOW
ON FIRST PAGE.
Click: OK
Then, CLOSE the dialogue box.

MISCELLANEOUS

One space after periods. One space after period, close quotation
mark. One space after colons.

Spell out numbers within dialogue.

Asterisk breaks (to indicate switch in POV, major time break or
location change within the same chapter):
One blank line, then CENTER *(followed by 5 blank spaces)*(5
blank spaces)* =

*   *   *

Ellipses: final word, space, period, space, period, space, period,
space, next word =
You know . . . what I mean?
Ellipses within quotes: final word, space, period, space, period,
space, period, end quote.
"You know . . ."
Ellipses within question/quotes: "You know . . .?"

Emdash = solid double line, no spaces: you know—what I mean?

Items that appear as printed items (signs, short notes): ALL
CAPITAL LETTERS, no quotation marks, no italics.

Present foreign words and words for emphasis *in italics*. NO
UNDERLINE.

Titles: Books, Movies, TV Programs, Radio Programs, Comic Strips, Websites, Plays, Newspapers, Pamphlets: *Italics*, no quotes.

Titles of other works: Songs, short stories, essays, short poems = Quotation marks, no italics

Fonts/Styles: Unless otherwise stated, TIMES NEW ROMAN, 12 POINT FONT, DOUBLE SPACED.

**Be certain to check websites of each and every agent/editor/publisher before you submit your work. They may have specifically preferred Submission Guidelines for you to adhere to.

SUBMITTING YOUR SHORT STORIES:

www.duotrope.com is a stellar site to research markets for you to submit your short stories. You can target your search by genre and submission process. Be sure to sign up for their weekly newsletter to receive call for submissions with themes and deadlines.

Be aware that it is ideal to submit your work only to print publications. Unless the E-zine is extremely reputable (such as: *GQ* or *Criminal Element*) agents, editors and publishers don't view this print credit nearly as favorable.

SEARCHING FOR AN AGENT/PUBLISHER:

www.agentquery.com is an ideal free search tool where you can research agents currently looking for clients. Target your search by genre and you will receive a full list of agents to research.

www.publishersmarketplace.com is the most reputable source for researching agents and editors. This is a pay service, however you have the ability to track sales, discover the latest deals, and research fully what agents and editors are currently accepting and looking for.

No reputable agents/editors/publishers require you to pay a fee for their services. The website Preditors & Editors is where you can check agents and book publishers to make sure there are no hidden fees or costs related to submitting or considering your work for representation or publication. Be certain to check this site before you submit your novel.

THE COPYRIGHT ISSUE: PROTECT YOUR WORK

You've created an original work of art. Hours, months, possibly years dedicated to stringing words together you and you alone can present to the world. So why risk the possibility of having your work invalidated or rejected merely due to the fact you weren't aware of the risks involved with sharing your words via the Internet.

Did you know that when you post anything online this work is considered "published"? Frightening, yet true. With the constant change in the publishing industry, agents and publishers are extremely cautious when selecting novels and stories for representation and publication. Any excuse to send a rejection seems to be the norm nowadays, so don't put your carefully crafted words at risk.

The agent or publisher you query will perform due diligence on you and the sample chapter or story you submit to them. There are word generating software programs that these professionals access. Essentially they cut and paste elements of your work to see if the words appear anywhere on the Internet. Even if you are the actual writer of theses words, your submission could be red-flagged as "previously published" and no longer eligible for consideration.

Also, be ever vigilant and aware of the many social sites and groups which allow you to share your work, ask for editing tips, offer your work for free critiques, etc. Don't be fooled into believing this is an ideal situation for you. These are not protected websites and unless the group is "private" anyone is privy to the work and conversations shared there.

Do not share your work with these online groups, however feel free to offer your input—this is an ideal opportunity to meet writers. Establish a relationship with a few writers, then start your own private creative writing group. And for even more protection, share your work via private email. By doing so, you are assuring that your words are not in any way put at risk.

Although there are few truly original stories, there are thousands of ideas and themes for novels and stories and writers are always looking for interesting ideas. And titles can't be copyrighted, so if you have a fantastic idea for a title, do not present this on the worldwide web.

As for copyrighting your work—be certain to retain your original First Draft Word file. There is a record imbedded into the file which verifies when the work was created. This way if there is ever any doubt the words are actually yours, there is irrefutable evidence as to when you began working on the draft, also when the file was altered.

Using the Copyright symbol (©) is not necessary and is the sign of an amateur or "newbie" in the eyes of industry professionals. Your work is copyrighted the moment you create a verifiable document, whether on your computer or with pen on paper.

However if you've written a screenplay, protect yourself in every way you can. Register your script for $20.00 with the Writer's Guild of America (www.wgaregistry.org).

Protect the words you've worked so hard to craft.

🦃

Deborah J Ledford's publishing credits include *SNARE*, The Hillerman Sky Award Finalist and the classical music-themed *STACCATO*, both presented by Second Wind Publishing. She is a three-time nominee for the Pushcart Prize and her award-winning stories appear in numerous print publications as well as mystery and literary anthologies. She is a member of the professional organizations: ITW, MWA (SoCal), Sisters in Crime (National and LA, CA), and current President of the Sisters in Crime Desert Sleuths Chapter (AZ). www.DeborahJLedford.com.

Writing Aids and Organizational Tools

By
Coco Ihle
Author of:
She Had to Know

🦃

This chapter is devoted to how I used organizational tools to help me prepare and write my book, *She Had to Know*.

As a reader, quite often I find in my hurry to get into a new book, I race over character names and then get confused later about who is doing what. When character's names start with the same letter, the confusion is compounded. I've had to discipline myself to take my time learning the names as they are introduced, thus avoiding backtracking. My reading experience is also enhanced by investing my thoughts in these people from the start.

As a writer, I decided to make it as easy as possible for readers to meet my characters in a way they would remember. To accomplish this, I introduced married people as a couple, gave some distinguished description for the lone individuals and made sure names were not similar. I also wrote out a background profile for characters who appeared, both major and minor. That way, their names fit their personalities and thus are easier to recall for the reader.

A really handy tool I used early on was a chart I made, divided into two vertical columns. The left heading read: "First Names of Characters." The right, "Last Names of Characters." I started with the letters of the alphabet on the extreme left, A-Z down the page and did the same for the right column. Next to the alphabet letters I filled in my character names, first names in the left column and last in the right column. This gave me a visual of what letters I used for my names. It's quite easy to repeat letters unconsciously and this is an easy way to catch those repetitions. I had to change character names as a result of this exercise, but it has eliminated problems for my readers. I even included page numbers (in parenthesis) next to a name of a lesser used character in order to find him/her later when rewriting or editing.

The background character profile helped me learn more about the people in my book. Each character had one and they were very detailed. I started with a form that I duplicated for as many characters as I needed. Then I filled in each form with all the information I had and added to it as I got to know my characters better.

<u>Character Profile</u>

- Name
- Height
- Age in the story
- Birthplace and date
- Physical description (hair color, length and style, eye color, build)
- Race/nationality
- Regional influences, accent (voice style of speech, slang, signature phrases or words),
- Religion
- Marital status
- Scars or notable physical attributes, handicaps
- Athletic? Inactive?
- Overall health
- Style of dress
- Favorite colors
- How character feels about his/her appearance
- Brothers/sisters
- Relationship with parents
- Memories about childhood
- Educational background
- Work experience, occupation
- Where character lives (describe home, emotional

atmosphere), neat or messy
- Sexual preference
- Morals
- Women/men friends
- Pets
- Enemies (why?)
- Basic nature
- Personality traits (shy, outgoing, domineering, doormat, honest, kind, sense of humor)
- Strongest trait, weakest trait
- What does character fear?
- What is character proud of?
- What is character ashamed of?
- Outlook on life
- Ambitions
- Politics
- How does character see himself or herself?
- How is character seen by others?
- Do you like this person? (why or why not)
- Will readers like or dislike?
- Most important thing to remember about character
- Present problem? How will it get worse?
- What is the characters goal in the story?
- What traits will help/hurt character in achieving this goal?
- What makes character different from similar characters?
- Why will readers remember this character vividly?

The more you know about the people in your book, the more realistic they will be to you and your readers. The background profile is a wonderful tool to accomplish that. It may take some time to fill in, but it pays off in the long run. I filled in as much of those blanks as I could, although some may not be necessary for you. For instance, I didn't need to have a political opinion for my characters, so I left that blank. This profile can also come in handy down the road when you are writing a series and have forgotten an eye color or age of a character or something of that sort.

The background profile can inform your reader about a

character. In my book, Arran Hart lives in New Jersey. Here is an excerpt:

When the alarm went off the next morning, she was jolted out of a heavy, dreamless sleep and it took her a few minutes to realize how late it was. Glad of her habit of setting an alarm in case she overslept, she raced to shower and dress.

This passage tells the reader Arran is conscientious in not wanting to be late for work. It also tells the reader she is a clean person. Minor information, but important for the reader to have without saying, "Arran was conscientious and she was clean."

Back to the chart of first and last names. In my book, *She Had to Know*, I had a unique situation in which I needed to use the same initials for several characters. This was tricky to deal with. To solve this dilemma, I placed a clue early on in the book and then I tried making each of those characters as distinct as possible so the reader would remember them. The tricky part was inserting the clue causally. I didn't want to reader to know this was a clue. The reason? I was being fair to the reader by including all the facts so that the diligent ones could collect them to figure out who the murderer was at the end.

Another organizational tool I used was a timeline of events in my book. I can't say enough about how this helped me, especially during rewrites and editing.

At the edge of my desk, a glass wall separates my home office from the solarium. The other walls in my office are filled with bookshelves, doors, window, so the glass wall serves as a temporary bulletin board when I am knee deep in organizing material and chapters for my work-in-progress.

In my book, the main part of the story took place over a period of 3 ½ weeks in November 1987. I found a calendar for that month and year and duplicated it on a piece of drawing paper 22"x 16". Like a regular calendar month, I put the days of the week along the top and then numbered each day. Because the calendar was so big, I had room to pencil-in a synopsis of each day's happenings, what the characters were doing and where they were, and indicate where chapters started and ended. If I moved an event or chapter, I cut an extra block(s) the size of the day(s) in question and pasted it in on top of the old. This was especially handy for editing, rewriting and when I needed to know exactly where something happened within the manuscript, so I didn't waste time finding it.

This was also tricky, because my characters were traveling between two countries with different time zones. It was quite a challenge to remember when it was nighttime in one country, it was daytime in the other. On my chart, I indicated that with a crescent moon or sun symbol.

Generally, the more organized you are with your material, the easier it will be for you to put your finger on whatever you need to complete your project.

Besides character profiles and a timeline, I have files for history and geography of my settings, legends and superstitions of the area, photos, articles I've saved, notes I've taken, etc. Some of these things get used, some don't, but I have on hand what I need.

Setting played a huge role in *She Had to Know* by creating information about characters and mood for the story. An example of setting providing information follows. Arran, one of the sisters has a meeting with a lady at the Family and Children's Society:

Arriving on time, Arran followed a circular gravel drive and parked under the canopy of a huge oak tree that she was sure must have been there since Washington crossed the Delaware. A crisp smell of fall was in the air and she felt acorns crunching under her shoes as she approached the wooden Gothic arched door. Before entering, she stood silently for a moment praying that whatever she learned would be good news. Then with a deep breath, she boldly opened the door.

Immediately she was struck by the combined scents of old fabrics, waxed floors, perked coffee and stale air resulting presumably from long stuck windows. A faded twenties-vintage floral papered the walls, and antique chairs edged the well-trod carpet.

These two paragraphs tell the reader that Arran is conscientious about arriving on time, the place has old oak trees in an expansive drive, it is fall, and she is a person who prays and is courageous. The building has been there a long time, business is more important than fancy décor, but it has quality furniture, and many people have been through its doors.

An example of setting creating mood in my story:

Off the Corniche Road amidst vast desolate moorland and gnarled groves of trees, stood the often fog shrouded Wraithmoor Castle, an early-seventeenth-century Scots Baronial manor house. Perched on a rocky cliff overlooking the Firth of Clyde, it lay dreamlike, as if a product of Morpheus, a few miles south of the village of Ballantrae.

Or:

Thunder rolled and grumbled outside, and for long seconds, cracks of lightning illuminated the room in bright-white reverberating shafts. . . . Rain lashed the glass in sheets, and the wind howled through the casement windows with an eerie singing sound.

Or:

Daylight dawned cold, and mist hung in the air like a shroud. The rain had gone, leaving behind a miserable dampness that bit through everything with its penetrating chill.

Can you feel the mood?

Research was paramount to my story, as well. Since my heritage is Scottish, I belong to several Scottish societies which have supplied me with a myriad of information about dress and customs. My trips to Scotland were opportunities to collect books, pamphlets and brochures, speak with the locals and take hundreds of photos. Bagpipe and harp lessons taught me a lot about the music and the instruments. I saved everything and have shelves full of useful material. If I needed something I didn't have, I had Scottish friends I could call or I used the Internet. For Forensic information, I relied on D.P. Lyle and David Ciambrone to get my murder weapon and murder scenes right. I contacted the Strathclyde Police in Scotland and the New York City Police Department for help with death notification and police procedural details. My travel agent helped me with flights to and from Scotland.

I sketched Wraithmoor Castle as I envisioned it, but before I could do that, I researched Scottish architecture to keep it authentic looking. That sketch appears in the beginning of the book. Just for my own use, I even sketched the inside of Wraithmoor, so I could move my characters around logically.

At one point, I needed a Scottish drinking toast. It took a while to find just the right one, but I found it in the notes collected on one of my trips. Reading up on legends helped me invent my legend behind the fictitious Standing Stones of Pengar. Talking with an architect helped me devise the mechanics for the treasure room.

Now it was up to me to make it all this accumulated information come alive on the page. Because I was organized and had my tools around me, I didn't have to waste much time looking for anything. Instead, I lived in Scotland with my characters for many months and loved every moment of it.

Interview with Coco Ihle

What is your book about?

She Had to Know has an autobiographical element to it and deals with two long lost sisters who reunite and nearly lose their lives searching for a hidden treasure and a murderer in a Scottish castle.

How long had the idea of your book been developing before you began to write the story?

I was a product of foster care and adoption, so my early life was spent fantasizing about finding my birth family with the thought of writing a book one day involving my search. It wasn't until my early thirties that my Scottish roots were uncovered and a tiny seed was planted. In my fifties, one of my sisters was located and the book started forming in my mind. What better story to write than a mystery?

How much of yourself is hidden in the main characters of this book?

She Had to Know has two protagonists, the two sisters. I found it interesting that both sisters in the book have multiple characteristics of my sister and me. That is to say, one isn't me and the other my sister, my fictional characters have traits that both my sister and I have, plus some. It just worked out that way. Does that make sense?

It does make sense. Tell me, did you do any research for this

book?

Yes, a great deal. Luckily, when I found out about my Scottish heritage years earlier, I joined a local Scottish society and met many Scots who shared with me stories of their lives and culture. My son and I joined the society's bagpipe band and traveled to Scotland to order our bagpipes and kilts and to discover more about my homeland. To make things interesting, we stayed in several castles all over Britain. That's when I knew one sister in my book would own a castle hotel. More trips were necessary for fact finding, and many hours of speaking with my wonderful Scottish friends helped me get the details down. I also used books and pamphlets that I gathered on my travels along with the phone and, toward the end, the internet. What can I say, I love research.

What challenges did you face when you wrote this book?

In part of the book I deal with reuniting the sisters. I already knew how I felt, but I needed to find out how my sister dealt with her questions of not knowing where she came from or why she was given up; that sort of thing. The questions were difficult to ask and the answers were tough to put on paper, because I wanted to emphasize the joy of the sister's reunion, not dwell on the sadness of our lost childhood together. In the end, I left out much of the negative, though in the future, I may touch on more of the problems the sisters faced.

Another challenge for me was in simplifying the Scottish dialect so that everyone could understand it. I tried to be consistent with it so the reader would get into the cadence of the characters. I thought adding a glossary might help, too.

Do you think writing this book changed your life? If so, how?

Absolutely. In a couple of ways. My sister and I talked in detail about our lives before we met, and how we felt about all the things that happened and didn't happen through the years. Our talks created a stronger bond between us.

Another way my life changed was, my adopted mother used to accuse me of starting projects and losing interest before finishing them. Well, I took that criticism to heart. I know she's up there smiling down at me, because I finish projects now.

Do you prefer to write at a particular time of day?

Mornings are my favorite time, because my mind is fresh, but sometimes late at night when there are no distractions. Often, I'll wake in the middle of the night with an idea or a phrase and have to write it down on a tablet I keep on my nightstand. And occasionally, I just have to get up and write that thought or idea in more detail.

Do you have a favorite snack food or beverage that you enjoy while you write?

Ha! That would be my famous cup of joe. I have a wonderful 16 oz. thermos mug that keeps my coffee hot, so I don't have to get up so often for a refill. My right hand seems to be permanently crooked into the mug holding position. Just kidding. Occasionally, I like to munch on roasted almonds, too.

Why did you set your book to begin in 1985?

I've always been told to "write what you know." Since my own search was done primarily before computers, I wanted to write my story before that era. As I continue to search for two more siblings, I'm finding the computer age has only complicated matters. Often, too much information can be as much of a hindrance as not enough. Also, found information is often incorrect, which can lead to wasted time and effort. If it hadn't been for the Alma Society, which helps in family searches, I may have given up years ago.

What is your goal for the book, i.e.: what do you want people to take with them after they finish reading the story?

When I read a story, I want to be swept into it and escape from my life issues and just be entertained. I hope my readers will feel that way with my book. I also hope, people will be reinforced in their thinking that persistence is a virtue which almost always has its rewards. It certainly has in my life.

What do you like to read?

Mostly mysteries since that's what I like to write, and I'm lucky to know some very excellent writers in my genre through conferences, conventions and listserves. Memoirs are another area I like and in which I have written. And there are some wonderful YA authors out there whose work in fantasy I enjoy. But, I like thrillers, too. Oh, dear, I just love to read and if it is well written, I'll read just about anything that isn't too violent or graphic.

Do you have a saying or motto for your life and/or as a writer?

Funny you should ask. My favorite is: "Aspire to inspire before you expire." Isn't that great?

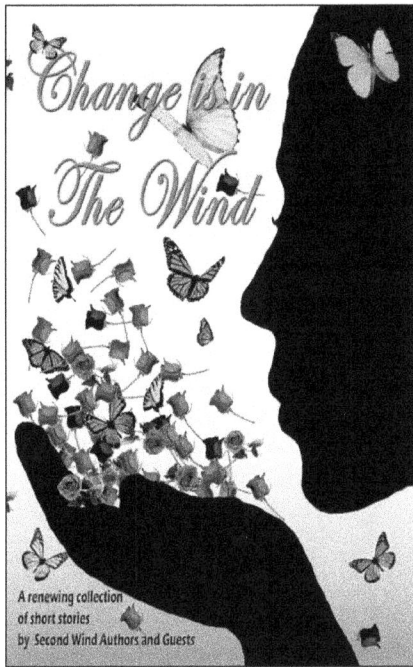

Change Is in The Wind is a fresh, challenging collection of short stories, all dealing with the theme of change and renewal. Virtually every major theme in modern literature, including romance, mystery, crime, science fiction, religion and even nature find their way into these stories. Featured are these stories by Second Wind Authors:

Salamander by Deborah J Ledford
Nerd of Prey by Noah Baird
Fifty-Two Years by J J Dare
Pain Killer by Dellani Oakes
Cache-22 by J. Conrad Guest
The Willow by Pat Bertram
Gratitude by Claire Collins
Apres Holiday by Susan Surman
Caddo Creek by Lazarus Barnhill

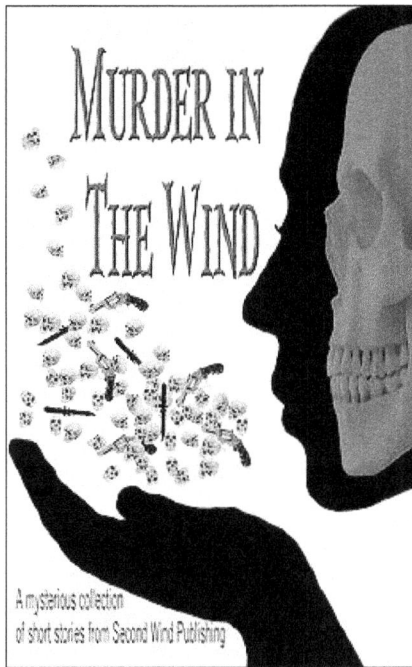

A Mysterious Collection of Short Stories from Second Wind Publishing. An anthology of crime/mystery short stories contributed by the outstanding authors of Second Wind Publishing. Murder, mayhem and the unexpected are rife in each riveting story. Included in this anthology are these crime and mystery stories:

A Whiff of Murder by Lazarus Barnhill
Hanging Around by JJ Dare
Murder at the Manor by Juliet Waldron
This Time by Claire Collins
Some Things You Can't Outrun by Mairead Walpole
The Fireplace by Christine Husom
The Spot by Deborah J Ledford
The Stygian Night by Pat Bertram
Window of Opportunity by Norm Brown

A little girl's body has been found in the desert near Rubicon Ranch. Was her death an accident? Or . . . murder! But who would want to kill a child? *Rubicon Ranch: Riley's Story* was the first collaborative novel written online by Second Wind Authors, and the book is now published.

The saga continues with *Rubicon Ranch: Necropieces*. Body parts are being found strewn about the desert. Everyone in this upscale community is hiding something, maybe even murder. But who committed the crime? No one knows yet, not even the authors!

You can find the ongoing story at:
www.rubiconranch.wordpress.com

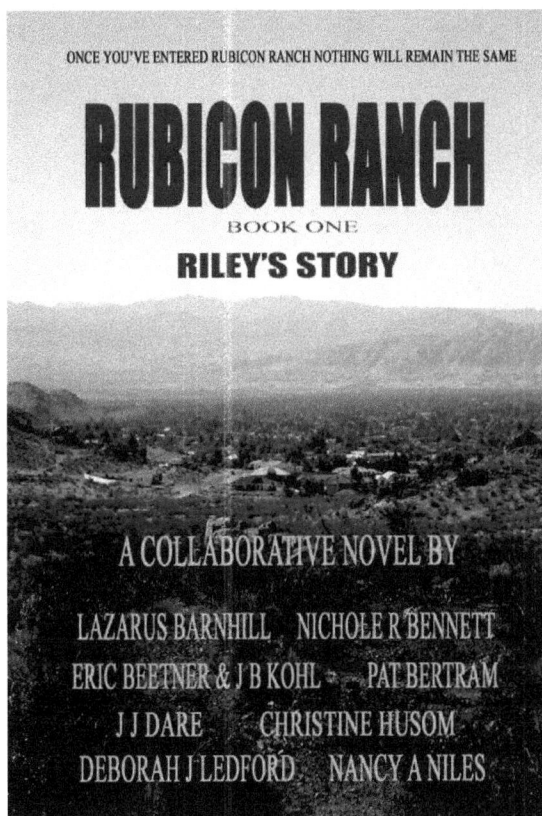

ONCE YOU'VE ENTERED RUBICON RANCH NOTHING WILL REMAIN THE SAME

RUBICON RANCH
BOOK ONE
RILEY'S STORY

A COLLABORATIVE NOVEL BY

LAZARUS BARNHILL   NICHOLE R BENNETT
ERIC BEETNER & J B KOHL   PAT BERTRAM
J J DARE   CHRISTINE HUSOM
DEBORAH J LEDFORD   NANCY A NILES